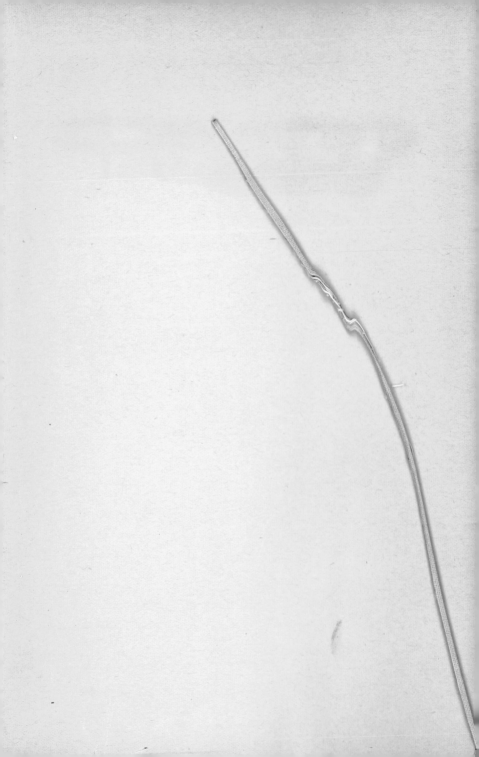

MY FOUR YEARS
IN GERMANY

BY

JAMES W. GERARD
LATE AMBASSADOR TO THE GERMAN IMPERIAL COURT

ILLUSTRATED

NEW YORK
GEORGE H. DORAN COMPANY

AMBASSADOR GERARD SAYING GOOD-BYE TO THE AMERICANS LEAVING
ON A SPECIAL TRAIN. AUGUST, 1914

TO MY SMALL BUT TACTFUL FAMILY OF ONE

MY WIFE

FOREWORD

I am writing what should have been the last chapter of this book as a foreword because I want to bring home to our people the gravity of the situation; because I want to tell them that the military and naval power of the German Empire is unbroken; that of the twelve million men whom the Kaiser has called to the colours but one million, five hundred thousand have been killed, five hundred thousand permanently disabled, not more than five hundred thousand are prisoners of war, and about five hundred thousand constitute the number of wounded or those on the sick list of each day, leaving at all times about nine million effectives under arms.

I state these figures because Americans do not grasp either the magnitude or the importance of this war. Perhaps the statement that over five million prisoners of war are held in the various countries will bring home to Americans the enormous mass of men engaged.

There have been no great losses in the German navy, and any losses of ships have been compensated for by the building of new ones. The nine million men, and more, for at leas four hundred thousand come of military age in Germany every year, because of their experience in two and a half years of war are better and more efficient soldiers than at the time when they were called to the colours. Their officers know far more of the science of this war and the men themselves now have the skill and bearing of veterans.

Nor should any one believe that Germany will break under starvation or make peace because of revolution.

The German nation is not one which makes revolutions. There will be scattered riots in Germany, but no simultaneous rising of the whole people. The officers of the army are all of one class, and of a class devoted to the ideals of autocracy. A revolution of the army is impossible; and at home there are only the boys and old men easily kept in subjection by the police.

There is far greater danger of the starvation of our Allies than of the starvation of the Germans. Every available inch of ground in Germany is cultivated, and cultivated by the aid of the old men, the boys and the women, and the two million prisoners of war.

The arable lands of Northern France and of Roumania are being cultivated by the German army with an efficiency never before known in these countries, and most of that food will be added to the food supplies of Germany. Certainly the people suffer; but still more certainly this war will not be ended because of the starvation of Germany.

Although thinking Germans know that if they do not win the war the financial day of reckoning will come, nevertheless, owing to the clever financial handling of the country by the government and the great banks, there is at present no financial distress in Germany; and the knowledge that, unless indemnities are obtained from other countries, the weight of the great war debt will fall upon the people, perhaps makes them readier to risk all in a final attempt to win the war and impose indemnities upon not only the nations of Europe but also upon the United States of America.

We are engaged in a war against the greatest military power the world has ever seen; against a people whose country was for so many centuries a theatre of devastating wars that fear is bred in the very marrow of their souls, making them ready to submit their lives and fortunes to an autocracy which for centuries has ground their faces, but which has promised them, as a result of the war, not only security but riches untold and the dominion of the world; a people which, as from a high mountain, has looked upon the cities of the world and the glories of them, and has been promised these cities and these glories by the devils of autocracy and of war.

We are warring against a nation whose poets and professors, whose pedagogues and whose parsons have united in stirring its people to a white pitch of hatred, first against Russia, then against England and now against America.

The U-Boat peril is a very real one for England. Russia may either break up into civil wars or become so ineffective that the millions of German troops engaged on the Russian front may be withdrawn and hurled against the Western lines. We stand in great peril, and only the exercise of ruthless realism can win this war for us. If Germany wins this war it means the triumph of the autocratic system. It means the triumph of those who believe not only in war as a national industry, not only in war for itself but also in war as a high and noble occupation. Unless Germany is beaten the whole world will be compelled to turn itself into an armed camp, until the German autocracy either brings every nation under its dominion or is forever wiped out as a form of government.

We are in this war because we were forced into it: because Germany not only murdered our citizens on the high seas, but also filled our country with spies and sought to incite our people to civil war. We were given no opportunity to dis-

cuss or negotiate. The forty-eight hour ultimatum given by Austria to Serbia was not, as Ber-
nard Shaw said, "A decent time in which to ask
a man to pay his hotel bill." What of the six-
hour ultimatum given to me in Berlin on the
evening of January thirty-first, 1917, when I was
notified at six that ruthless warfare would commence at twelve? Why the German government,
which up to that moment had professed amity
and a desire to stand by the *Sussex* pledges,
knew that it took almost two days to send a cable
to America! I believe that we are not only
justly in this war, but prudently in this war. If
we had stayed out and the war had been drawn
or won by Germany we should have been attacked, and that while Europe stood grinning
by: not directly at first, but through an attack on
some Central or South American State to which
it would be at least as difficult for us to send
troops as for Germany. And what if this powerful nation, vowed to war, were once firmly estab-
lised in South or Central America? What of
our boasted isolation then?

It is only because I believe that our people
should be informed that I have consented to
write this book. There are too many thinkers,
writers and speakers in the United States; from
now on we need the doers, the organisers, and

the realists who alone can win this contest for us, for democracy and for permanent peace!

Writing of events so new, I am, of course, compelled to exercise a great discretion, to keep silent on many things of which I would speak, to suspend many judgments and to hold for future disclosure many things, the relation of which now would perhaps only serve to increase bitterness or to cause internal dissension in our own land.

The American who travels through Germany in summer time or who spends a month having his liver tickled at Homburg or Carlsbad, who has his digestion restored by Dr. Dapper at Kissingen or who relearns the lost art of eating meat at Dr. Dengler's in Baden, learns little of the real Germany and its rulers; and in this book I tell something of the real Germany, not only that my readers may understand the events of the last three years but also that they may judge of what is likely to happen in our future relations with that country.

CONTENTS

xiii

CONTENTS

ILLUSTRATIONS

ILLUSTRATIONS

MY FOUR YEARS IN GERMANY

MY FOUR YEARS IN GERMANY

CHAPTER I

MY FIRST YEAR IN GERMANY

THE second day out on the *Imperator,* headed
for a summer's vacation, a loud knocking
woke me at seven A. M. The radio, handed in
from a friend in New York, told me of my appointment as Ambassador to Germany.

Many friends were on the ship. Henry Morgenthau, later Ambassador to Turkey, Colonel
George Harvey, Adolph Ochs and Louis Wiley
of the *New York Times,* Clarence Mackay, and
others.

The *Imperator* is a marvellous ship of fifty-four thousand tons or more, and at times it is
hard to believe that one is on the sea. In addition to the regular dining saloon, there is a grill
room and Ritz restaurant with its palm garden,
and, of course, an Hungarian Band. There are
also a gymnasium and swimming pool, and,
nightly, in the enormous ballroom dances are

given, the women dressing in their best just as they do on shore.

Colonel Harvey and Clarence Mackay gave me a dinner of twenty-four covers, something of a record at sea. For long afterwards in Germany, I saw everywhere pictures of the *Imperator* including one of the tables set for this dinner. These were sent out over Germany as a sort of propaganda to induce the Germans to patronise their own ships and indulge in ocean travel. I wish that the propaganda had been earlier and more successful, because it is by travel that peoples learn to know each other, and consequently to abstain from war.

On the night of the usual ship concert, Henry Morgenthau translated a little speech for me into German, which I managed to get through after painfully learning it by heart. Now that I have a better knowledge of German, a cold sweat breaks out when I think of the awful German accent with which I delivered that address.

A flying trip to Berlin early in August to look into the house question followed, and then I returned to the United States.

In September I went to Washington to be "instructed," talked with the President and Secretary, and sat at the feet of the Assistant Secretary of State, Alvey A. Adee, the revered Sage of the Department of State.

On September ninth, 1913, having resigned as Justice of the Supreme Court of the State of New York, I sailed for Germany, stopping on the way in London in order to make the acquaintance of Ambassador Page, certain wise people in Washington having expressed the belief that a personal acquaintance of our Ambassadors made it easier for them to work together.

Two cares assail a newly appointed Ambassador. He must first take thought of what he shall wear and where he shall live. All other nations have beautiful Embassies or Legations in Berlin, but I found that my two immediate predecessors had occupied a villa originally built as a two-family house, pleasantly enough situated, but two miles from the centre of Berlin and entirely unsuitable for an Embassy.

There are few private houses in Berlin, most of the people living in apartments. After some trouble I found a handsome house on the Wilhelm Platz immediately opposite the Chancellor's palace and the Foreign Office, in the very centre of Berlin. This house had been built as a palace for the Princes Hatzfeld and had later passed into the possession of a banking family named von Schwabach.

The United States Government, unlike other nations, does not own or pay the rent of a suitable Embassy, but gives allowance for offices, if the house is large enough to afford office room for the office force of the Embassy. The von Schwabach palace was nothing but a shell. Even the gas and electric light fixtures had been removed; and when the hot water and heating system, bath-rooms, electric lights and fixtures, etc., had been put in, and the house furnished from top to bottom, my first year's salary had far passed the minus point.

The palace was not ready for occupancy until the end of January, 1914, and, in the meantime, we lived at the Hotel Esplanade, and I transacted business at the old, two-family villa.

There are more diplomats in Berlin than in any other capital in the world, because each of the twenty-five States constituting the German Empire sends a legation to Berlin; even the free cities of Hamburg, Lübeck and Bremen have a resident minister at the Empire's capital.

Invariable custom requires a new Ambassador in Berlin to give two receptions, one to the Diplomatic Corps and the other to all those people who have the right to go to court. These are the officials, nobles and officers of the army and navy, and such other persons as have been presented at court. Such people are called *hoffähig*, meaning that they are fit for court.

It is interesting here to note that Jews are not admitted to court. Such Jews as have been en-

AMBASSADOR GERARD ON HIS WAY TO PRESENT HIS LETTERS OF
CREDENCE TO THE EMPEROR

THE HOUSE ON THE WILHELM PLATZ, RENTED FOR USE AS THE EMBASSY

nobled and allowed to put the coveted "von" before their names have first of all been required to submit to baptism in some Christian church. Examples are the von Schwabach family, whose ancestral house I occupied in Berlin, and Friedlaender-Fuld, officially rated as the richest man in Berlin, who made a large fortune in coke and its by-products.

These two receptions are really introductions of an Ambassador to official and court society.

Before these receptions, however, and in the month of November, I presented my letters of credence as Ambassador to the Emperor. This presentation is quite a ceremony. Three coaches were sent for me and my staff, coaches like that in which Cinderella goes to her ball, mostly glass, with white wigged coachmen, outriders in white wigs and standing footmen holding on to the back part of the coach. Baron von Roeder, introducer of Ambassadors, came for me and accompanied me in the first coach; the men of the Embassy staff sat in the other two coaches. Our little procession progressed solemnly through the streets of Berlin, passing on the way through the centre division of the arch known as the Brandenburger Thor, the gateway that stands at the head of the Unter den Linden, a privilege given only on this occasion.

We mounted long stairs in the palace, and in

a large room were received by the aides and the officers of the Emperor's household, of course all in uniform. Then I was ushered alone into the adjoining room where the Emperor, very erect and dressed in the black uniform of the Death's Head Hussars, stood by a table. I made him a little speech, and presented my letters of credence and the letters of recall of my predecessor. The Emperor then unbent from his very erect and impressive attitude and talked with me in a very friendly manner, especially impressing me with his interest in business and commercial affairs. I then, in accordance with custom, asked leave to present my staff. The doors were opened. The staff came in and were presented to the Emperor, who talked in a very jolly and agreeable way to all of us, saying that he hoped above all to see the whole of the Embassy staff riding in the Tier Garten in the mornings.

The Emperor is a most impressive figure, and, in his black uniform surrounded by his officers, certainly looked every inch a king. Although my predecessors, on occasions of this kind, had worn a sort of fancy diplomatic uniform designed by themselves, I decided to abandon this and return to the democratic, if unattractive and uncomfortable, dress-suit, simply because the newspapers of America and certain congressmen, while they have had no objection to the wearing of uniforms by the army and navy, police and postmen, and do not expect officers to lead their troops into battle in dress-suits, have, nevertheless, had a most extraordinary prejudice against American diplomats following the usual custom of adopting a diplomatic uniform.

Some days after my presentation to the Emperor, I was taken to Potsdam, which is situated about half an hour's train journey from Berlin, and, from the station there, driven to the new palace and presented to the Empress. The Empress was most charming and affable, and presented a very distinguished appearance. Accompanied by Mrs. Gerard, and always, either by night or by day, in the infernal dress-suit, I was received by the Crown Prince and Princess, and others of the royal princes and their wives. On these occasions we sat down and did not stand, as when received by the Emperor and Empress, and simply made "polite conversation" for about twenty minutes, being received first by the ladies-in-waiting and aides. These princes were always in uniform of some kind.

At the reception for the *hoffähig* people Mrs. Gerard stood in one room and I in another, and with each of us was a representative of the Emperor's household to introduce the people of the court, and an army officer to introduce the people of the army. The officer assigned to me had the extraordinary name of der Pfortner von der Hoelle, which means the "porter of Hell." I have often wondered since by what prophetic instinct he was sent to introduce me to the two years and a half of world war which I experienced in Berlin. This unfortunate officer, a most charming gentleman, was killed early in the war.

The Berlin season lasts from about the twentieth of January for about six weeks. It is short in duration because, if the *hoffähig* people stay longer than six weeks in Berlin, they become liable to pay their local income tax in Berlin, where the rate is higher than in those parts of Germany where they have their country estates.

The first great court ceremonial is the *Schleppencour,* so-called from the long trains or *Schleppen* worn by the women. On this night we "presented" Mr. and Mrs. Robert K. Cassatt of Philadelphia, Mrs. Ernest Wiltsee, Mrs. and Miss Luce and Mrs. Norman Whitehouse. On the arrival at the palace with these and all the members of the Embassy Staff and their wives, we were shown up a long stair-case, at the top of which a guard of honour, dressed in costume of the time of Frederick the Great, presented arms to all Ambassadors, and ruffled kettle-drums. Through long lines of cadets from the military schools, dressed as pages, in white, with short breeches and powdered wigs, we passed

24

through several rooms where all the people to pass in review were gathered. Behind these, in a room about sixty feet by fifty, on a throne facing the door were the Emperor and Empress, and on the broad steps of this throne were the princes and their wives, the court ladies-in-waiting and all the other members of the court. The wives of the Ambassadors entered the room first, followed at intervals of about twenty feet by the ladies of the Embassy and the ladies to be presented. As they entered the room and made a change of direction toward the throne, pages in white straightened out the ladies' trains with long sticks. Arrived opposite the throne and about twenty feet from it, each Ambassador's wife made a low curtsey and then stood on the foot of the throne, to the left of the Emperor and Empress, and as each lady of the Embassy, not before presented, and each lady to be presented stopped beside the throne and made a low curtsy, the Ambassadress had to call out the name of each one in a loud voice; and when the last one had passed she followed her out of the room, walking sideways so as not to turn her back on the royalties,—something of a feat when towing a train about fifteen feet long. When all the Ambassadresses had so passed, it was the turn of the Ambassadors, who carried out substantially the same programme, substituting low bows

for curtsies. The Ambassadors were followed
by the Ministers' wives, these by the Ministers
and these by the dignitaries of the German
Court. All passed into the adjoining hall, and
there a buffet supper was served. The whole affair began at about eight o'clock and was over
in an hour.

At the court balls, which also began early in
the evening, a different procedure was followed.
There the guests were required to assemble before eight-twenty in the ball-room. As in the
Schleppencour, on one side of the room was the
throne with seats for the Emperor and Empress,
and to the right of this throne were the chairs
for the Ambassadors' wives who were seated in
the order of their husbands' rank, with the ladies
of their Embassy, and any ladies they had
brought to the ball standing behind them. After
them came the Ministers' wives, sitting in similar
fashion; then the Ambassadors, standing with
their staffs behind them on raised steps, with any
men that they had asked invitations for, and the
Ministers in similar order. To the left of the
throne stood the wives of the Dukes and dignitaries of Germany and then their husbands.
When all were assembled, promptly at the time
announced, the orchestra, which was dressed in
mediæval costume and sat in a gallery, sounded
trumpets and then the Emperor and Empress

entered the room, the Emperor, of course, in uniform, followed by the ladies and gentlemen of the household all in brilliant uniforms, and one or two officers of the court regiment, picked out for their great height and dressed in the kind of uniform Rupert of Hentzau wears on the stage,—a silver helmet surmounted by an eagle, a steel breast-plate, white breeches and coat, and enormous high boots coming half way up the thigh. The Grand Huntsman wore a white wig, three-cornered hat and a long green coat.

On entering the room, the Empress usually commenced on one side and the Emperor on the other, going around the room and speaking to the Ambassadors' wives and Ambassadors, etc., in turn, and the Empress in similar fashion, chatting for a moment with the German dignitaries and their wives lined up on the opposite side of the room. After going perhaps half way around each side, the Emperor and Empress would then change sides. This going around the room and chatting with people in turn is called "making the circle", and young royalties are practised in "making the circle" by being made to go up to the trees in a garden and address a few pleasant words to each tree, in this manner learning one of the principal duties of royalty.

The dancing is only by young women and young officers of noble families who have practised the dances before. They are under the superintendence of several young officers who are known as *Vortänzer* and when any one in Berlin in court society gives a ball these *Vortänzer* are the ones who see that all dancing is conducted strictly according to rule and manage the affairs of the ball-room with true Prussian efficiency. Supper is about ten-thirty at a court ball and is at small tables. Each royalty has a table holding about eight people and to these people are invited without particular rule as to precedence. The younger guests and lower dignitaries are not placed at supper but find places at tables to suit themselves. After supper all go back to the ball-room and there the young ladies and officers, led by the *Vortänzer,* execute a sort of lancers, in the final figure of which long lines are formed of dancers radiating from the throne; and all the dancers make bows and curtsies to the Emperor and Empress who are either standing or sitting at this time on the throne. At about eleven-thirty the ball is over, and as the guests pass out through the long hall, they are given glasses of hot punch and a peculiar sort of local Berlin bun, in order to ward off the lurking dangers of the villainous winter climate.

At the court balls the diplomats are, of course, in their best diplomatic uniform. All Germans are in uniform of some kind, but the women do not wear the long trains worn at the *Schleppen-cour*. They wear ordinary ball dresses. In connection with court dancing it is rather interesting to note that when the tango and turkey trot made their way over the frontiers of Germany in the autumn of 1913, the Emperor issued a special order that no officers of the army or navy should dance any of these dances or should go to the house of any person who, at any time, whether officers were present or not, had allowed any of these new dances to be danced. This effectually extinguished the turkey trot, the bunny hug and the tango, and maintained the waltz and the polka in their old estate. It may seem ridiculous that such a decree should be so solemnly issued, but I believe that the higher authorities in Germany earnestly desired that the people, and, especially, the officers of the army and navy, should learn not to enjoy themselves too much. A great endeavour was always made to keep them in a life, so far as possible, of Spartan simplicity. For instance, the army officers were forbidden to play polo, not because of anything against the game, which, of course, is splendid practice for riding, but because it would make a distinction in the army between rich and poor.

The Emperor's birthday, January twenty-seventh, is a day of great celebration. At nine-thirty in the morning the Ambassadors, Ministers and all the dignitaries of the court attend Divine Service in the chapel of the palace. On this day in 1914, the Queen of Greece and many of the reigning princes of the German States were present. In the evening there was a gala performance in the opera house, the entire house being occupied by members of the court. Between the acts in the large foyer, royalties "made the circle," and I had quite a long conversation with both the Emperor and Empress and was "caught" by the King of Saxony. Many of the Ambassadors have letters of credence not only to the court at Berlin but also to the rulers of the minor German States. For instance, the Belgian Minister was accredited to thirteen countries in Germany and the Spanish Ambassador to eleven. For some reason or other, the American and Turkish Ambassadors are accredited only to the court at Berlin. Some of the German rulers feel this quite keenly, and the King of Saxony, especially. I had been warned that he was very anxious to show his resentment of this distinction by refusing to shake hands with the American Ambassador. He was in the foyer on the occasion of this gala performance and said that he would like to have me presented to him. I,

A SALON IN THE AMERICAN EMBASSY

THE BALLROOM OF THE EMBASSY. THIS WAS AFTERWARD TURNED INTO A
WORKROOM FOR THE RELIEF OF AMERICANS IN WAR DAYS

of course, could not refuse, but forgot the warning of my predecessors and put out my hand, which the King ostentatiously neglected to take. A few moments later the wife of the Turkish Ambassador was presented to the King of Saxony and received a similar rebuff; but, as she was a daughter of the Khedive of Egypt, and therefore a Royal Highness in her own right, she went around the King of Saxony, seized his hand, which he had put behind him, brought it around to the front and shook it warmly, a fine example of great presence of mind.

Writing of all these things and looking out from a sky-scraper in New York, these details of court life seem very frivolous and far away. But an Ambassador is compelled to become part of this system. The most important conversations with the Emperor sometimes take place at court functions, and the Ambassador and his secretaries often gather their most useful bits of information over tea cups or with the cigars after dinner.

Aside from the short season, Berlin is rather dull; Bismarck characterised it as a "desert of bricks and newspapers."

In addition to making visits to the royalties, custom required me to call first upon the Imperial Chancellor and the Minister of Foreign Affairs. The other ministers are supposed to call first, although I believe the redoubtable von Tirpitz claimed a different rule. So, during the first winter I gradually made the acquaintance of those people who sway the destinies of the German Empire and its seventy millions.

I dined with the Emperor and had long conversations with him on New Year's Day and at the two court balls.

All during this winter Germans from the highest down tried to impress me with the great danger which they said threatened America from Japan. The military and naval attachés and I were told that the German information system sent news that Mexico was full of Japanese colonels and America of Japanese spies. Possibly much of the prejudice in America against the Japanese was cooked up by the German propagandists whom we later learned to know so well.

It is noteworthy that during the whole of my first winter in Berlin I was not officially or semi-officially afforded an opportunity to meet any of the members of the Reichstag or any of the leaders in the business world. The great merchants, whose acquaintance I made, as well as the literary and artistic people, I had to seek out; because most of them were not *hoffähig* and I did not come in contact with them at any court functions, official dinners or even in the houses of the court nobles or those connected with the government.

32

A very interesting character whom I met during the first winter and often conversed with, was Prince Henkel-Donnersmarck. Prince Donnersmarck, who died December, 1916, at the age of eighty-six years, was the richest male subject in Germany, the richest subject being Frau von Krupp-Böhlen, the heiress of the Krupp cannon foundry. He was the first governor of Lorraine during the war of 1870 and had had a finger in all of the political and commercial activities of Germany for more than half a century. He told me, on one occasion, that he had advocated exacting a war indemnity of thirty milliards from France after the war of 1870, and said that France could easily pay it—and that that sum or much more should be exacted as an indemnity at the conclusion of the World War of 1914. He said that he had always advocated a protective tariff for agricultural products in Germany as well as encouragement of the German manufacturing interests: that agriculture was necessary to the country in order to provide strong soldiers for war, and manufacturing industries to provide money to pay for the army and navy and their equipment. He made me promise to take his second son to America in order that he might see American life, and the great iron and coal districts of Pennsylvania. Of course, most of these conversations took place

before the World War. After two years of that
war and, as prospects of paying the expenses of
the war from the indemnities to be exacted from
the enemies of Germany gradually melted away,
the Prince quite naturally developed a great
anxiety as to how the expenses of the war should
be paid by Germany; and I am sure that this
anxiety had much to do with his death at the
end of the year, 1916.

Custom demanded that I should ask for an
appointment and call on each of the Ambassadors on arrival. The British Ambassador was
Sir Edward Goschen, a man of perhaps sixty-
eight years, a widower. He spoke French, of
course, and German; and, accompanied by his
dog, was a frequent visitor at our house. I am
very grateful for the help and advice he so gen-
erously gave me—doubly valuable as coming
from a man of his fame and experience. Jules
Cambon was the Ambassador of France. His
brother, Paul, is Ambassador to the Court of St.
James. Jules Cambon is well-known to Americans, having passed five years in this country.
He was Ambassador to Spain for five years, and,
at the time of my arrival, had been about the
same period at Berlin. In spite of his long residence in each of these countries, he spoke only
French; but he possessed a really marvellous insight into the political life of each of these na-

tions. Bollati, the Italian Ambassador, was a great admirer of Germany; he spoke German well and did everything possible to keep Italy out of war with her former Allies in the Triple Alliance.

Spain was represented by Polo de Bernabe, who now represents the interests of the United States in Germany, as well as those of France, Russia, Belgium, Serbia and Roumania. It is a curious commentary on the absurdity of war that, on leaving Berlin, I handed over the interests of the United States to this Ambassador, who, as Spanish minister to the United States, was handed his passports at the outbreak of the Spanish-American war! I am sure that not only he, but all his Embassy, will devotedly represent our interests in Germany. Sverbeeu represented the interests of Russia; Soughimoura, Japan; and Mouktar Pascha, Turkey. The wife of the latter was a daughter of the Khedive of Egypt, and Mouktar Pascha himself a general of distinction in the Turkish army.

An Ambassador must keep on intimate terms with his colleagues. It is often through them that he learns of important matters affecting his own country or others. All of these Ambassadors and most of the Ministers occupied handsome houses furnished by their government.

35

They had large salaries and a fund for entertaining.

During this first winter before the war, I saw a great deal of the German Crown Prince as well as of several of his brothers.

I cannot subscribe to the general opinion of the Crown Prince. I found him a most agreeable man, a sharp observer and the possessor of intellectual attainments of no mean order. He is undoubtedly popular in Germany, excelling in all sports, a fearless rider and a good shot. He is ably seconded by the Crown Princess. The mother of the Crown Princess is a Russian Grand Duchess, and her father was a Duke of Mecklenburg-Schwerin. She is a very beautiful woman made popular by her affable manners. The one defect of the Crown Prince has been his eagerness for war; but, as he has characterised this war as the most stupid ever waged in history, perhaps he will be satisfied, if he comes to the throne, with what all Germany has suffered in this conflict.

The Crown Prince was very anxious, before the war, to visit the United States; and we had practically arranged to make a trip to Alaska in search of some of the big game there, with stops at the principal cities of America.

The second son of the Kaiser, Prince Eitel Fritz, is considered by the Germans to have distinguished himself most in this war. He is given credit for great personal bravery.

Prince Adalbert, the sailor prince, is quite American in his manners. In February, 1914, the Crown Prince and Princes Eitel Fritz and Adalbert came to our Embassy for a very small dance to which were asked all the pretty American girls then in Berlin.

It is never the custom to invite royalties to an entertainment. They invite themselves to a dance or a dinner, and the list of proposed guests is always submitted to them. When a royalty arrives at the house, the host (and the hostess, if the royalty be a woman) always waits at the front door and escorts the royalties up-stairs.

Allison Armour also gave a dance at which the Crown Prince was present, following a dinner at the Automobile Club. Armour has been a constant visitor to Germany for many years, usually going in his yacht to Kiel in summer and to Corfu, where the Emperor goes, in winter. As he has never tried to obtain anything from the Emperor, he has become quite intimate with him and with all the members of the royal family.

The Chancellor, von Bethmann-Hollweg, is an enormous man of perhaps six feet five or six. He comes of a banking family in Frankfort. It is too soon to give a just estimate of his acts in this war. When I arrived in Berlin and until November, 1916, von Jagow was Minister of Foreign Affairs. In past years he had occupied the post of Ambassador to Italy, and with great reluctance took his place at the head of the Foreign Office. Zimmermann was an Under Secretary, succeeding von Jagow when the latter was practically forced out of office. Zimmermann, on account of his plain and hearty manners and democratic air, was more of a favourite with the Ambassadors and members of the Reichstag than von Jagow, who, in appearance and manner, was the ideal old-style diplomat of the stage.

Von Jagow was not a good speaker and the agitation against him was started by those who claimed that, in answering questions in the Reichstag, he did not make a forceful enough appearance on behalf of the government. Von Jagow did not cultivate the members of the Reichstag and his delicate health prevented him from undertaking more than the duties of his office.

As a matter of fact, I believe that von Jagow had a juster estimate of foreign nations than Zimmermann, and more correctly divined the thoughts of the American people in this war than did his successor. I thought that I enjoyed the personal friendship of both von Jagow and Zimmermann and, therefore, was rather unpleasantly surprised when I saw in the papers that Zimmermann had stated in the Reichstag that he had been compelled, from motives of policy, to keep on friendly terms with me. I sincerely hope that what he said on this occasion was incorrectly reported. Von Jagow, after his fall, took charge of a hospital at Libau in the occupied portion of Russia. This shows the devotion to duty of the Prussian noble class, and their readiness to take up any task, however humble, that may help their country.

CHAPTER II

MY commission read, "Ambassador to Germany."

It is characteristic of our deep ignorance of all foreign affairs that I was appointed Ambassador to a place which does not exist. Politically, there is no such place as "Germany." There are the twenty-five States, Prussia, Bavaria, Württemberg, Saxony, etc., which make up the "German Empire," but there is no such political entity as "Germany."

These twenty-five States have votes in the Bundesrat, a body which may be said to correspond remotely to our United States Senate. But each State has a different number of votes. Prussia has seventeen, Bavaria six, Württemberg and Saxony four each, Baden and Hesse three each, Mecklenburg-Schwerin and Brunswick two each, and the rest one each. Prussia controls Brunswick.

The Reichstag, or Imperial Parliament, corresponds to our House of Representatives. The members are elected by manhood suffrage of those over twenty-five. But in practice the Reichstag is nothing but a debating society because of the preponderating power of the Bundesrat, or upper chamber. At the head of the ministry is the Chancellor, appointed by the Emperor; and the other Ministers, such as Colonies, Interior, Education, Justice and Foreign Affairs, are but underlings of the Chancellor and appointed by him. The Chancellor is not responsible to the Reichstag, as Bethmann-Hollweg clearly stated at the time of the Zabern affair, but only to the Emperor.

It is true that an innovation properly belonging only to a parliamentary government was introduced some seven years ago, viz., that the ministers must answer questions (as in Great Britain) put them by the members of the Reichstag. But there the likeness to a parliamentary government begins and ends.

The members of the Bundesrat are named by the Princes of the twenty-five States making up the German Empire. Prussia, which has seventeen votes, may name seventeen members of the Bundesrat or one member, who, however, when he votes casts seventeen votes. The votes of a State must always be cast as a unit. In the usual procedure bills are prepared and adopted in the Bundesrat and then sent to the Reichstag whence, if passed, they return to the Bundesrat where the final approval must take place. Therefore, in practice, the Bundesrat makes the laws with the assent of the Reichstag. The members of the Bundesrat have the right to appear and make speeches in the Reichstag. The fundamental constitution of the German Empire is not changed, as with us, by a separate body but is changed in the same way that an ordinary law is passed; except that if there are fourteen votes against the proposed change in the Bundesrat the proposition is defeated, and, further, the constitution cannot be changed with respect to rights expressly granted by it to any one of the twenty-five States without the assent of that State.

In order to pass a law a majority vote in the Bundesrat and Reichstag is sufficient if there is a quorum present, and a quorum is a majority of the members elected in the Reichstag: in the Bundesrat the quorum consists of such members as are present at a regularly called meeting, providing the Chancellor or the Vice-Chancellor attends.

The boundaries of the districts sending members to the Reichstag have not been changed since 1872, while, in the meantime, a great shifting of population, as well as great increase of population has taken place. And because of this, the Reichstag to-day does not represent the people of Germany in the sense intended by the framers of the Imperial Constitution.

Much of the legislation that affects the every-day life of a German emanates from the parliaments of Prussia, Bavaria and Saxony, etc., as with us in our State Legislatures. The purely legislative power of the ministers and Bundesrat is, however, large. These German States have constitutions of some sort. The Grand Duchies of Mecklenburg have no constitution whatever. It is understood that the people themselves do not want one, on financial grounds, fearing that many expenses now borne by the Grand Duke out of his large private income, would be saddled on the people. The other States have Constitutions varying in form. In Prussia there are a House of Lords and a House of Deputies. The members of the latter are elected by a system of circle votes, by which the vote of one rich man voting in circle number one counts as much as thousands voting in circle number three. It is the recognition by Bethmann-Hollweg that this vicious system must be changed that brought down on him the wrath of the Prussian country squires, who for so long have ruled the German Empire, filling places, civil and military, with their children and relatives.

In considering Germany, the immense influence of the military party must not be left out of account; and, with the developments of the navy, that branch of the service also claimed a share in guiding the policy of the Government.

The administrative, executive and judicial officers of Prussia are not elected. The country is governed and judged by men who enter this branch of the government service exactly as others enter the army or navy. These are gradually promoted through the various grades. This applies to judges, clerks of courts, district attorneys and the officials who govern the political divisions of Prussia, for Prussia is divided into circles, presidencies and provinces. For instance, a young man may enter the government service as assistant to the clerk of some court. He may then become district attorney in a small town, then clerk of a larger court, possibly attached to the police presidency of a large city; he may then become a minor judge, etc., until finally he becomes a judge of one of the higher courts or an over-president of a province. Practically the only elective officers who have any power are members of the Reichstag and the Prussian Legislature, and there, as I have shown, the power is very small. Mayors and City Councillors are elected in Prussia, but have little power; and are elected by the vicious system of circle voting.

Time and again during the course of the Great War when I made some complaint or request af-

fecting the interests of one of the various nations I represented, I was met in the Foreign Office by the statement, "We can do nothing with
the military. Please read Bismarck's memoirs
and you will see what difficulty he had with the
military." Undoubtedly, owing to the fact that
the Chancellor seldom took strong ground, the
influence which both the army and navy claimed
in dictating the policy of the Empire was greatly
increased.

Roughly speaking there are three great political divisions or parties in the German Reichstag.
To the right of the presiding officer sit the Conservatives. Most of these are members from the
Prussian Junker or squire class. They are strong
for the rights of the crown and against any extension of the suffrage in Prussia or anywhere
else. They form probably the most important
body of conservatives now existing in any country in the world. Their leader, Heydebrand, is
known as the uncrowned king of Prussia. On
the left side the Social Democrats sit. As they
evidently oppose the kingship and favour a republic, no Social Democratic member has ever
been called into the government. They represent
the great industrial populations of Germany.
Roughly, they constitute about one-third of the
Reichstag, and would sit there in greater numbers if Germany were again redistricted so that

proper representation were given to the cities, to which there has been a great rush of population since the time when the Reichstag districts were originally constituted.

In the centre, and holding the balance of power, sit the members of the Centrum or Catholic body. Among them are many priests. It is noteworthy that in this war Roman Catholic opinion in neutral countries, like Spain, inclines to the side of Germany; while in Germany, to protect their religious liberties, the Catholic population vote as Catholics to send Catholic members to the Reichstag, and these sit and vote as Catholics alone.

Germans high in rank in the government often told me that no part of conquered Poland would ever be incorporated in Prussia or the Empire, because it was not desirable to add to the Roman Catholic population; that they had troubles enough with the Catholics now in Germany and had no desire to add to their numbers. This, and the desire to lure the Poles into the creation of a national army which could be utilised by the German machine, were the reasons for the creation by Germany (with the assent of Austria) of the new country of Poland.

This Catholic party is the result in Germany of the *Kulturkampf,* or War for Civilisation, as it was called by Bismarck, a contest dating from

1870 between the State in Germany and the Roman Catholic Church.

Prussia has always been the centre of Protestantism in Germany, although there are many Roman Catholics in the Rhine Provinces of Prussia, and in that part of Prussia inhabited principally by Poles, originally part of the Kingdom of Poland.

Baden and Bavaria, the two principal South German States, and others are Catholic. In 1870, on the withdrawal of the French garrison from Rome, the Temporal Power of the Pope ended, and Bismarck, though appealed to by Catholics, took no interest in the defence of the Papacy. The conflict between the Roman Catholics and the Government in Germany was precipitated by the promulgation by the Vatican Council, in 1870, of the Dogma of the Infallibility of the Pope.

A certain number of German pastors and bishops refused to subscribe to the new dogma. In the conflict that ensued these pastors and bishops were backed by the government. The religious orders were suppressed, civil marriage made compulsory and the State assumed new powers not only in the appointment but even in the education of the Catholic priests. The Jesuits were expelled from Germany in 1872. These measures, generally known as the May Laws, because passed in May, 1873, 1874 and 1875, led to the creation and strengthening of the Centrum or Catholic party. For a long period many churches were vacant in Prussia. Finally, owing to the growth of the Centrum, Bismarck gave in. The May Laws were rescinded in 1886 and the religious orders, the Jesuits excepted, were permitted to return in 1887. Civil marriage, however, remained obligatory in Prussia.

Ever since the *Kulturkampf* the Centrum has held the balance of power in Germany, acting sometimes with the Conservatives and sometimes with the Social Democrats.

In addition to these three great parties, there are minor parties and groups which sometimes act with one party and sometimes with another, the National Liberals, for example, and the Progressives. Since the war certain members of the National Liberal party were most bitter in assailing President Wilson and the United States. In the demand for ruthless submarine war they acted with the Conservatives. There are also Polish, Hanoverian, Danish and Alsatian members of the Reichstag.

There are three great race questions in Germany. First of all, that of Alsace-Lorraine. It is unnecessary to go at length into this well-known question. In the chapter on the affair at Zabern, something will be seen of the attitude of the troops toward the civil population. At the outbreak of the war several of the deputies, sitting in the Reichstag as members from Alsace-Lorraine, crossed the frontier and joined the French army.

If there is one talent which the Germans superlatively lack, it is that of ruling over other peoples and inducing other people to become part of their nation.

It is now a long time since portions of the Kingdom of Poland, by various partitions of that kingdom, were incorporated with Prussia, but the Polish question is more alive to-day than at the time of the last partition.

The Poles are of a livelier race than the Germans, are Roman Catholics and always retain their dream of a reconstituted and independent Kingdom of Poland.

It is hard to conceive that Poland was at one time perhaps the most powerful kingdom of Europe, with a population numbering twenty millions and extending from the Baltic to the Carpathians and the Black Sea, including in its territory the basins of the Warta, Vistula, Dwina, Dnieper and Upper Dniester, and that it had under its dominion besides Poles proper and the Baltic Slavs, the Lithuanians, the White Russians and the Little Russians or Ruthenians.

The Polish aristocracy was absolutely incapable of governing its own country, which fell an easy prey to the intrigues of Frederick the Great and the two Empresses, Maria Theresa of Austria and Catherine of Russia. The last partition of Poland was in the year 1795.

Posen, at one time one of the capitals of the old kingdom of Poland, is the intellectual centre of that part of Poland which has been incorporated into Prussia. For years Prussia has alternately cajoled and oppressed the Poles, and has made every endeavour to replace the Polish inhabitants with German colonists. A commission has been established which buys estates from Poles and sells them to Germans. This commission has the power of condemning the lands of Poles, taking these lands from them by force, compensating them at a rate determined by the commission and settling Germans on the lands so seized. This commission has its headquarters in Posen. The result has not been successful. All the country side surrounding Posen and the city itself are divided into two factions. By going to one hotel or the other you announce that you are pro-German or pro-Polish. Poles will not deal in shops kept by Germans or in shops unless the signs are in Polish.

The sons of Germans who have settled in Poland under the protection of the commission often marry Polish women. The invariable result of these mixed marriages is that the children are Catholics and Poles. Polish deputies voting as Poles sit in the Prussian legislature and in the Reichstag, and if a portion of the old Kingdom of Poland is made a separate country at the end of this war, it will have the effect of making the Poles in Prussia more restless and more aggressive than ever.

In order to win the sympathies of the Poles, the Emperor caused a royal castle to be built within recent years in the city of Posen, and appointed a popular Polish gentleman who had served in the Prussian army and was attached to the Emperor, the Count Hutten-Czapski, as its lord-warden. In this castle was a very beautiful Byzantine chapel built from designs especially selected by the Emperor. In January, 1914, we went with Allison Armour and the Cassatts, Mrs. Wiltsee and Mrs. Whitehouse on a trip to Posen to see this chapel.

Some of our German friends tried to play a joke on us by telling us that the best hotel was the hotel patronised by the Poles. To have gone there would have been to declare ourselves anti-German and pro-Polish, but we were warned in time. The castle has a large throne room and ball-room; in the hall is a stuffed aurochs killed by the Emperor. The aurochs is a species of buffalo greatly resembling those which used to roam our western prairies. The breed has been preserved on certain great estates in eastern Germany and in the hunting forests of the Czar in the neighbourhood of Warsaw.

Some of the Poles told me that at the first attempt to give a court ball in this new castle the Polish population in the streets threw ink through the carriage windows on the dresses of the ladies going to the ball and thus made it a failure. The chapel of the castle is very beautiful and is a great credit to the Emperor's taste as an architect.

While being shown through the Emperor's private apartments in this castle, I noticed a saddle on a sort of elevated stool in front of a desk. I asked the guide what this was for: he told me that the Emperor, when working, always sits in a saddle.

In Posen, in a book-store, the proprietor brought out for me a number of books caricaturing the German rule of Alsace-Lorraine. It is curious that a community of interests should make a market for these books in Polish Posen.

Although not so well advertised, the Polish question is as acute as that of Alsace-Lorraine.

After its successful war in 1866 against Austria, Bavaria, Saxony, Baden, Hanover, etc., Prussia became possessed of the two duchies of Schleswig-Holstein, which are to the south of

Denmark on the Jutland Peninsula. Here, strangely enough, there is a Danish question. A number of Danes inhabit these duchies and have been irritated by the Prussian officials and officers into preserving their national feeling intact ever since 1866. Galling restrictions have been made, the very existence of which intensifies the hatred and prevents the assimilation of these Danes. For instance, Amundsen, the Arctic explorer, was forbidden to lecture in Danish in these duchies during the winter of 1913-14, and there were regulations enforced preventing more than a certain number of these Danish people from assembling in a hotel, as well as regulations against the employment of Danish servants.

In 1866, after its successful war, Prussia wiped out the old kingdom of Hanover and drove its king into exile in Austria. To-day there is still a party of protest against this aggression. The Kaiser believes, however, that the ghost of the claim of the Kings of Hanover was laid when he married his only daughter to the heir of the House of Hanover and gave the young pair the vacant Duchy of Brunswick. That this young man will inherit the great Guelph treasure was no drawback to the match in the eyes of those in Berlin.

There is a hatred of Prussia in other parts of Germany, but coupled with so much fear that it will never take practical shape. In Bavaria, for example, even the comic newspapers have for years ridiculed the Prussians and the House of Hohenzollern. The smashing defeat by Prussia of Austria and the allied German States, Bavaria, Saxony, Hesse, Hanover, etc., in 1866, and the growth of Prussianism since then in all of these countries, keep the people from any overt act. It is a question, perhaps, as to how these countries, especially Bavaria, would act in case of the utter defeat of Germany. But at present they must be counted on only as faithful servants, in a military way, of the German Emperor.

Montesquieu, the author of the "Esprit des Lois," says, "All law comes from the soil," and it has been claimed that residence in the hot climate of the tropics in some measure changes Anglo-Saxon character. It is, therefore, always well in judging national character to know something of the physical characteristics and climate of the country which a nation inhabits.

The heart of modern Germany is the great north central plain which comprises practically all of the original kingdom of Prussia, stretching northward from the Saxon and Hartz mountains to the North and Baltic seas. It is from this dreary and infertile plain that for many centuries conquering military races have poured over Europe. The climate is not so cold in winter as that of the northern part of the United States. There is much rain and the winter skies are so dark that the absence of the sun must have some effect upon the character of the people. The Saxons inhabit a more mountainous country; Württemberg and Baden are hilly; Bavaria is a land of beauty, diversified with lovely lakes and mountains. The soft outlines of the vine-covered hills of the Rhine Valley have long been the admiration of travellers.

The inhabitants of Prussia were originally not Germanic, but rather Slavish in type; and, indeed, to-day in the forest of the River Spree, on which Berlin is situated, and only about fifty miles from that city, there still dwell descendants of the original Wendish inhabitants of the country who speak the Wendish language. The wet-nurses, whose picturesque dress is so noticeable on the streets of Berlin, all come from this Wendish colony, which has been preserved through the many wars that have swept over this part of Germany because of the refuge afforded in the swamps and forests of this district.

The inhabitants of the Rhine Valley drink wine instead of beer. They are more lively in their disposition than the Prussians, Saxons and Bavarians, who are of a heavy and phlegmatic nature. The Bavarians are noted for their prowess as beer drinkers, and it is not at all unusual for

55

prosperous burghers of Munich to dispose of thirty large glasses of beer in a day; hence the cures which exist all over Germany and where the average German business man spends part, at least, of his annual vacation.

In peace times the Germans are heavy eaters. As some one says, "It is not true that the Germans eat all the time, but they eat all the time except during seven periods of the day when they take their meals." And it is a fact that prosperous merchants of Berlin, before the war, had seven meals a day; first breakfast at a comfortably early hour; second breakfast at about eleven, of perhaps a glass of milk or perhaps a glass of beer and sandwiches; a very heavy lunch of four or five courses with wine and beer; coffee and cakes at three; tea and sandwiches or sandwiches and beer at about five; a strong dinner with several kinds of wines at about seven or seven-thirty; and a substantial supper before going to bed.

The Germans are wonderful judges of wines, and, at any formal dinner, use as many as eight varieties. The best wine is passed in glasses on trays, and the guests are not expected, of course, to take this wine unless they actually desire to drink it. I know one American woman who was stopping at a Prince's castle in Hungary and who, on the first night, allowed the butler to fill her glasses with wine which she did not drink. The second evening the butler passed her sternly by, and she was offered no more wine during her stay in the castle.

Many of the doctors who were with me thought that the heavy eating and large consumption of wine and beer had unfavourably affected the German national character, and had made the people more aggressive and irritable and consequently readier for war. The influence of diet on national character should not be under-estimated. Meat-eating nations have always ruled vegetarians.

CHAPTER III

DURING this first winter in Berlin, I spent each morning in the Embassy office, and, if I had any business at the Foreign Office, called there about five o'clock in the afternoon. It was the custom that all Ambassadors should call on Tuesday afternoons at the Foreign Office, going in to see the Foreign Minister in the order of their arrival in the waiting-room, and to have a short talk with him about current diplomatic affairs.

In the previous chapter I have given a detailed account of the ceremonies of court life, because a knowledge of this life is essential to a grasp of the spirit which animates those ruling the destinies of the German Empire.

My first winter, however, was not all cakes and ale. There were several interesting bits of diplomatic work. First, we were then engaged in our conflict with Huerta, the Dictator of Mexico, and it was part of my work to secure from Germany promises that she would not recognise this Mexican President.

I also spent a great deal of time in endeavouring to get the German Government to take part officially in the San Francisco Fair, but, so far as I could make out, Great Britain, probably at the instance of Germany, seemed to have entered into some sort of agreement, or at any rate a tacit understanding, that neither country would participate officially in this Exposition.

After the lamentable failure of the Jamestown Exposition, the countries of Europe were certainly not to be blamed for not spending their money in aid of a similar enterprise. But I believe that the attitude of Germany had a deeper significance, and that certain, at least, of the German statesmen had contemplated a *rapprochement* with Great Britain and a mutual spanking of America and its Monroe Doctrine by these two great powers. Later I was informed, by a man high in the German Foreign Office, that Germany had proposed to Great Britain a joint intervention in Mexico, an invasion which would have put an end forever to the Monroe Doctrine, of course to be followed by the forceful colonisation of Central and South America by European Powers. I was told that Great Britain refused. But whether this proposition and refusal in fact were made, can be learned from the archives of the British Foreign Office.

During this period of trouble with Mexico,

the German Press, almost without exception, and especially that part of it controlled by the Government and by the Conservatives or Junkers, was most bitter in its attitude towards America.

The reason for this was the underlying hatred of an autocracy for a successful democracy, envy of the wealth, liberty and commercial success of America, and a deep and strong resentment against the Monroe Doctrine which prevented Germany from using her powerful fleet and great military force to seize a foothold in the Western hemisphere.

Germany came late into the field of colonisation in her endeavour to find "a place in the sun." The colonies secured were not habitable by white men. Togo, Kameroons, German East Africa, are too tropical in climate, too subject to tropical diseases, ever to become successful German colonies. German Southwest Africa has a more healthy climate but is a barren land. About the only successful industry there has been that of gathering the small diamonds that were discovered in the sands of the beaches and of the deserts running back from the sea.

On the earnest request of Secretary Bryan, I endeavoured to persuade the German authorities to have Germany become a signatory to the so-called Bryan Peace Treaties. After many efforts and long interviews, von Jagow, the Foreign Minister, finally told me that Germany would not sign these treaties because the greatest asset of Germany in war was her readiness for a sudden assault, that they had no objection to signing the treaty with America, but that they feared they would then be immediately asked to sign similar treaties with Great Britain, France and Russia, that if they refused to sign with these countries the refusal would almost be equivalent to a declaration of war, and, if they did sign, intending in good faith to stand by the treaty, that Germany would be deprived of her greatest asset in war, namely, her readiness for a sudden and overpowering attack.

✓I also, during this first winter, studied and made reports on the commercial situation of Germany and especially the German discriminations against American goods. To these matters I shall refer in more detail in another chapter.

Opposition and attention to the oil monopoly project also occupied a great part of my working hours. Petroleum is used very extensively in Germany for illuminating purposes by the poorer part of the population, especially in the farming villages and industrial towns. This oil used in Germany comes from two sources of supply, from America and from the oil wells of Galicia and Roumania. The German American Oil Company there, through which the American oil was dis-

tributed, although a German company, was controlled by American capital, and German capital
was largely interested in the Galician and Roumanian oil fields. The oil from Galicia and Roumania is not so good a quality as that imported
from America.

Before my arrival in Germany the government had proposed a law creating the oil monopoly; that is to say, a company was to be created, controlled by the government for the purpose of carrying on the entire oil business of
Germany, and no other person or company, by
its provisions, was to be allowed to sell any illuminating oil or similar products in the Empire.
The bill provided that the business of those engaged in the wholesale selling of oil, and their
plants, etc., should be taken over by this government company, condemned and paid for. The
German American Company, however, had also
a retail business and plant throughout Germany
for which it was proposed that no compensation
should be given. The government bill also contained certain curious "jokers"; for instance, it
provided for the taking over of all plants
"within the customs limit of the German Empire," thus leaving out of the compensation a refinery which was situated in the free port of
Hamburg, although, of course, by operation of
this monopoly bill the refinery was rendered use-

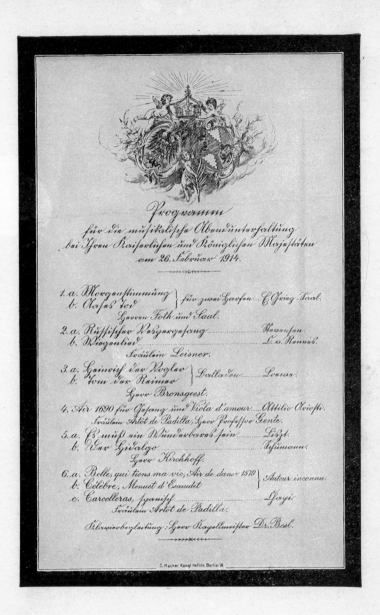

PROGRAMME OF THE MUSIC AFTER DINNER WITH THE KAISER
AT THE ROYAL PALACE, BERLIN

less to the American controlled company which owned it.

In the course of this investigation it came to light that the Prussian state railways were used as a means of discriminating against the American oil. American oil came to Germany through the port of Hamburg, and the Galician and Roumanian oil through the frontier town of Oderberg. Taking a delivery point equally distant between Oderberg and Hamburg, the rate charged on oil from Hamburg to this point was twice as great as that charged for a similar quantity of oil from Oderberg.

I took up this fight on the line that the company must be compensated for all of its property, that used in retail as well as in wholesale business, and, second, that it must be compensated for the good-will of its business, which it had built up through a number of years by the expenditure of very large sums of money. Of course where a company has been in operation for years and is continually advertising its business, its good-will often is its greatest asset and has often been built up by the greatest expenditure of money. For instance, in buying a successful newspaper, the value does not lie in the real-estate, presses, etc., but in the good-will of the newspaper, the result of years of work and expensive advertising.

63

I made no objection that the German government did not have a perfect right to create this monopoly and to put the American controlled company entirely out of the field, but insisted upon a fair compensation for all their property and good-will. Even a fair compensation for the property and good-will would have started the government monopoly company with a large debt upon which it would have been required to pay interest, and this interest, of course, would have been added to the cost of oil to the German consumers. In my final conversation on the subject with von Bethmann-Hollweg, he said, "You don't mean to say that President Wilson and Secretary Bryan will do anything for the Standard Oil Company?" I answered that every one in America knew that the Standard Oil Company had neither influence with nor control over President Wilson and Secretary Bryan, but that they both could and would give the Standard Oil Company the same measure of protection which any American citizen doing business abroad had a right to expect from his government. I also said that I thought they had done enough for the Germans interested in the Galician and Roumanian oil fields when they had used the Prussian state railways to give these oil producers an unfair advantage over those importing American oil.

Shortly after this the question of the creation

of this oil monopoly was dropped and naturally has not been revived during the war, and I very much doubt whether, after the war, the people of liberalised Germany will consent to pay more for inferior oil in order to make good the investments of certain German banks and financiers in Galicia and Roumania. I doubt whether a more liberal Germany will wish to put the control of a great business in the hands of the government, thereby greatly increasing the number of government officials and the weight of government influence in the country. Heaven knows there are officials enough to-day in Germany, without turning over a great department of private industry to the government for the sole purpose of making good bad investments of certain financiers and adding to the political influence of the central government.

In May, 1914, Colonel House and his beautiful wife arrived to pay us a visit in Berlin. He was, of course, anxious to have a talk with the Emperor, and this was arranged by the Emperor inviting the Colonel and me to what is called the *Schrippenfest,* at the new palace at Potsdam.

For many years, in fact since the days of Frederick the Great, the learning (*Lehr*) battalion, composed of picked soldiers from all the regiments of Prussia, has been quartered at Pots-

dam, and on a certain day in April this battalion
has been given a dinner at which they eat white
rolls (*Schrippen*) instead of the usual black
bread. This feast has been carried on from these
older days and has become quite a ceremony.

The Colonel and I motored to Potsdam, arrayed in dress-suits, and waited in one of the
salons of the ground floor of the new palace.
Finally the Emperor and the Empress and several of the Princes and their wives and the usual
dignitaries of the Emperor's household arrived.
The Colonel was presented to the royalties and
then a Divine Service was held in the open air
at one end of the palace. The Empress and
Princesses occupied large chairs and the Emperor
stood with his sons behind him and then the various dignitaries of the court. The Lehr Battalion
was drawn up behind. There were a large band
and the choir boys from the Berlin cathedral.
The service was very impressive and not less so
because of a great Zeppelin which hovered over
our heads during the whole of the service.

After Divine Service, the Lehr Battalion
marched in review and then was given food and
beer in long arbours constructed in front of the
palace. While the men were eating, the Emperor
and Empress and Princes passed among the tables, speaking to the soldiers. We then went to
the new palace where in the extraordinary hall

studded with curious specimens of minerals from all countries, a long table forming three sides of a square was set for about sixty people. Colonel House and I sat directly across the table from the Emperor, with General Falkenhayn between us. The Emperor was in a very good mood and at one time, talking across the table, said to me that the Colonel and I, in our black dress-suits, looked like a couple of crows, that we were like two undertakers at a feast and spoiled the picture. After luncheon the Emperor had a long talk with Colonel House, and then called me into the conversation.

On May twenty-sixth, I arranged that the Colonel should meet von Tirpitz at dinner in our house. We did not guess then what a central figure in this war the great admiral was going to be. At that time and until his fall, he was Minister of Marine, which corresponds to our Secretary of the Navy Department, and what is called in German *Reichsmarineamt*. The Colonel also met von Bethmann-Hollweg, von Jagow, Zimmermann and many others.

There are two other heads of departments, connected with the navy, of equal rank with the Secretary of the Naval Department and not reporting to him. These are the heads of the naval staff and the head of what is known as the Marine Cabinet. The head of the naval staff is supposed to direct the actual operations of warfare in the navy, and the head of the Marine Cabinet is charged with the personnel of the navy, with determining what officers are to be promoted and what officers are to take over ships or commands.

While von Tirpitz was Secretary of the Navy, by the force of his personality, he dominated the two other departments, but since his fall the heads of these two other departments have held positions as important, if not more important, than that of Secretary of the Navy.

On May thirty-first, we took Colonel and Mrs. House to the aviation field of Joachimsthal. Here the Dutch aviator Fokker was flying and after being introduced to us he did some stunts for our benefit. Fokker was employed by the German army and later became a naturalised German. The machines designed by him, and named after him, for a long time held the mastery of the air on the West front.

The advice of Colonel House, a most wise and prudent counsellor, was at all times of the greatest value to me during my stay in Berlin. We exchanged letters weekly, I sending him a weekly bulletin of the situation in Berlin and much news and gossip too personal or too indefinite to be placed in official reports.

War with Germany seemed a thing not even

to be considered when in this month of May, 1914, I called on the Foreign Office, by direction, to thank the Imperial Government for the aid given the Americans at Tampico by German ships of war.

Early in February, Mr. S. Bergmann, a German who had made a fortune in America and who had returned to Germany to take up again his German citizenship, invited me to go over the great electrical works which he had established. Prince Henry of Prussia, the brother of the Emperor, was the only other guest and together we inspected the vast works, afterwards having lunch in Mr. Bergmann's office. Prince Henry has always been interested in America since his visit here. On that visit he spent most of his time with German societies, etc. Of course, now we know he came as a propagandist with the object of welding together the Germans in America and keeping up their interest in the Fatherland. He made a similar trip to the Argentine just before the Great War, with a similar purpose, but I understand his excursion was not considered a great success, from any standpoint. A man of affable manners, no one is better qualified to go abroad as a German propagandist than he. If all Germans had been like him there would have been no World War in 1914.

On March eighteenth, we were invited to a

fancy-dress ball at the palace of the Crown
Prince. The guests were mostly young people
and officers. The Crown Princess wore a beautiful Russian dress with its characteristic high
front piece on the head. The Crown Prince and
all the officers present were in the picturesque
uniforms of their respective regiments of a
period of one hundred years ago. Prince Oscar,
the fifth son of the Kaiser, looked particularly
well.

The hours for balls in Berlin, where officers
attended, were a good example for hostesses in
this country. The invitations read for eight
o'clock and that meant eight o'clock. A cold dinner of perhaps four courses is immediately served
on the arrival of the guests, who, with the exception of a very few distinguished ones, are not
given any particular places. At a quarter to nine
the dancing begins, supper is at about eleven and
the guests go home at twelve, at an hour which
enables the officers to get to bed early.

During the season there were balls at the British and French Embassy and performances by
the Russian Ballet, then in Berlin, at the Russian
Embassy.

The wonderful new Royal Library, designed
by Ihne, was opened on March twenty-second.
The Emperor attended, coming in with the beautiful Queen of Roumania walking by his side.

She is an exceedingly handsome woman, half English and half Russian. Some days later I was presented to her at a reception held at the Roumanian Minister's and found her as pleasant to talk to as good to look upon.

At the end of March there was a Horse Show. The horses did not get prizes for mere looks and manners in trotting and cantering, as here. They must all do something, for the horse is considered primarily as a war horse; such, for instance, as stopping suddenly and turning at a word of command. The jumping was excellent, officers riding in all the events. It was not a function of "society," but all "society" was there and most keenly interested; for in a warlike country, just as in the Middle Ages, the master's life may depend upon the qualities of his horse.

I have always been fond of horses and horse-racing, and the race-tracks about Berlin were always an attraction for me.

Many of the drivers and jockeys were Americans. Taral was a successful jockey for my father-in-law, Marcus Daly. He is now the trainer of one of the best racing stables in Germany, that of the brothers Weinberg, who made a fortune in dye-stuffs. "Pop" Campbell, who trained Mr. Daly's Ogden, a Futurity winner, is also a Berlin trainer. The top notch jockey was Archibald of California. McCreery, who once trained for one of my brothers, had the stable which rivalled the Weinbergs', that of Baron Oppenheim, a rich banker of Cologne.

The German officers are splendid riders and take part in many races. The Crown Prince himself is a successful jockey and racing stable owner.

On June fifth, at the annual hunt race, the big steeplechase of the year, the Emperor himself appeared at the Grünewald track, occupying his private box, a sort of little house beyond the finish.

Bookmakers are not allowed in Germany. The betting is in mutual pools. About seventeen per cent of the money paid is taken by the Jockey Club, the State and charities, so that the bettor, with this percentage running always against him, has little chance of ultimate success.

Many of the races are confined to horses bred in Denmark and the Central Empires.

All of us in the Embassy joined the Red White Tennis Club situated in the Grünewald about five miles from the centre of Berlin. The Crown Prince was a member and often played there. He is an excellent player, not quite up to championship form, but he can give a good account of himself in any company short of the top class. He has the advantage of always finding that the best players are only too glad to have an opportunity to play with him. At this Tennis Club during all the period of the feeling of hatred against America we were treated with extreme courtesy by all our German fellow members.

We saw a great deal of the two exchange professors in the winter of 1913-14, Professor Paul Shorey of the University of Chicago and Professor Archibald Coolidge of Harvard. These exchange professors give courses and lectures in the universities and their first appearance is quite an event. On this first day in 1913, they each delivered a lecture in the University of Berlin, and on this lecture day Prince August Wilhelm, representing the Kaiser, attended. The Kaiser used invariably to attend, but of late years I am afraid has rather lost interest in this enterprise at first so much favoured by him.

The *Cologne Gazette* at one time after the commencement of the war, in an article, expressed great surprise that America should permit the export of munitions of war to the Allies and said, quite seriously, that Germany had done everything possible to win the favour of America, that Roosevelt had been offered a review of German troops, that the Emperor had invited Americans who came to Kiel on their yachts to dine with him, and that he had even sat through the lectures given by American exchange professors.

Before the war there was but one cable direct from Germany to America. This cable was owned by a German company and reached America *via* the Azore Islands. I endeavoured to obtain permission for the Western Union Company to land a cable in Germany, but the opposition of the German company, which did not desire to have its monopoly interfered with, caused the applications of the Western Union to be definitely pigeon-holed. In August, 1914, after the outbreak of the war, when I told this to Ballin of the Hamburg American Line and von Gwinner, head of the Deutsche Bank, and when they thought of how much they could have saved for themselves and Germany and their companies if there had been an American owned cable landing in Germany, their anger at the delay on the part of official Germany knew no bounds. Within a very short time I received an answer from the Foreign Office granting the application of the Western Union Company, providing the cable went direct to America. This concession, however, came too late and, naturally, the Western Union did not take up the matter during the war.

CHAPTER IV

MILITARISM IN GERMANY AND THE ZABERN
AFFAIR

IN 1913-1914 occurred a series of events
known as the "Zabern Affair," which to my
mind decided the "system"—the military autocracy—for a speedy war. In this affair the German people appeared at last to be opening their
eyes, to recover in some degree from the panic
fear of their neighbours which had made them
submit to the arrogance and exactions of the
military caste and to be almost ready to demili-
tarise themselves, a thing abhorrent to the upholders of caste, the system, the army and the
Hohenzollerns.

This writing on the wall—these letters forming the word "Zabern"—the actions of the Social
Democrats and their growing boldness, all were
warnings to the autocracy of its waning power,
and impelled that autocracy towards war as a
bloodletting cure for popular discontent.

Prussia, which has imposed its will, as well as
its methods of thought and life on all the rest
of Germany, is undoubtedly a military nation.

More than one hundred and twenty-five years ago Mirabeau, the great French orator at the commencement of the Revolution, said, "War is the national industry of Prussia." Later, Napoleon remarked that Prussia "was hatched from a cannon ball," and shortly before the Franco-Prussian war of 1870 the French military *attaché,* in reporting to his government, wrote that "other countries possessed an army, but in Prussia the army possessed the country."

In practice the class of nobles in Prussia owns the army. Officers may enter the army in two ways, either by enlisting in the regiment, first as private and then being rapidly promoted to the position of non-commissioned officer, and then probationary ensign, or *avantageur;* or the young aspirant may come directly from a two years' course in one of the cadet schools and enter the regiment as probationary ensign. In both cases the young officer is observed by the officers during a period of probation and can become an officer of that regiment only by the consent of the regimental officers. In other words, each regiment is like a club, the officers having the right of black-ball.

This system has practically confined the professional officers to a class of nobles. It is not at all unusual to find in a regiment officers whose

ancestors were officers of the same regiment two
hundred years or more ago.

In addition to these officers who make the army
their career, a certain number of Germans, after
undergoing an enlistment in the army of one
year and two periods of training thereafter, are
made reserve officers. These reserve officers are
called to the colours for manœuvres and also, of
course, when the whole nation is arrayed in war.
These reserve officers seldom attain a rank higher
than that of captain. They may, however, while
exercising civil functions, be promoted, and in
this manner the Chancellor, while occupying civil
positions, has gradually been promoted to the
rank of General and von Jagow, during the war,
to the rank of Major. As a rule reserve officers
are the one-yearers, or *Einjähriger,* who, because they have attained a certain standard of
education, serve only one year with the army
instead of the two required from others. The
Bavarian army is in a sense independent of Prussia, but is modelled on the same system.

For years officers of the army, both in the discharge of their duties and outside, have behaved
in a very arrogant way toward the civil population. Time and again, while I was in Germany
waiting in line at some ticket office, an officer has
shoved himself ahead of all others without even
a protest from those waiting. On one occasion,

I went to the races in Berlin with my brother-in-law and bought a box. While we were out looking at the horses between the races, a Prussian officer and his wife seated themselves in our box. I called the attention of one of the ushers to this, but the usher said that he did not dare ask a Prussian officer to leave, and it was only after sending for the head usher and showing him my Jockey Club badge and my pass as Ambassador, that I was able to secure possession of my own box.

There have been many instances in Germany where officers having a slight dispute with civilians have instantly cut the civilian down. Instances of this kind and the harsh treatment of the Germans by officers and under-officers, while serving in the army, undoubtedly created in Germany a spirit of antagonism not only to the army itself but to the whole military system of Prussia. Affairs were brought to a head by the so-called Zabern Affair. In this affair the internal antagonism between the civil population and professional soldiers, which had assumed great proportions in a period of long peace, seemed to reach its climax. Of course this antagonism had increased with the increase in 1913-14 of the effective strength of the standing army, bringing a material increase in the numbers of officers and non-commissioned officers who represent military professionalism.

The Imperial Provinces or Reichsland, as Alsace and Lorraine are called, had been in a peculiar position within the body politic of Germany since their annexation in 1870. The Reichsland, as indicated by its name, was to be considered as common property of the German Empire and was not annexed to any one German State. Its government is by an Imperial Viceroy, with a kind of cabinet consisting of one Secretary of State, Civil and Under Secretaries and Department heads, assisted by a legislative body of two chambers, one elected by popular vote and the other consisting of members partly elected by municipal bodies, universities, churches and so forth, and partly appointed by the Imperial Government. The Viceroy and his cabinet are appointed by the Emperor in his capacity of the sovereign of the Reichsland. Until the thirty-first of May, 1911, the Reichsland had no constitution of its own, the form of its government being regulated by the Reichstag and Federal Council (Bundesrat) in about the same way as the territories of the United States are ruled by Congress and the President. In 1911, Alsace-Lorraine received a constitution which gave it representation in the Federal Council, representation in the Reichstag having already been granted as early as 1871.

The sympathy of Alsace-Lorraine for France had been increased by the policy of several of the German viceroys,—von Manteuffel, Prince Hohenlohe, Prince Münster and Count Wedel, who had, in their administrations, alternated severe measures with great leniency and had not improved conditions, so that the population, essentially South German, was undoubtedly irritated by the tone and manner of the North German officials.

Great industries had been developed by the Imperial Government, especially textile and coal mining, and the industrial population centering in Mülhausen was hotly and thoroughly Social Democratic. The upper or well-to-do classes were tied to France by family connections and by religion. The bourgeois remained mildly anti-German, more properly speaking, anti-government, for similar reasons, and the working men were opposed to the government on social and economic grounds. The farming population, not troubling much about the politics, but being affected by the campaign of the nationalistic press, were in sympathy with France; so the atmosphere was well prepared for the coming storm.

Zabern, or in French, Saverne, is a little town of between eight and nine thousand inhabitants, beautifully situated at the foot of the Vosges Mountains on the banks of the Rhine-Marne

Canal. Its garrison comprised the staff and two battalions of Infantry Regiment, Number Ninety-nine, commanded by von Reuter, and among its officers was a Lieutenant von Forstner, a young man only twenty years old, whose boyish appearance had excited the school children and boys working in nearby iron factories to ridicule him. It became known that this young officer, while instructing his men, had insulted the French flag and had called the Alsatian recruits *Wackes,* a nick-name meaning "square-head," and frequently used by the people of Alsace-Lorraine in a jocular way, but hotly resented by them if used towards them by others. It was further reported that he had promised his men a reward of ten marks if one of them, in case of trouble, should bring down a Social Democrat. Forstner had told his men to beware, and warned them against listening to French foreign agents, whom the Germans claimed were inducing French soldiers to desert in order to join the French legion. It is probable that Forstner, in talking to his men of the French Foreign Legion, used language offensive to French ears. He admitted that he had used the word *Wackes* in defiance of an order of the commanding general, and for this he had been punished with several days' confinement in a military prison. Lieutenant von Forstner, who was ordered to instruct his squad about the regulations in case of trouble with the civil population, claimed that he had only added to the usual instructions a statement that every true soldier should do his best to suppress any disturbances and that he, Forstner, would give a special reward to any of his men who would arrest one of "those damned Social Democrats."

Reports of the acts of Forstner and other officers were rapidly spread among the population. The two newspapers of Zabern published articles. The excitement grew, and there were demonstrations against the officials and especially against Forstner. Finally, conditions became so bad that Colonel von Reuter requested the head of the local civil administration, Director Mahler, to restore order, stating that he would take the matter into his own hands if order was not restored. The director, a native of a small village near Zabern, replied coolly that he saw no necessity for interfering with peace loving and law abiding people. On November twenty-ninth, 1913, a large crowd assembled in front of the barracks. Colonel von Reuter ordered Lieutenant Schad, commanding the Guard as officer of the day, to disperse the crowd. Accordingly Lieutenant Schad called the Guard to arms and three times summoned the crowd to disperse and go home. The soldiers charged and drove the multitude across the Square and into a side street and arrested about fifteen persons, among them the President, two Judges and the State Attorney of the Zabern Supreme Court, who had just come out from the court building and who were caught in the crowd. They were subsequently released. The rest of the persons arrested were kept in the cellar of the barracks over night.

The report of these occurrences caused immense excitement throughout Germany. A great outcry went up against militarism, even in quarters where no socialistic tendencies existed. This feeling was not helped by the fact that the General commanding the fifteenth army to which the Zabern regiment belonged was an exponent of extreme militaristic ideas; a man, who several years before, as Colonel of the Colonial troops, representing the war ministry before the Reichstag and debating there the question of the number of troops to be kept in German South West Africa, had most clearly shown his contempt for the Reichstag.

Colonel von Reuter and Lieutenant Schad, when court-martialled for their acts in ordering the troops to move against the civil population, claimed the benefit of a Prussian law of 1820, which provided that in any city, town or village, the highest military officer in command must assume the authority, usually vested in the civil government, whenever for any reason the civil administration neglects to keep order. The Colonel and Lieutenant were subsequently acquitted on the ground that they had acted under the provisions of this law.

The excitement throughout Germany was further increased by other circumstances. The Emperor remained during these critical days at Donaueschingen, the princely estate of his friend and favourite, Prince Fürstenberg, enjoying himself with fox-hunting, torch-light processions and cabaret performances. Of course, all this had been arranged long before any one dreamed of any trouble in Zabern, and the Emperor could scarcely be expected to realise the gravity of the situation which suddenly arose. But this very fact created a bad impression. It was even rumoured that the Empress, alarmed by the situation, had ordered a train to be made ready in order to go to him and try to convince him of the necessity of returning to Berlin.

The newly appointed minister of war, Falkenhayn, went to Donaueschingen, where he was joined by von Deimling. This action aggravated the situation, because the public concluded that the Emperor would hear the advice and report of military officers only. The sudden death, by heart failure, of the Emperor's closest friend, von Hulsen, chief of the Emperor's Military Cabinet, during a banquet at Donaueschingen, gave

THE GLORY WHICH IS POTSDAM. SUMMER RESIDENCE OF THE KAISER
IN THE PARK OF SANS SOUCI

DEMONSTRATION OF SYMPATHY FOR THE AMERICANS, AT THE
TOWN HALL, AUGUST, 1914 (PAGE 146)

the rapidly developing events a tragic and mysterious colouring, and these conferences in Donaueschingen resulted in the tendering of their resignations by the Viceroy, von Wedel, and Secretary of State Zorn von Bulach, Viceroy and Secretary of State of Alsace-Lorraine, who felt that the military party had gained an upper hand in the conflict with the civil authorities. The Chancellor then hurried to Donaueschingen, arriving a few hours before the departure of the Emperor; and a subsequent order of the Emperor to General von Deimling to see to it that the military officers did not overstep their authority and directing him to investigate the occurrences and take measures to punish all guilty parties, somewhat quieted the nation and caused the two highest civil officials of Alsace-Lorraine to withdraw their resignations.

Zabern, where a brigadier-general had been sent by von Deimling to restore civil government, had begun to quiet down. But the Chancellor had hardly returned to Berlin when another incident stirred Germany. While practising field service in the neighbourhood of Zabern and marching through a village, Lieutenant von Forstner had an altercation with a lame shoemaker and cut him down. This brutal act of militarism caused a new outburst throughout Germany. Forstner was tried by a court-martial for hitting and wounding an unarmed civilian, and sentenced by the lower court to one year's imprisonment, but acquitted by the higher court as having acted in "supposed self-defence."

No less than three parties, the Centrum, the Progressives and the Social Democrats, addressed interpellations to the Chancellor about this occurrence at Zabern. I was present at the debate in the Reichstag, which took place on the fourth, fifth and sixth of December, 1913. Three South Germans, a member of the Centrum, Hauss, a Progressive named Roser, and the Socialist deputy from Mülhausen in Alsace, Peirotes, commenced by moving and seconding the interpellation and related in vehement language the occurrences at Zabern. The Chancellor replied in defence of the government. Unfortunately he had that morning received family news of a most unpleasant character, which added to his nervousness. He spoke with a low voice and looked like a downhearted and sick man. It was whispered afterwards in the lobbies that he had forgotten the most important part of his speech. The unfavourable impression which he made was increased by von Falkenhayn, appearing for the first time before the Reichstag. If the Reichstag members had been disappointed by the Chancellor, they were stirred to the highest pitch of bitterness by the speech of the War Minister. In

a sharp, commanding voice he told them that the
military officers had only done their duty, that
they would not be swerved from their path by
press agents or hysterical individuals, that Forstner was a very young officer who had been severely punished, but that this kind of courageous
young officer was the kind that the country
needed, etc. Immediately after this speech the
Progressive party moved that the attitude of the
Chancellor did not meet the approval of the representatives of the people, and it became evident
that, for the first time in the history of the German Empire, a vote of censure directed against
the government would be debated. The debate
was continued all the next day, the Chancellor
making another speech and saying what he probably had intended to say the day before. He related what he had achieved at Donaueschingen;
that the Emperor had issued a cabinet order
saying that the military authorities should be
kept within legal bounds, that all the guilty persons would be punished, that the Regiment, Number Ninety-nine, had been removed from Zabern,
that the absolute law of 1820 had been abolished
for Alsace-Lorraine, and that no Chancellor
should for one moment tolerate disregard of law
by any government officials, civil or military, and
remain in his position.

This second speech of the Chancellor made a

better impression and somewhat affected the more extreme members of the Reichstag, but it came too late to prevent the passage of the vote of censure by the remarkable majority of two hundred and ninety-three to fifty-four. Only the Conservatives voted against it. A few days later, when the Social Democrats demanded that the Chancellor take the consequence of the vote of distrust and resign, the attitude of the members of all the other parties, who had been favourably impressed by the second speech of the Chancellor, showed that they were not yet prepared to go the length of holding that a vote of distrust in the Reichstag must necessarily mean the resignation of the Chancellor.

Public excitement gradually calmed down, and a complete change of the officials at Zabern helped to bring about a normal condition of affairs. The Viceroy, Count Wedel, and Secretary of State Zorn von Bulach, resigned and were replaced by von Dallwitz and Count Rödern.

However, the everlasting question came up again a little later during the regular budget debate of the Reichstag. The Chancellor made his speech, giving a review of the political international situation. He was followed by Herr Scheidemann, leader of the Social Democrats, who mercilessly attacked the Chancellor and stated that if the Chancellor still thought that he

was the right man at the helm, he, Scheidemann,
would show that the contrary was the case. He
then enumerated what he called the many political failures of the Chancellor, the failure of the
bill to amend the Prussian franchise law, and
stated that the few bills which had been passed,
such as the bill giving Alsace-Lorraine a real
constitution, had been carried only with the help
of the Social Democratic party. The speaker
then once more rehashed the incidents of the Zabern matter, referred to the attitude of the Emperor, who, he said, had evidently been too busy
with hunting and festivities to devote time to such
trivial matters as the Zabern Affair, and also said
that, if the Chancellor had refused to withdraw,
the only possible conclusion from the vote of the
two hundred and ninety-three Reichstag members, who were certainly not influenced by personal feelings against the Chancellor, was that
the Chancellor must be sticking to his post only
because of the mistaken idea of the Emperor's
authority and because he must believe in the
fetish of personal government. Scheidemann
begged that the same majority which had passed
the vote of censure should now follow it up by
voting down the Chancellor's salary and thus
force him out of office.

The Chancellor immediately replied, saying
that he needed no advice from Herr Scheidemann,

and that when the government had consented
to change the rules of the Reichstag he had
expressly reserved the authority either to regard or disregard any resolution passed after
an interpellation, and that formerly, after discussing an interpellation and the answer of
the government, no vote could be taken to
approve or reject a resolution expressing its opinion of such course of action. Such resolutions
might be considered as valuable material, but it
had been agreed that they could have no binding
effect either upon the government or any member
of it, and that nobody had ever dreamed that by
a mere change of business rules the whole constitution of the Empire was being changed and
authority given to the Reichstag to dismiss ministers at will; that in France and Great Britain
conditions were different, but that parliamentary
government did not exist in Germany; that it was
the constitutional privilege of the Emperor to
appoint the Chancellor without any assistance or
advice from the Reichstag; that he, the Chancellor, would resist with all his might every attempt to change this system; and that he, therefore, refused to resign because the resolution had
no other effect than to make it evident that a difference of opinion existed between the Reichstag
and the government.

This debate took place on December ninth, 1913, and, with the exception of the Social Democrats and the Polish deputies, the leaders of all parties supported the view of the Chancellor. The motion to strike out the Chancellor's salary was voted down, only the Social Democrats and Poles voting in favour of it.

It is unquestioned, however, that this Zabern Affair and the consequent attitude of the whole nation, as well as the extraordinary vote in the Reichstag, greatly alarmed the military party.

It was perhaps the final factor which decided the advocates of the old military system of Germany in favour of a European war. Usually in past years when the Reichstag in adjournments had risen and cheered the name of the Emperor, the Social Democrats absented themselves from the Chamber, but when the Reichstag adjourned on May twentieth, 1914, these members remained in the Chamber and refused either to rise or to cheer the Emperor. The President of the Reichstag immediately called attention to this breach of respect to the Emperor, upon which the Socialists shouted, "That is our affair," and tried to drown the cheers with hoots and hisses at which the other parties applauded tumultuously.

This occurrence I know greatly incensed the Emperor and did much, I believe, to win his consent to the war.

CHAPTER V

TO the outsider, the Germans seem a fierce
and martial nation. But, in reality, the
mass of the Germans, in consenting to the great
sacrifice entailed by their enormous preparations
for war, have been actuated by fear.

This fear dates from the Thirty Years' War,
the war which commenced in 1618 and was ter-
minated in 1648. In 1648, when the Treaty of
Westphalia was concluded, Germany was almost
a desert. Its population had fallen from twenty
millions to four millions. The few remaining
people were so starved that cannibalism was
openly practised. In the German States polyg-
amy was legalised, and was a recognised institution for many years thereafter.

Of thirty-five thousand Bohemian villages,
only six thousand were left standing. In the
lower Palatinate only one-tenth of the population
survived; in Württemberg, only one-sixth. Hundreds of square miles of once fertile country were
overgrown with forests inhabited only by wolves.

A picture of this horrible period is found in the curious novel, "The Adventurous Simplicissimus," written by Grimmelshausen, and published in 1669, which describes the adventures of a wise peasant who finally leaves his native Germany and betakes himself to a desert island which he refuses to leave when offered an opportunity to go back to the Fatherland. He answers those who wish to persuade him to go back with words which seem quite appropriate to-day: "My God, where do you want to carry me? Here is peace. There is war. Here I know nothing of the arts of the court, ambitions, anger, envy, deceit, nor have I cares concerning my clothing and nourishment. . . . While I still lived in Europe everything was (O, woe that I must appear witness to such acts of Christians!) filled with war, burning, murder, robbery, plundering and the shame of women and virgins." The Munich weekly, "Simplicissimus," whose powerful political cartoons have often startled Europe, takes its name from this character.

After the conclusion of the Thirty Years' War, Germany was again and again ravaged by smaller wars, culminating in the Seven Years' War of Frederick the Great and the humbling of Germany under the heel of Napoleon. In the wars of Frederick the Great, one tenth of the population was killed. Even the great Battle of the

Nations at Leipsic in 1813 did not free Germany from wars, and in 1866 Prussia and the smaller North German States, with Italy, defeated Austria, assisted by Bavaria, Hesse-Cassel, Hesse-Darmstadt, Nassau, Saxony, Baden, Württemberg and Hanover.

I am convinced that the fear of war induced by a hereditary instinct, caused the mass of the Germans to become the tools and dupes of those who played upon this very fear in order to create a military autocracy. On the other hand, and, especially, in the noble class, we have in Germany a great number of people who believe in war for its own sake. In part, these nobles are the descendants of the Teutonic Knights who conquered the Slav population of Prussia, and have ever since bound that population to their will.

The Prussian army was created by the father of Frederick the Great, who went to the most ridiculous extremes in obtaining tall men at all costs for his force.

The father of Frederick the Great gave the following written instructions to the two tutors of his son. "Above all let both tutors exert themselves to the utmost to inspire him with a love of soldiery and carefully impress upon his mind that, as nothing can confer honour and fame upon a prince except the sword, the monarch who seeks not his sole satisfaction in it must ever appear a contemptible character in the eyes of the world."

Frederick the Great left, by the death of that father who had once threatened to execute him, at the head of a marvellous army with a full treasury, finally decided upon war, as he admits in his own letters, "in order to be talked about," and his desire to be talked about led to the Seven Years' War.

The short war against Denmark in 1864, against Austria, Bavaria, etc., in 1866 and against France in 1870, enormously increased both the pride and prestige of the Prussian army. It must not be forgotten that at all periods of history it seems as if some blind instinct had driven the inhabitants of the inhospitable plains of North Germany to war and to conquest. The Cimbri and Teutones—the tribes defeated by Marius; Ariovistus, who was defeated by Julius Caesar; the Goths and the Visi-Goths; the Franks and the Saxons; all have poured forth from this infertile country, for the conquest of other lands. The Germans of to-day express this longing of the North Germans for pleasanter climes in the phrase in which they demand "a place in the sun."

The nobles of Prussia are always for war. The business men and manufacturers and ship-owners desire an increasing field for their activities. The German colonies were uninhabitable by Europeans. All his life the glittering Emperor and his generals had planned and thought of war; and the Crown Prince, surrounded by his remarkable collection of relics and reminders of Napoleon, dreamed only of taking the lead in a successful war of conquest. Early in the winter of 1913-14, the Crown Prince showed his collection of Napoleana to a beautiful American woman of my acquaintance, and said that he hoped war would occur while his father was alive, but, if not, he would start a war the moment he came to the throne.

Since writing the above, the American woman who had this conversation with the Crown Prince wrote out for me the exact conversation in her own words, as follows: "I had given him Norman Angell's book, 'The Great Illusion,' which seeks to prove that war is unprofitable. He (the Crown Prince) said that whether war was profitable or not, when he came to the throne there would be war, if not before, just for the fun of it. On a previous occasion he had said that the plan was to attack and conquer France, then England, and after that my country (the United States of America); Russia was also to be conquered, and Germany would be master of the world."

The extraordinary collection of relics, statues,

busts, souvenirs, etc., of the first Napoleon, collected by the Crown Prince, which he was showing at the time of the first of these conversations
to this American lady, shows the trend of his
mind and that all his admiration is centred upon
Napoleon, the man who sought the mastery of the
world, and who is thought by admirers like the
Crown Prince to have failed only because of
slight mistakes which they feel, in his place, they
would not have made.

If the Germans' long preparations for war
were to bear any fruit, countless facts pointed to
the summer of 1914 as the time when the army
should strike that great and sudden blow at the
liberties of the world.

It was in June, 1914, that the improved Kiel
Canal was reopened, enabling the greatest warships to pass from the Baltic to the North Sea.

In the Zeppelins the Germans had arms not
possessed by any other country and with which
they undoubtedly believed that they could do
much more damage to Great Britain than was the
case after the actual outbreak of hostilities. They
had paid great attention to the development of
the submarine. Their aeroplanes were superior
to those of other nations. They believed that in
the use of poison gas, which was prepared before
the outbreak of the war, they had a prize that
would absolutely demoralise their enemy. They

had their flame throwers and the heavy artillery and howitzers which reduced the redoubtable forts of Liège and Namur to fragments within a few hours, and which made the holding of any fortresses impossible.

On their side, by the imposition of a heavy tax called the *Wehrbeitrag* or supplementary defence tax, they had, in 1913, increased their army by a number of army corps. On the other hand, the law for three years' military service voted in France had not yet gone into effect, nor had the law for universal military service voted by the Belgian Chambers. Undoubtedly the Germans based great hopes upon the Bagdad railway which was to carry their influence to the East, and even threatened the rule of Great Britain in Egypt and India. Undoubtedly there was talk, too, of a Slav railroad to run from the Danube to the Adriatic which would cut off Germany from access to the Southern Sea. Francis Deloisi, the Frenchman, in his book published before the great war, called "De la Guerre des Balkans à la Guerre Européenne," says, "In a word, the present war (Balkan) is the work of Russia, and the Danube Asiatic railway is a Russian project. If it succeeds, a continuous barrier of Slav peoples will bar the way to the Mediterranean of the path of Austro-German expansion from the Black Sea to the Adriatic. But here again the

Romanoffs confront the Hapsburgs, the Austro-Serb conflict becomes the Austro-Russian conflict, two great groups are formed, and the Balkan conflict becomes the European conflict."

Another reason for an immediate war was the loan by France to Russia made on condition that additional strategic railways were to be constructed by the Russians in Poland. Although this money had been received, the railways had not been constructed at the time of the opening of the Great War. Speaking of this situation, the Russian General Kuropatkin, in his report for the year 1900, said, "We must cherish no illusions as to the possibility of an easy victory over the Austrian army," and he then went on to say, "Austria had eight railways to transport troops to the Russian frontier while Russia had only four; and, while Germany had seventeen such railways running to the German-Russian frontier, the Russians had only five." Kuropatkin further said, "The differences are too enormous and leave our neighbours a superiority which cannot be overcome by the numbers of our troops, or their courage."

Comparing the two armies, he said, "The invasion of Russia by German troops is more probable than the invasion of Germany by Russian troops"; and, "Our Western frontier, in the event of a European war, would be in such danger as it never has known in all the history of Russia."

Agitation by workmen in Russia was believed in Germany to be the beginning of a revolution.

Illuminating figures may be seen in the gold purchase of the German Imperial Bank: in 1911, 174,000,000 marks; in 1912, 173,000,000 marks; but in 1913, 317,000,000 marks.

There was a belief in Germany that the French nation was degenerate and corrupt and unprepared for war. This belief became conviction when, in the debates of the French Senate, Senator Humbert, early in 1914, publicly exposed what he claimed to be the weakness and unpreparedness of France.

Prince Lichnowsky, the German Ambassador in London, certainly reported to his government that England did not wish to enter the war. He claims now that he did not mean that Great Britain would not fight at all events, but undoubtedly the German Foreign Office believed that Great Britain would remain out of the war. The raising of the Ulster army by Sir Edward Carson, one of the most gigantic political bluffs in all history, which had no more revolutionary or military significance than a torchlight parade during one of our presidential campaigns, was reported by the German spies as a real and serious revolutionary movement; and, of course, it was believed by the

Germans that Ireland would rise in general rebellion the moment that war was declared. In the summer of 1914 Russia was believed to be on the edge of revolution.

As I have said in a previous chapter, the movement against militarism, culminating in the extraordinary vote in the Reichstag against the government at the time of the Zabern Affair, warned the government and military people that the mass of Germans were coming to their senses and were preparing to shake off the bogy of militarism and fear, which had roosted so long on their shoulders like a Prussian old-man-of-the-sea. The Pan-Germans and the Annexationists were hot for war. The people alive could recall only three wars, the war against Denmark in 1864, which was settled in a few days and added the duchies of Schleswig and Holstein to the Prussian crown, and the war of 1866 in which Bavaria, Baden, Württemberg, Hesse-Darmstadt, and Saxony were defeated, when the Austrian kingdom of Hanover disappeared and the territories of Hesse-Cassel and Nassau, and the free city of Frankfort were added to Prussia. This war, from its declaration to the battle of Königgratz in which the Austrians were completely defeated, lasted only two weeks. In 1870, France was defeated within a month and a half after the opening of hostilities; so that the Kaiser

was implicitly believed when, on the first day of
the war, he appeared on the balcony of the palace
and told the crowds who were keen for war, that
"before the leaves have fallen from the trees you
will be back in your homes." The army and all
Germany believed him and believed, too, that a
few short weeks would see the destruction of
France and the consequent seizure of her rich
colonies; that Russia could then be struck a good
quick blow before she could concentrate her army
and resources; that Great Britain would remain
neutral; and that Germany would consequently
become, if not the actual owner, at least the dictator of the world. Some one has since said that
the Emperor must have meant pine trees.

Working ever in the dark, either owning or
influencing newspapers, the great munition and
arms factory of the Krupp's insidiously poisoned
the minds of the people with the microbe of war.

Prince Lichnowsky, the German Ambassador
to London, called upon me often after the outbreak of the war, and insisted that he had correctly reported the sentiments of Great Britain in
saying that Great Britain did not want war. After his return to Germany the Germans quite unfairly treated him as a man who had failed and
seemed to blame him because Great Britain had
taken the only possible course open to her and
ranged herself on the side of France and Russia.

The dedication at Leipzig, in the year 1913, of the great monument to celebrate what is called the "War of Liberation," and the victory of Leipzig in the War of the Nations, 1813, had undoubtedly kindled a martial spirit in Germany. To my mind, the course which really determined the Emperor and the ruling class for war was the attitude of the whole people in the Zabern Affair and their evident and growing dislike of militarism. The fact that the Socialists, at the close of the session of the Reichstag, boldly remained in the Chamber and refused to rise or to cheer the name of the Emperor indicated a new spirit of resistance to autocracy; and autocracy saw that if it was to keep its hold upon Germany it must lead the nation into a short and successful war.

This is no new trick of a ruling and aristocratic class. From the days when the patricians of Rome forced the people into war whenever the people showed a disposition to demand their rights, autocracies have always turned to war as the best antidote against the spirit of democracy.

CHAPTER VI

KIEL, situated on the Baltic, on the eastern side of the peninsula of Jutland near the Baltic entrance of the Kiel Canal, is the principal naval centre of Germany.

When the Germans decided to build up a great fleet the Emperor used every means to encourage a love of yachting and of the sea, and endeavoured to make the Kiel Week a rival of the week at Cowes, the British yachting centre.

With this end in view, the rich Germans were encouraged and almost commanded to build and race yachts; and Americans and others who visited Kiel in their yachts were entertained by the Emperor in an intimacy impossible if they had come to Berlin merely as tourists, residing in a hotel.

In June, 1914, we went to Kiel as guests of Allison Armour of Chicago, on his yacht, the *Utowana*. I was detained by business in Berlin and Mrs. Gerard preceded me to Kiel. I arrived there on Saturday, the twenty-seventh of June, and that night went with Armour to dine with the Emperor on board the Emperor's yacht, *Hohenzollern.*

In the harbour were a fair number of German yachts, mostly sailing yachts, taking part in the races; the fine old yacht of Lord Brassey, *The Sunbeam,* and the yacht of the Prince of Monaco, in which he conducts his scientific voyages. A great British fleet, comprising some of the most powerful dreadnoughts, had also arrived, sent as an earnest of the good will and kindly feeling then supposed to exist between Great Britain and Germany. The redoubtable von Tirpitz was present on a German battleship, and the Hamburg American Line had an old transatlantic steamer, the *Deutschland,* rechristened the *Victoria Luise,* filled with guests, most of whom were invited on a hint from the Emperor.

At dinner on the *Hohenzollern* a number of British were present. The Kaiser had on one side of him the wife of the British Admiral, Lady Maud Warrender, and on the other side, the Countess of March, whose husband is heir to the Duke of Richmond. I sat between Princess Münster and the Countess of March, and after dinner the Emperor drew me over to the rail of the ship, and talked to me for some time. I wish that diplomatic etiquette would permit me to reveal what he said, but even in war time I do not think I ought to violate the confidence that hospitality seals. However important and interesting, especially to the tame Socialists of Germany, I do not give this conversation with the Emperor, nor the conversation with him and Colonel House at the *Schrippenfest,* because I was his guest. Conversations with the Emperor which I had on later occasions were at official audiences and to these the same rule does not apply. He also invited me to sail with him in his yacht, the *Meteor,* in the races from Kiel to Eckernfjord on the coming Tuesday.

Sunday afternoon Prince Henry and his wife, who reside in the castle at Kiel, were to give an afternoon reception and garden party; but on arriving at the gates we were told that the party would not take place. After going on board the *Utowana,* Frederick W. Wile, the celebrated correspondent of the *London Daily Mail,* ranged up alongside in a small launch and informed us that the Arch Duke Franz Ferdinand, the heir to the Austrian throne, and his wife had been assassinated at Sarajevo. There was much rushing to and fro in fast launches, the Emperor himself being summoned from the race which was in progress. That night we dined on board the yacht of the Prince of Monaco. All the diplomats and notables whom I met during the afternoon and evening seemed to think that there was

THE EMPEROR'S RACING YACHT, AND OTHERS, AT KIEL

THE "HOHENZOLLERN"

no chance that the tragedy at Sarajevo would lead to war. The next morning the Emperor left early for Berlin, but expressly directed that the festivities and races at Kiel should be carried out as arranged.

Monday afternoon there was a *Bierabend* in the large hall of the yacht club at Kiel. The Emperor was to have presided at this dinner, but his place was taken by his brother, Prince Henry. Sir Edward Goschen, the British Ambassador, who was living on one of the British battleships, sat on his right and I sat on his left. During the evening a curious incident happened. The Prince and I were talking of the dangers of after-dinner speaking and what a dangerous sport it was. In the midst of our conversation some one whispered to the Prince and he rose to his feet, proposed the health of the visiting British Admiral and fleet, and made a little speech. As he concluded, he said, addressing the officers of the British fleet: "We are sorry you are going and we are sorry you came." It is remarkable as showing the discipline of the German nation and their respect for authority that thereafter no German ever referred to this curious slip of the tongue. The night was rather mild and after dinner we walked about the gardens of the yacht club. I had a long and interesting conversation with the Prince of Monaco. That Prince, who receives such a large income from the company which carries on the gambling rooms at Monte Carlo, is a man of the world intensely interested in scientific research: there is practically no corner of the seven seas into which his yacht has not poked her nose in the search for material for the Sea Museum which he has established at Monaco.

On Tuesday Armour and I boarded the Emperor's sailing yacht, the new *Meteor*. The race was a beautiful run from Kiel to Eckernfjord and was won by the *Meteor*. As the Emperor was not on board, I did not get one of the souvenir scarf-pins always given to guests who sail with him on a winning race. Among our crew was Grand Admiral von Köster, subsequently an advocate of the ruthless submarine war.

Eckernfjord is a little fishing and bathing town. Near by is the country residence of Prince Henry, a rather modest house, built in brick in English Elizabethan style. The wife of Prince Henry was a Princess of Hesse-Darmstadt and is the sister of the Czarina of Russia. We had tea with Prince and Princess Henry, their family, the Duke of Sonderburg-Glücksburg and several others of his family. The billiard room of the house is decorated with the large original caricatures made by McCutcheon of the Prince's stay in America. Prince and Princess Henry came out to dine on the *Utowana,* and Armour

and the Prince went ashore to attend another
Bierabend, but I dodged the smoke and beer and
remained on board. Before he left the yacht,
I had a talk with Prince Henry. He seemed
most exercised over the dislike of the Germans
by all other peoples and asked me why I thought
it existed. I politely told him that I thought
it existed because of the success which the Germans had had in all fields of endeavour, particularly in manufacturing and commerce. He said,
with great truth, that he believed a great deal
of it came from the bad manners of the travelling
Germans. Prince Henry is an able and reasonable man with a most delightful manner. He
speaks English with a perfect English accent,
and I think would be far happier as an English
country gentleman than as the Grand Admiral
of the German Baltic Fleet. He has been devoted to automobiling and has greatly encouraged
that industry in Germany. The Automobile Club
of Berlin is his particular pet.

On returning to Kiel next day we spent several
days longer there. I lunched on board his battleship with Grand Admiral von Tirpitz, sitting
next to him at the table. He struck me then as
an amiable sea dog, combining much political and
worldly wisdom with his knowledge of the sea.
From Kiel we motored one night to dine with a
Count and Countess in their country house. This

house had been built perhaps two hundred years, and was on one side of a square, the other three sides being formed by the great stone barns in which the produce of the estate was stored. Although the first floor of the house was elevated about eight feet above the ground, the family, on account of the dampness of that part of the world, lived in the second story, and the dining room was on this story. An ancestor of the Count had, at a time when this part of the country was part of Denmark and about the year 1700, lent all his available money to the King of Denmark. A crude painting in the hall showed him sitting in the hall of this particular house, smoking a long pipe and surrounded by three or four sisters who were all spinning. Our hostess told us that this picture represented the lending ancestor being supported by his sisters while waiting the return of the loan which he had made to the Danish king, an early example of the situation disclosed by the popular song which runs: "Everybody works but father." Of course, no one ever expected a Prussian nobleman to do any work except in the line of war or in governing the inferior classes of the country.

CHAPTER VII

THE SYSTEM

PEOPLE of other countries have been wondering why it is that the German government is able so easily to impose its will upon the German people. I have set out in another chapter, in detail, the political system from which you have seen that the Reichstag is nothing but a debating society; that the Prussians do not really have universal suffrage but, by reason of the vicious circle system of voting, the elective franchise remains in the hands of the few; and that the government of the country through the *Landräte, Regierungspräsidenten* and *Oberpräsidenten* is a central system from above downwards and not the election of the rulers by the people; and, in the chapter on militarism and Zabern, I have told by what means the control of the army is kept in the hands of the class of nobles.

These are not the only means by which the system controls the country. These alone would not suffice. From the time when he is four years old, the German is disciplined and taught that his government is the only good and effective form. The teachers in the schools are all government paid and teach the children only the principles desired by the rulers of the German people. There are no Saturday holidays in the German schools and their summer holidays are for only three to five weeks. You never see gangs of small boys in Germany. Their games and their walks are superintended by their teachers who are always inculcating in them reverence and awe for the military heroes of the past and present. On Saturday night the German boy is turned over by the State paid school teacher to the State paid pastor who adds divine authority to the principles of reverence for the German system.

There is a real system of caste in Germany. For instance, I was playing tennis one day with a man and, while dressing afterwards, I asked him what he was. He answered that he was a *Kaufmann,* or merchant. For the German this answer was enough. It placed him in the merchant class. I asked him what sort of a *Kaufmann* he was. He then told me he was president of a large electrical company. Of course, with us he would have answered first that he was president of the electrical company, but being a German he simply disclosed his caste without going into details. It is a curious thing on the registers of guests in a German summer resort to see Mrs. Manufactory-Proprietor Schultze registered with Mrs. Landrat Schwartz and Mrs. Second Lieutenant von Bing. Of course, there is no doubt as to the relative social positions of Mrs. Manufactory-Proprietor Schultze and Mrs. Second Lieutenant von Bing. Mrs. Manufactory-Proprietor Schultze may have a steam yacht and a tiara, an opera box and ten million marks. She may be an old lady noted for her works of charity. Her husband may have made discoveries of enormous value to the human race, but she will always be compelled to take her place behind Mrs. Second Lieutenant von Bing, even if the latter is only seventeen years old.

Of course, occasionally, officers of the army and navy condescend to marry into the merchant caste, and if a girl has a choice of three equally attractive young men, one a doctor, earning ten thousand dollars a year; one a manufacturer, earning the same amount; and one an army officer with a "von" before his name and three thousand dollars a year, there is no hesitation on her part: she takes the noble and the army officer.

For years all the highest official positions of the government have been held by members of the Prussian noble class, and when Zimmermann, of a substantial family in East Prussia, but not of noble birth, was made Foreign Minister, the most intense surprise was exhibited all over Germany at this innovation.

One of the most successful ways of disciplining the people is by the *Rat* system. *Rat* means councillor, and is a title of honour given to any one who has attained a certain measure of success or standing in his chosen business or profession. For instance, a business man is made a commerce *Rat;* a lawyer, a justice *Rat;* a doctor, a sanitary *Rat;* an architect or builder, a building *Rat;* a keeper of the archives, an archive *Rat;* and so on. They are created in this way: first, a man becomes a plain *Rat,* then, later on, he becomes a secret *Rat* or privy councillor; still later, a court secret *Rat* and, later still, a *wirklicher,* or really and truly secret court *Rat* to which may be added the title of Excellency, which puts the man who has attained this absolutely at the head of the *Rat* ladder.

But see the insidious working of the system. By German custom the woman always carries the husband's title. The wife of a successful builder is known as Mrs. Really Truly Secret Court Building *Rat* and her social precedence over the other women depends entirely upon her husband's position in the *Rat* class. Titles of nobility alone do not count when they come in contact with a high government position. Now if a lawyer gets to be about forty years old and is not some sort of a *Rat,* his wife begins to nag him and his friends and relations look at him with suspicion. There must be something in his life which prevents his obtaining the coveted distinction and if there is anything in a man's past, if he has shown at any time any spirit of opposition to the government, as disclosed by the police registers, which are kept written up to date about every German citizen, then he has no chance of obtaining any of these distinctions which make up so much of the social life of Germany. It is a means by which the government keeps a far tighter hold on the intellectual part of its population than if they were threatened with torture and the stake. The Social Democrats, who, of course, have declared themselves against the existing system of government and in favour of a republic, can receive no distinctions from the government because they dared to lift their voices and their pens in criticism of the existing order. For them there is the fear of the law. Convictions for the crime of *Lèse-Majesté* are of almost daily occurrence and, at the opening of the war, an amnesty was granted in many of these cases, the ministry of war withdrawing many prosecutions against poor devils waiting their trial in jail because they had dared to speak disrespectfully of the army. The following quotation from a German book, written since the war, shows very clearly that this state of affairs existed: "In the beneficent atmosphere of general amnesty came the news that the Minister of War had withdrawn pending prosecutions against newspapers on account of their insults to the army or its members." (Dr. J. Jastrow, "Im Kriegszustand.")

Besides the *Rat* system and the military system, there exists the enormous mass of Prussian officials. In a country where so many things are under government control these officials are almost immeasurably more numerous than in other countries. In Prussia, for example, all the railways are government-owned, with the exception of one road about sixty miles long and a few small branch roads. This army of officials are retainers of the government, and not only, of course, themselves refrain from criticising the system, but also use their influence upon the members of their own family and all with whom they come in contact. They are subject to trial in special secret courts and one of them who dared in any way to criticise the existing system would not for long remain a member of it. Of course, the members of the Reichstag have the privilege of free speech without responsibility, and there are occasional Socialists, who know that they

116

have nothing to expect from the government, who
dare to speak in criticism.

All the newspapers are subject to control as in
no other country. In the first place their proprietors are subject to the influence of the *Rat*
system as is every other German, and the newspaper proprietor, whose sons perhaps enter the
army, whose daughters may be married to naval
officers or officials, and who seeks for his sons
promotion as judge, state's attorney, etc., has
to be very careful that the utterances of his newspaper do not prevent his promotion in the social
scale or interfere with the career of his family
and relations.

Since the war while a preventive censure does
not exist in Germany nevertheless a newspaper
may be suppressed at will; a fearful punishment
for a newspaper, which, by being suppressed for,
say, five days or a week, has its business affairs
thrown into the utmost confusion and suffers an
enormous direct loss.

Many of the larger newspapers are either
owned or influenced by concerns like the Krupps'.
For instance, during this war, all news coming
from Germany to other countries has been furnished by either the Over-Seas or Trans-Ocean
service, both news agencies in which the Krupps
are large stockholders. The smaller newspapers
are influenced directly by the government.

In the Middle Ages there was often declared a sort of truce to prevent fighting in a city, which was called the *Burgfrieden* or "peace of the city," and, at the beginning of this war, all political parties were supposed to declare a sort of *Burgfrieden* and not try to obtain any political advantage.

There was, therefore, intense indignation among the Social Democrats of Germany when it was discovered, in the spring of 1916, that the Minister of the Interior was making arrangements to send out news service to be furnished free to the smaller newspapers, and that he was engaged in instructing the various *Landräte* and other officials of the Interior Department how effectively to use this machinery in order to gull the people to the advantage of the government, and to keep them in ignorance of anything which might tend to turn them against the system.

Besides the *Rat* system there is, of course, the system of decorations. Countless orders and decorations are given in Germany. At the head is the Order of the Black Eagle; there are the Order of the Red Eagle, the Prussian Order of the Crown, the orders, *"Pour le Mérite,"* the Order of the House of Hohenzollern, and many others, and in each of the twenty-five States there are also orders, distinctions and decorations. These orders in turn are divided into numerous classes.

For instance, a man can have the Red Eagle order of the first, second, third or fourth class, and these may be complicated with a laurel crown, with an oak crown, with swords and with stars, etc. Even domestic servants, who have served a long time in one family, receive orders; and faithful postmen and other officials who have never appeared on the police books for having made statements against the government or the army are sure of receiving some sort of order.

Once a year in Berlin a great festival is held called the *Ordensfest,* when all who hold orders or decorations of any kind are invited to a great banquet. The butler, who has served for twenty-five years, there rubs shoulders with the diplomat who has received a Black Eagle for adding a colony to the German Empire, and the faithful cook may be seated near an officer who has obtained *"Pour le Mérite"* for sinking an enemy warship. All this in one sense is democratic, but in its effect it tends to induce the plain people to be satisfied with a piece of ribbon instead of the right to vote, and to make them upholders of a system by which they are deprived of any opportunity to make a real advance in life.

This system is the most complete that has ever existed in any country, because it has drawn so many of the inhabitants of the country into its meshes. Practically, the industrial workers of the great towns and the stupid peasants in the country are the only people in Germany left out of its net.

I had a shooting place very near Berlin, in fact I could reach it in three quarters of an hour by motor from the Embassy door, and there I had an opportunity of studying the conditions of life of the peasant class.

Germany is still a country of great proprietors. Lands may be held there by a tenure which was abolished in Great Britain hundreds of years ago. In Great Britain, property may only be tied up under fixed conditions during the lives of certain chosen people, in being at the death of the testator. In the State of New York, property may only be tied up during the lives of two persons, in being at the death of the person making the will, and for twenty-one years (the minority of an infant) thereafter. But in the Central Empires, property still may be tied up for an indefinite period under the feudal system, so that great estates, no matter how extravagant the life tenant may be, are not sold and do not come into the market for division among the people.

For instance, to-day there exist estates in the Central Empires which must pass from oldest son to oldest son indefinitely and, failing that, to the next in line, and so on; and conditions have

AMBASSADOR GERARD ON THE WAY TO HIS SHOOTING PRESERVE

A KEEPER AND BEATERS ON THE SHOOTING PRESERVE. IT SHOWS THE EARLY
INOCULATION OF DISCIPLINE INTO THE GERMAN SMALL BOY

even been annexed by which children cannot inherit if their father has married a woman not of a stated number of quarterings of nobility. There is a Prince holding great estates in Hungary. He is a bachelor and if he desires his children to inherit these estates there are only thirteen girls in the world whom he can marry, according to the terms of the instrument by which some distant ancestor founded this inheritance.

This vicious system has prevented extensive peasant proprietorship. The government, however, to a certain extent, has encouraged peasant proprietorship, but only with very small parcels of land; and it would be an unusual thing in Germany, especially in Prussia, to find a peasant owning more than twenty or thirty acres of land, most of the land being held by the peasants in such small quantities that after working their own lands they have time left to work the lands of the adjoining landed proprietor at a very small wage.

All the titles of the nobility are not confined to the oldest son. The "Pocketbook of Counts," published by the same firm which publishes the "Almanac de Gotha," contains the counts of Austria, Germany and Hungary together, showing in this way the intimate personal relation between the noble families of these three countries. All the sons of a count are counts, and so on, ad infinitum. Thus in Hungary there are probably seventy Counts Szecheny and about the same number of Zichy, etc. Some of the German noble families are not far behind. In fact it may be said that almost any person, in what is known as "society" in the Central Empires, has a title of some sort. The prefix "von" shows that the person is a noble and is often coupled with names of people who have no title. By custom in Germany, a "von" when he goes abroad is allowed to call himself Baron. But in Germany he could not do so. These noble families in the Central Empires, by the system of *Majorat* which I have described, hold large landed estates, and naturally exert a great influence upon their labourers. As a rule the system of tenant farming does not exist; that is, estates are not leased to small farmers as was the custom in Ireland and is still in Great Britain, but estates are worked as great agricultural enterprises under superintendents appointed by the proprietor. This system, impossible in America or even in Great Britain, is possible in the Central Empires where the villages are full of peasants who, not so many generations ago, were serfs attached to the land and who lived in wholesome fear of the landed proprietors.

This is the first method by which influence is exercised on the population. There is also the restricted franchise or "circle voting" which gives the control of the franchise to a few rich proprietors.

As a rule, the oldest son enters the army as an officer and may continue, but if he has not displayed any special aptitude for the military profession he retires and manages his estate. These estates are calculated by their proprietors to give at least four per cent interest income on the value of the land. Many younger sons after a short term of service in the army, usually as officers and not as *Einjähriger* leave the army and enter diplomacy or some other branch of the government service. The offices of judge, district attorney, etc., not being elective, this career as well as that leading to the position of *Landrat* and over-president of a province is open to those who, because they belong to old Prussian landed families, find favour in the eyes of the government. Much is heard in Germany and out of Germany of the Prussian Squire or Junker.

There is no leisure class among the Junkers. They are all workers, patriotic, honest and devoted to the Emperor and the Fatherland. If it is possible that government by one class is to be suffered, then the Prussian Junkers have proved themselves more fit for rule than any class in all history. Their virtues are Spartan, their minds narrow but incorruptible, and their bravery and patriotism undoubted. One can but admire them and their stern virtues. This class, largely because of its poverty and its constant occupation, does not travel; nor does the casual tourist or health seeker in Germany come in contact with these men. The Junkers will fight hard to keep their privileges, and the throne will fight hard for the Junkers because they are the greatest supporters of the Hohenzollerns.

The workingmen in the cities are hard workers and probably work longer and get less out of life than any workingmen in the world. The laws so much admired and made ostensibly for their protection, such as insurance against unemployment, sickness, injury, old age, etc., are in reality skilful measures which bind them to the soil as effectively as the serfs of the Middle Ages were bound to their masters' estates.

I have had letters from workingmen who have worked in America begging me for a steerage fare to America, saying that their insurance payments were so large that they could not save money out of their wages. Of course, after having made these payments for some years, the workingman naturally hesitates to emigrate and so lose all the premiums he has paid to the State. In peace times a skilled mechanic in Germany received less than two dollars a day, for which he was compelled to work at least ten hours.

Agricultural labourers in the Central Empires are poorly paid. The women do much of the work done here by men. For instance, once when staying at a nobleman's estate in Hungary, I noticed that the gardeners were all women, and, on inquiring how much they received, I was told they were paid about twenty cents a day. The women in the farming districts of Germany are worked harder than the cattle. In summer time they are out in the fields at five or six in the morning and do not return until eight or later at night. For this work they are sometimes paid as high as forty-eight cents a day in harvest time. Nevertheless, these small wages tempt many Russians to Germany during the harvest season. At the outbreak of the war there were perhaps fifty thousand Russians employed in Germany; men, women and girls. These the Germans retained in a sort of slavery to work the fields. I spoke to one Polish girl who was working on an estate over which I had shooting rights, near Berlin. She told me that at the commencement of the war she and her family were working in Germany and that since the war they all desired to return to Poland but that the Germans would not permit it.

This hard working of women in agricultural pursuits tends to stupefy and brutalise the rural population and keeps them in a condition of subjection to the Prussian Church and the Prussian system, and in readiness for war. Both Prussian Junkers and the German manufacturers look with favour upon the employment of so many women in farm work because the greater the number of the labourers, the smaller their wages throughout the country.

When I first came to Germany I, of course, was filled with the ideas that prevailed in America that the German workingman had an easy time. My mind was filled with pictures of the German workingmen sitting with their families at tables, drinking beer and listening to classical music. After I had spent some time in Germany, I found that the reason that the German workingmen sat about the tables was because they were too tired to do anything else.

I sincerely hope that after the war the workingmen of this country will induce delegates of their German brothers to make a tour of America. For when the German workingmen see how much better off the Americans are, they will return to Germany and demand shorter hours and higher wages; and the American will not be brought into competition with labour slaves such as the German workingmen of the period before the war.

As one goes through the streets of Berlin there are no evidences of poverty to be seen; but over fifty-five per cent of the families in Berlin are families living in one room.

The Germans are taken care of and educated very much in the same way that the authorities here look after the inmates of a poor-house or penitentiary. Such a thing as a German railway conductor rising to be president of the road is an impossibility in Germany; and the list of self-made men is small indeed,—by that I mean men who have risen from the ranks of the working-men.

The Socialists, representing the element opposed to the Conservatives, elect a few members to the Prussian Lower House and about one-third of the members to the Reichstag, but otherwise have no part whatever in the government. No Socialist would have any chance whatever if he set out to enter the government service with the ambition of becoming a district attorney or judge. Jews have not much chance in the government service. A few exceptions have been made. At one time Dernburg, who carried on the propaganda in America during the first year of the war, and who is a Jew, was appointed Colonial Minister of the Empire.

In my opinion, the liberalisation of Prussia has been halted by the fact that there has been no party of protest except that of the Socialists, and the Socialists, because they have, in effect, demanded abolition of the monarchy and the establishment of a republic as part of their programme, have been unable to do anything in the obtaining of the reforms.

Up to the beginning of the war there was great dissatisfaction. The people were irritated by certain direct taxes such as the tax upon matches, and because every Protestant in Prussia was compelled to pay a tax for the support of the church, unless he made a declaration that he was an atheist.

The only class in Germany which knows something of the outside world is the *Kaufmann* class. Prussian nobles of the ruling class are not travellers. They are always busy with the army and navy, government employments or their estates; and, as a rule, too poor to travel. The poor, of course, do not travel, and the *Kaufmann,* although he learns much in his travels in other countries to make him dissatisfied with the small opportunity which he has in a political way in Germany, is satisfied to let things stand because of the enormous profits which he makes through the low wages and long hours of the German workingman.

Lawyers and judges amount to little in Germany and we do not find there a class of political lawyers who, in republics, always seem to get the management of affairs in their own hands.

CHAPTER VIII

AFTER my return from Kiel to Berlin a period of calm ensued. No one seemed to think that the murders at Sarajevo would have any effect upon the world.

The Emperor had gone North on his yacht, but, as I believe, not until a certain line of action had been agreed upon.

Most of the diplomats started on their vacations. Sir Edward Goschen, British Ambassador, as well as the Russian Ambassador, left Berlin. This shows, of course, how little war was expected in diplomatic circles.

I went on two visits to German country-houses in Silesia, where the richest estates are situated. One of these visits was to the country-house of a Count, one of the wealthiest men in Germany, possessed of a fortune of about twenty to thirty million dollars. He has a great estate in Silesia, farmed, as I explained, not by tenant farmers, but by his own superintendents. In the centre is a beautiful country house or castle. We were thirty-two guests in the house-party. This Count

129

and his charming wife had travelled much and evidently desired to model their country life on that of England. Our amusements were tennis, swimming and clay-pigeon shooting, with dancing and music at night. Life such as this, and especially, the lavish entertainment of so many guests, is something very exceptional in Prussian country life and quite a seven months' wonder for the country side.

Some days after my return to Berlin the ultimatum of Austria was sent to Serbia. Even then there was very little excitement, and, when the Serbian answer was published, it was believed that this would end the incident, and that matters would be adjusted by dilatory diplomats in the usual way.

On the twenty-sixth of July, matters began to boil. The Emperor returned on this day and, from the morning of the twenty-seventh, took charge. On the twenty-seventh, also, Sir Edward Goschen returned to Berlin. I kept in touch, so far as possible, with the other diplomats, as the German officials were exceedingly uncommunicative, although I called on von Jagow every day and tried to get something out of him. On the night of the twenty-ninth, von Bethmann-Hollweg and Sir Edward had their memorable conversation in which the Chancellor, while making no promises about the French colonies, agreed, if

Great Britain remained neutral, to make "no territorial aggressions at the expense of France."

Von Bethmann-Hollweg further stated to Sir Edward, that ever since he had been Chancellor the object of his policy had been to bring about an understanding with Great Britain and that he had in mind a general neutrality agreement between Germany and Great Britain.

On the thirtieth, Sir Edward Grey refused the bargain proposed, namely that Great Britain should engage to stand by while the French colonies were taken and France beaten, so long as French territory was not taken. Sir Edward Grey said that the so-called bargain at the expense of France would constitute a disgrace from which the good name of Great Britain would never recover. He also refused to bargain with reference to the neutrality of Belgium.

Peace talk continued, however, on both the thirtieth and thirty-first, and many diplomats were still optimistic. On the thirty-first I was lunching at the Hotel Bristol with Mrs. Gerard and Thomas H. Birch, our minister to Portugal, and his wife. I left the table and went over and talked to Mouktar Pascha, the Turkish Ambassador, who assured me that there was no danger whatever of war. But in spite of his assurances and judging by the situation and what I learned from other diplomats, I had cabled to the State

Department on the morning of that day saying that a general European war was inevitable. On the thirty-first, *Kriegsgefahrzustand* or "condition of danger of war" was proclaimed at seven P. M., and at seven P. M. the demand was made by Germany that Russia should demobilise within twelve hours. On the thirtieth, I had a talk with Baron Beyens, the Minister of Belgium, and Jules Cambon, the French Ambassador, in the garden of the French Embassy in the afternoon. They both agreed that nothing could prevent war except the intervention of America.

Both Ambassador Cambon and Minister Beyens were very sad and depressed. After leaving them I met Sir Edward Goschen upon the street and had a short conversation with him. He also was very depressed.

Acting on my own responsibility, I sent the following letter to the Chancellor:

"Your Excellency:

Is there nothing that my country can do? Nothing that I can do towards stopping this dreadful war?

I am sure that the President would approve any act of mine looking towards peace.

Yours ever,

(Signed)   JAMES W. GERARD."

To this letter I never had any reply.

On the first of August at five P. M. the order
for mobilisation was given, and at seven-ten
P. M. war was declared by Germany on Russia,
the Kaiser proclaiming from the balcony of the
palace that "he knew no parties more."

Of course, during these days the population of
Berlin was greatly excited. Every night great
crowds of people paraded the streets singing
"Deutschland Ueber Alles" and demanding war.
Extras, distributed free, were issued at frequent
intervals by the newspapers, and there was a
general feeling among the Germans that their
years of preparation would now bear fruit, that
Germany would conquer the world and impose
its *Kultur* upon all nations.

On the second of August, I called in the morning to say good-bye to the Russian Ambassador.
His Embassy was filled with unfortunate Russians who had gone there to seek protection and
help. Right and left, men and women were
weeping and the whole atmosphere seemed that
of despair.

On the day the Russian Ambassador left, I
sent him my automobile to take him to the station. The chauffeur and footman reported to
me that the police protection was inadequate,
that the automobile was nearly overturned by
the crowd, and that men jumped on the running
board and struck the Ambassador and the ladies

with him in the face with sticks. His train was
due to leave at one-fifteen P. M. At about ten
minutes of one, while I was standing in my room
in the Embassy surrounded by a crowd of Americans, Mrs. James, wife of the Senator from
Kentucky and Mrs. Post Wheeler, wife of our
Secretary to the Embassy in Japan, came to me
and said that they were anxious to get through
to Japan *via* Siberia and did not know what to
do. I immediately scribbled a note to the Russian Ambassador asking him to take them on the
train with him. This, and the ladies, I confided
to the care of a red-headed page boy of the Embassy who spoke German. By some miracle he
managed to get them to the railroad station before the Ambassador's train left, the Ambassador
kindly agreeing to take them with him. His
train, however, instead of going to Russia, was
headed for Denmark; and from there the two
ladies crossed to Sweden, thence to England, and
so home, it being perhaps as well for them that
they did not have an opportunity to attempt the
Siberian journey during this period of mobilisation.

The Russian Ambassador reciprocated by con-
fiding to me a Russian Princess who had intended to go out with him but who, intimidated,
perhaps, by the scenes on the way to the station,
had lost her nerve at the railway station and

refused to depart with the Ambassador. She remained for a while in Berlin, and after some weeks recovered sufficient courage to make the trip to Denmark.

On the morning of August fourth, having received an invitation the day before, I "attended" at the Palace in Berlin. In the room where the court balls had been held in peace times, a certain number of the members of the Reichstag were assembled. The diplomats were in a gallery on the west side of the room. Soon the Emperor, dressed in field grey uniform and attended by several members of his staff and a number of ladies, entered the room. He walked with a martial stride and glanced toward the gallery where the diplomats were assembled, as if to see how many were there. Taking his place upon the throne and standing, he read an address to the members of the Reichstag. The members cheered him and then adjourned to the Reichstag where the Chancellor addressed them, making his famous declaration about Belgium, stating that "necessity knew no law," and that the German troops were perhaps at that moment crossing the Belgian frontier. Certain laws which had been prepared with reference to the government of the country, and which I will give in more detail in another place, as well as the war credit, were voted upon by the Reichstag.

The Socialists had not been present in the Palace, but joined now in voting the necessary credits.

On the afternoon of August fourth, I went to see von Jagow to try and pick up any news. The British Ambassador sat in the waiting-room of the Foreign Office. Sir Edward told me that he was there for the purpose of asking for his passports. He spoke in English, of course, and I am sure that he was overheard by a man sitting in the room who looked to me like a German newspaper man, so that I was not surprised when, late in the afternoon, extra sheets appeared upon the street announcing that the British Ambassador had asked for his passports and that Great Britain had declared war.

At this news the rage of the population of Berlin was indescribable. The Foreign Office had believed, and this belief had percolated through all classes in the capital, that the British were so occupied with the Ulster rebellion and unrest in Ireland that they would not declare war.

After dinner I went to the station to say good-bye to the French Ambassador, Jules Cambon. The route from the French Embassy by the Branderburg Thor to the Lehrter railway station was lined with troops and police, so that no accident whatever occurred. There was no one at the station except a very inferior official from the

CROWDS IN FRONT OF THE EMBASSY AWAITING BULLETINS
AUGUST, 1914

THE AMERICAN EMBASSY WAS THE CENTRE OF INTEREST TO MANY
IN THOSE EARLY DAYS OF THE WAR

German Foreign Office. Cambon was in excellent spirits and kept his nerve and composure admirably. His family, luckily, were not in Berlin at the time of the outbreak of the war. Cambon instead of being sent out by way of Switzerland, whence of course the road to France was easy, was sent North to Denmark. He was very badly treated on the train, and payment for the special train, in gold, was exacted from him by the German government.

Then I went for a walk about Berlin, soon becoming involved in the great crowd in front of the British Embassy on the Wilhelm Strasse. The crowd threw stones, etc., and managed to break all the windows of the Embassy. The Germans charged afterwards that people in the Embassy had infuriated the crowd by throwing pennies to them. I did not see any occurrences of this kind. As the Unter den Linden and the Wilhelm Platz are paved with asphalt the crowd must have brought with them the missiles which they used, with the premeditated design of smashing the Embassy windows. A few mounted police made their appearance but were at no time in sufficient numbers to hold the crowd in check.

Afterwards I went around to the Unter den Linden where there was a great crowd in front of the Hotel Adlon. A man standing on the outskirts of the crowd begged me not to go into the hotel, as he said the people were looking for British newspaper correspondents.

So threatening was the crowd towards the British correspondents that Wile rang up the porter of the Embassy after we had gone to bed and, not wishing to disturb us, he occupied the lounge in the porter's rooms.

Believing that possibly the British Embassy might be in such a condition that Sir Edward Goschen, the British Ambassador, might not care to spend the night there, I ordered an automobile and went up through the crowd which still choked the Wilhelm Strasse, with Roland Harvey, the Second Secretary, to the British Embassy. Sir Edward and his secretaries were perfectly calm and politely declined the refuge which I offered them in our Embassy. I chatted with them for a while, and, as I was starting to leave, a servant told me that the crowds in the street had greatly increased and were watching my automobile. I sent out word by the servant to open the automobile, as it was a landau, and to tell the chauffeur, when I got in, to drive very slowly.

I drove slowly through the crowd, assailed only by the peculiar hissing word that the Germans use when they are especially angry and which is supposed to convey the utmost contempt. This word is *"Pfui"* and has a peculiar effect when hissed out from thousands of Teutonic throats.

As we left the outskirts of the crowd, a man of respectable appearance jumped on the running board of the automobile, spit at me, saying *"Pfui,"* and struck Harvey in the face with his hat. I stopped the automobile, jumped out and chased this man down the street and caught him. My German footman came running up and explained that I was the American Ambassador and not an Englishman. The man who struck Harvey thereupon apologised and gave his card. He was a Berlin lawyer who came to the Embassy next morning and apologised again for his "mistake."

The following day, August fifth, I spent part of the time taking over from Sir Edward the British interests. Joseph C. Grew, our First Secretary, and I went to the British Embassy; seals were placed upon the archives, and we received such instructions and information as could be given us, with reference to the British subjects in Germany and their interests. The British correspondents were collected in the Embassy and permission was obtained for them to leave on the Embassy train.

During the day British subjects, without distinction as to age or sex, were seized, wherever found, and sent to the fortress of Spandau. I remonstrated with von Jagow and told him that that was a measure taken only in the Middle

Ages, and I believe that he remonstrated with the authorities and arranged for a cessation of the arbitrary arrests of women.

Frederick W. Wile, the well-known American correspondent of the *London Daily Mail,* was to go out also with the British party, on the ground that he had been a correspondent of a British newspaper. In the evening I went to the Foreign Office to get his passport, and, while one of the department chiefs was signing the passport, he stopped in the middle of his signature, threw down the pen on the table, and said he absolutely refused to sign a passport for Wile because he hated him so and because he believed he had been largely instrumental in the bringing about of the war. Of course this latter statement was quite ridiculous, but it took me some time before I could persuade this German official to calm his hate and complete his signature.

I have heard a few people say that Wile was unduly fearful of what the Germans might do to him, but the foregoing incident shows that his fears were well grounded, and knowing of this incident, which I did not tell him, I was very glad to have him accept the hospitality of the Embassy for the night preceding his departure. He was perfectly cool, although naturally much pleased when I informed him that his departure had been arranged.

Sir Edward and his staff and the British correspondents left next morning early, about six A. M. No untoward incidents occurred at the time of their departure which was, of course, unknown to the populace of Berlin.

During these first days there was a great spy excitement in Germany. People were seized by the crowds in the streets and, in some instances, on the theory that they were French or Russian spies, were shot. Foreigners were in a very dangerous situation throughout Germany, and many Americans were subjected to arrest and indignities.

A curious rumour spread all over Germany to the effect that automobiles loaded with French gold were being rushed across the country to Russia. Peasants and gamekeepers and others turned out on the roads with guns, and travelling by automobile became exceedingly dangerous. A German Countess was shot, an officer wounded and the Duchess of Ratibor was shot in the arm. It was sometime before this excitement was allayed, and many notices were published in the newspapers before this mania was driven from the popular brain.

There were rumours also that Russians had poisoned the Muggelsee, the lake from whence Berlin draws part of its water supply. There were constant rumours of the arrest of Russian spies disguised as women throughout Germany.

Many Americans were detained under a sort of arrest in their hotels; among these were Archer Huntington and his wife; Charles H. Sherrill, formerly our minister to the Argentine and many others.

CHAPTER IX

OF course, as soon as there was a prospect of war, the Embassy was overrun with Americans. Few Americans had taken the precaution of travelling with passports, and passports had become a necessity. All of the Embassy force and all the volunteers that I could prevail upon to serve, even a child of eleven years old, who was stopping in the house with us, were taking applications of the Americans who literally in thousands crowded the Wilhelm Platz in front of the Embassy.

The question of money became acute. Travellers who had letters of credit and bank checks for large sums could not get a cent of money in Germany. The American Express Company, I believe, paid all holders of its checks. When, with Mr. Wolf, President of the American Association of Commerce and Trade in Berlin, I called upon the director of the Imperial Bank and begged him to arrange something for the relief of American travellers in Germany, he refused to do anything; and I then suggested to him that he might give paper money, which they were then printing in Germany, to the Americans for good American credits such as letters of credit and bank checks, and that they would then have a credit in America which might become very valuable in the future. He, however, refused to see this. Director Herbert Gutmann of the Dresdener Bank was the far-seeing banker who relieved the situation. Gutmann arranged with me that the Dresdener Bank, the second largest bank in Germany, would cash the bank checks, letters of credit and the American Express Company's drafts and international business checks, etc., of Americans for reasonable amounts, provided the Embassy seal was put on the letter of credit or check to show that the holder was an American, and, outside of Berlin, the seal of the American Consulate. This immediately relieved the situation.

With the exception of Mr. Wolf who was, however, quite busy with his own affairs, I had no American Committees such as were organised in London and Paris to help me in Berlin. In Munich, however, the Americans there organised themselves into an efficient committee.

Mr. and Mrs. Ralph Pulitzer were in Berlin and immediately went to work in our Embassy.

Mr. Pulitzer busied himself at giving out passports and Mrs. Pulitzer proved herself a very
efficient worker. She and Mrs. Ruddock, wife
of our Third Secretary, and Mrs. Gherhardi, wife
of the Naval Attaché, with Mrs. Gerard formed
a sort of relief committee to look after the Americans who were without help or resources.

I arranged, with the very efficient help of
Lanier Winslow, for special trains to carry the
Americans in Germany to Holland. Trains were
run from Switzerland, Munich and Carlsbad
across Germany to Holland, and from Berlin
were run a number of trains to Holland.

The first room on entering the Embassy was
the ticket-office, and there, first Mr. Winslow,
and afterwards Captain Fenton, sold tickets, giving tickets free to those who were certified to be
without funds by the committee of Mrs. Pulitzer
and Mrs. Gerard. This committee worked on the
second floor of the Embassy in the ballroom, part
of it being roped off to keep the crowds back
from the ladies.

Each week I bought a numl r of steerage passages from the Holland American Line and the
ladies resold them in the ballroom. We had to
do this because the Holland American Line had
no licence to sell steerage tickets in Germany;
but by buying two or three hundred at a time
direct from the Company, I was enabled to ped-

dle them out in our ballroom to those Americans who, in their eagerness to reach their own country, were willing to endure the discomforts of travel in the steerage.

Winslow accompanied one special train to Holland, and I must say that I sympathised with him when I learned of what he had to do in the way of chasing lost hand-baggage and finding milk for crying babies.

These special trains were started from the Charlottenburg station, in a quiet part of Berlin so that no crowd was attracted by the departure of the Americans. The Carlsbad train went through very successfully, taking the Americans who had been shut up in Carlsbad since the commencement of the war.

One of the curious developments of this time was a meeting of sympathy for the Americans stranded in Germany, held in the town hall of Berlin on the eleventh of August. This meeting was commenced in one of the meeting rooms of the town hall, but so many people attended that we were compelled to adjourn to the great hall. There speeches were made by the over-Burgomaster, von Gwinner, Professor von Harnack and me. Another professor, who spoke excellent English, with an English accent, made a bitter attack upon Great Britain. In the pamphlet in which the speeches of Harnack and the over-

146

Burgomaster were published this professor's speech was left out. In his speech stating the object of the meeting, the over-Burgomaster said: "Since we hear that a large number of American citizens in the German Empire, and, especially, in Berlin, find themselves in embarrassments due to the shutting off of means of return to their own country, we here solemnly declare it to be our duty to care for them as brethren to the limit of our ability, and we appeal to all citizens of Berlin and the whole of the German Empire to co-operate with us to this end."

Professor von Harnack, head of the Royal Library in Berlin, is one of the ablest of the German professors. In his speech he gave expression to the feeling that was prevalent in the first days of the war that Germany was defending itself against a Russian invasion which threatened to blot out the German *Kultur*. He said, after referring to Western civilisation: "But in the face of this civilisation, there arises now before my eyes another civilisation, the civilisation of the tribe, with its patriarchal organisation, the civilisation of the horde that is gathered and kept together by despots,—the Mongolian Muscovite civilisation. This civilisation could not endure the light of the eighteenth century, still less the light of the nineteenth century, and now in the twentieth century it breaks loose and threatens us. This unorganised Asiatic mass, like the desert with its sands, wants to gather up our fields of grain."

Nothing was done for the Americans stranded in Germany by the Germans with the exception of the arrangements for the payment of funds by the Dresdener Bank on the letters of credit and the dispatching of special trains by the railroad department of the German government. As a matter of fact, nothing more could have been required of the Germans, as it was naturally the duty of the American government to take care of its citizens stranded abroad.

Almost the instant that war was declared, I cabled to our government suggesting that a ship should be sent over with gold because, of course, with gold, no matter what the country, necessaries can always be bought. Rumours of the dispatch of the *Tennessee* and other ships from America, reached Berlin and a great number of the more ignorant of the Americans got to believe that these ships were being sent over to take Americans home.

One morning an American woman spoke to me and said she would consent to go home on one of these ships provided she was given a state-room with a bath and Walker-Gordon milk for her children, while another woman of German ex-

WORKING IN THE EMBASSY BALLROOM AT THE OUTBREAK
OF HOSTILITIES, AUGUST, 1914

WAR DAYS IN BERLIN.   AMBASSADOR GERARD AND HIS STAFF

traction used to sit for hours in a corner of the ballroom, occasionally exclaiming aloud with much feeling, "O God, will them ships never come?"

In these first days of the war we also made a card index of all the Americans in Berlin, and, so far as possible, in Germany; in order to weed out those who had received the passports in the first days when possibly some people not entitled to them received them, and to find the deserving cases. All Americans were required to present themselves at the Embassy and answer a few questions, after which, if everything seemed all right, their passports were marked "recommended for transportation to America."

I sent out circulars from time to time to the consuls throughout Germany giving general instructions with regard to the treatment of Americans. The following circular sent out on August twelfth is a sample:

"AMERICAN EMBASSY,
BERLIN, August 12, 1914.
*"To the Consular Representatives
of the United States in Germany,
and for the general information of
American Citizens.*

"A communication will to-morrow be published in the *Berlin Lokal Anzeiger* regarding the sending of a special train to the Dutch frontier for the special conveyance of Americans. Other trains will probably be arranged for from time to time. No further news has been received regarding the sending of transports from the United States, but applications for repatriation are being considered by the Embassy and the various consular offices throughout Germany according to the Embassy's last circular and the announcements published in the *Lokal Anzeiger*.

"All Americans leaving Berlin must have their passports stamped by the Foreign Office, for which purpose they should apply to *Geheimer Legationsrat* Dr. Eckhardt at Wilhelmstrasse 76. Americans residing outside of Berlin should ascertain from their respective consular representatives what steps they should take in this regard.

"Letters for the United States may be sent to the Embassy and will be forwarded at the first opportunity.

"German subjects who desire to communicate with friends in Great Britain, Russia, France or Belgium, or who desire to send money, should make their requests to the Imperial Foreign Office. Americans are permitted to enter Italy. The steamers of the Italian lines are running at present, but are full for some time in advance. The Embassy is also informed that the steamer from

Vlissingen, Holland, runs daily at 11 A. M. The Ambassador cannot, however, recommend Americans to try to reach Holland by the ordinary schedule trains, as he has received reports of delays *en route,* owing to the fact that all civil travellers are ejected from trains when troops require accommodations. It is better to wait for special trains arranged for by the Embassy.

"The Dresdener Bank and its branches throughout Germany will cash *for Americans only* letters of credit and checks issued by good American banks in limited amounts. Included in this category are the checks of the Bankers' Association, Bankers' Trust Company, International Mercantile Marine Company, and American Express Company. All checks and letters of credit must, however, be stamped by American consuls, and consuls must see that the consular stamp is affixed to those checks and letters of credit only as are the bona fide property of American citizens. The Commerz & Disconto Bank makes the same offer and the Deutsche Bank will cash checks and letters of credit drawn by its correspondents.

"American consular officers may also draw later on the Dresdener Bank for their salaries and the official expenses of their consulates. Before drawing such funds from the bank, however, all consular officers should submit their expense accounts to me for approval. These expense accounts should be transmitted to the Embassy at the earliest opportunity.

"THE AMBASSADOR."

It will be noticed from the above circular that all Americans were required to have their passports stamped at the Foreign Office. One American did not receive back his passport, although he had left it at the Foreign Office. The Foreign Office claimed that it had delivered the passport to some one from the Embassy, but we were not very much surprised when this identical passport turned up later in the possession of Lodi, the confessed German spy, who was shot in the Tower of London.

After a time the American Government cabled me to advance money to destitute Americans; and the ladies in the ballroom, with their assistants, attended to this branch, advancing money where needed or so much as a person needed to make up the balance of passage on steerage tickets from Holland to the United States. At the same time we gradually built up a banking system. Those in the United States who had friends or relatives in Germany sent them money by giving the money to our State Department, and the State Department in turn cabled me to make a payment. This payment was made by my drawing a draft for the amount stated on the State Department, the recipient selling this draft at a fixed rate to the Deutsche Bank in Berlin. This business assumed great proportions, and after the Americans who were in a hurry to go home had disappeared, the ones remaining were kept in funds by their friends and relatives through this sort of bank under our management.

On August twenty-third, Assistant Secretary of War Breckenridge, who had come from America on the warship *Tennessee,* bringing gold with him, and a certain number of army officers, arrived in Berlin and took over our relief organisation in so far as it applied to the repatriation of Americans, housing it in rooms hired in a nearby hotel, the Kaiserhoff. This commission was composed of Majors J. A. Ryan, J. H. Ford and G. W. Martin and Captains Miller and Fenton, but the relief committee and the banking office were still continued in the Embassy ballroom.

A bulletin was published under the auspices of the American Association of Commerce and Trade and the advice there given was that all Americans having the means to leave should do so when the opportunity for leaving by special trains was presented, and proceed direct to London whence they could obtain transportation to the United States. All Americans without means were directed to apply to the relief commission which was authorized to pay for the transportation and subsistence of stranded Americans in order to enable them to return home.

The enormous quantity of baggage left behind by Americans in Germany was a problem requiring solution.

In spite of repeated advice to leave, many Americans insisted on remaining in Germany. Few of them were business people; there were many song-birds, piano players, and students. We had much trouble with these belated Americans. For example, one woman and her daughter refused to leave when advised, but stayed on and ran up bills for over ten thousand marks; and as arrest for debt exists in Germany, they could not leave when they finally decided to go. All of us in the Embassy had to subscribe the money necessary to pay their most pressing debts and they finally left the country, leaving an added prejudice against Americans.

CHAPTER X

PRISONERS OF WAR

DURING the period of the first months of the war, in addition to other work, it became necessary to look after those subjects of other nations who had been confided to my care.

At first the British were allowed considerable liberty, although none were permitted to leave the country. They were required to report to the police at stated times during the day and could not remain out late at night.

The Japanese had received warning from their Embassy as to the turn that events might take and, before sending its ultimatum, the Japanese government had warned its citizens, so that a great number of them had left Germany. After the declaration of war by Japan, all the Japanese in Germany were immediately imprisoned. This was stated to be in order to save them from the fury of the population and certainly the people seemed to be greatly incensed against the Japanese. When I finally obtained permission for their release and departure from Germany

I had to send some one with the parties of Japanese to the Swiss frontier in order to protect them from injury. They were permitted to leave only through Switzerland and, therefore, had to change cars at Munich. Before sending any of them to Munich I invariably telegraphed our Consul there to notify the Munich police so that proper protection could be provided at the railway station.

On one occasion a number of Japanese were waiting in the Embassy in order to take the night train for Munich. I sent a servant to take them out in order that they might get something to eat in a restaurant, but as no restaurant in Berlin would sell them food, arrangements were made to give them meals in the Embassy.

The members of the Siamese Legation, who in appearance greatly resemble the Japanese, were often subjected to indignities, and for a long time did not dare move about freely in Berlin, or even leave their houses.

The Japanese were marvels of courtesy. After I visited some of them at the civilian camp of Ruhleben, they wrote me a letter thanking me for the visit. Nearly every Japanese leaving Germany on his arrival in Switzerland wrote me a grateful letter.

When I finally left Germany, as I stepped from the special train at Zürich, a Japanese woman, who had been imprisoned in Germany and whose husband I had visited in a prison, came forward to thank me. A Japanese man was waiting in the hotel office in Berne when I arrived there, for a similar purpose, and the next morning early the Japanese Minister called and left a beautiful clock for Mrs. Gerard as an expression of his gratitude for the attention shown to his countrymen. It was really a pleasure to be able to do something for these polite and charming people.

On August twentieth I paid my first visit to a German prison camp. This was to the camp at Doeberitz situated about eight miles west of Berlin, a sort of military camp with permanent barracks. Some of these barracks were used for the confinement of such British civilians as the Germans had arrested in the first days of the war. There were only a few British among the prisoners, with a number of Russian and French. I was allowed to converse freely with the prisoners and found that they had no complaints. As the war went on, however, a number of British prisoners of war were taken by the Germans during the course of the great retreat of the British in Northern France. Then officers and privates began to come into Germany and were distributed in various camps. Finally, in the autumn of 1914, the British Government decided on interning a great number of Germans in Great Britain; and the German government immediately, and as a reprisal, interned all the British civilian men who, up to this time, had enjoyed comparative freedom in Berlin and other cities of the Empire. The British civilians were shut up in a race track about five miles from the centre of Berlin, called Ruhleben. This race track in peace times was used for contests of trotting horses and on it were the usual grandstands and brick stable buildings containing box stalls with hay lofts above, where the race horses were kept.

On August twentieth I paid my first visit to the police presidency in Berlin where political prisoners, when arrested, were confined. A small number of British prisoners subject to especial investigation were there interned. This prison, which I often subsequently visited, was clean and well kept, and I never had any particular complaints from the prisoners confined there, except, of course, as the war progressed, concerning the inadequacy of the food.

I had organised a special department immediately on the breaking out of the war to care for the interests of the British. At first Mr. Boylston Beal, a lawyer of Boston, assisted by Mr. Rivington Pyne of New York, was at the head of this department, of which later the Honourable John B. Jackson, formerly our Minister to the Balkan States, Greece and Cuba, took charge.

He volunteered to give his assistance at the commencement of the war and I was glad of his help, especially as he had been twelve years secretary in the Berlin Embassy and, therefore, was well acquainted not only with Germany but with German official life and customs. Mr. Jackson was most ably assisted by Charles H. Russell, Jr., of New York, and Lithgow Osborne. Of course, others in the Embassy had much to do with this department.

The first privates, prisoners of war, came to the camp of Doeberitz near Berlin. Early in the war Mr. Grew, our First Secretary, and Consul General Lay visited the camp for officers at Torgau. The question of the inspection of prisoners of the camps and the rights of Ambassadors charged with the interests of hostile powers was quite in the clouds. So many reports came to Germany about the bad treatment in England of German prisoners of war that I finally arranged to have Mr. Jackson visit them and report. This was arranged by my colleague, our Ambassador to Great Britain, and in the first winter Mr. Jackson made his trip there. His report of conditions there did much to allay the German belief as to the ill-treatment of their subjects who were prisoners in Great Britain and helped me greatly in bringing about better conditions in Germany. After vainly endeavouring to get the German government to agree to some definite plan for the inspection of the prisoners, after my notes to the Foreign Office had remained unanswered for a long period of time, and after sending a personal letter to von Jagow calling his attention to the fact that the delay was injuring German prisoners in other countries, I finally called on von Bethmann-Hollweg and told him that my notes concerning prisoners were sent by the Foreign Office to the military authorities: that, while I could talk with officials of the Foreign Office, I never came into contact with the people who really passed upon the notes sent by me, and who made the decisions as to the treatment of prisoners of war and inspection of their camps; and I begged the Chancellor to break down diplomatic precedent and allow me to speak with the military authorities who decided these questions. I said, "If I cannot get an answer to my proposition about prisoners, I will take a chair and sit in front of your palace in the street until I receive an answer."

The result was a meeting in my office.

I discussed the question involved with two representatives from the Foreign Office, two from the General Staff, two from the War Department and with Count Schwerin who commanded the civilian camp at the Ruhleben race track. In twenty minutes we managed to reach an agree-

ment which I then and there drew up: the substance of which, as between Great Britain and
Germany, was that the American Ambassador
and his representatives in Germany and the
American Ambassador and his representatives in
Great Britain should have the right to visit the
prison camps on giving reasonable notice, which
was to be twenty-four hours where possible, and
should have the right to converse with the prisoners, within sight but out of hearing, of the camp
officials; that an endeavour should be made to ad-
just matters complained of with the camp authorities before bringing them to the notice of higher
authorities; that ten representatives should be
named by our Ambassador and that these should
receive passes enabling them to visit the camps
under the conditions above stated. This agreement was ratified by the British and German
Governments and thereafter for a long time we
worked under its provisions and in most questions
dealt direct with the War Department.

Of course, before this meeting I had managed
to get permission to visit the camps of Ruhleben
and Doeberitz near Berlin; and Mr. Michaelson,
our consul at Cologne, and Mr. Jackson and
others at the Embassy had been permitted to visit
certain camps. But immediately preceding the
meeting on the fourth of March and while
matters were still being discussed we were com-

pelled to a certain extent to suspend our visits.

In the first days of the war it was undoubtedly and unfortunately true that prisoners of war taken by the Germans, both at the time of their capture and in transit to the prison camps, were often badly treated by the soldiers, guards or the civil population.

The instances were too numerous, the evidence too overwhelming, to be denied. In the prison camps themselves, owing to the peculiar system of military government in Germany, the treatment of the prisoners varied greatly. As I have, I think, stated in another place, Germany is divided into army corps districts. Over each of these districts is, in time of war, a representative corps commander who is clothed with absolute power in that district, his orders superseding those of all civilian officials. These corps commanders do not report to the war department but are in a measure independent and very jealous of their rights. For instance, to show the difficulty of dealing with these corps commanders, after my arrangements concerning the inspection of prisoners of war had been ratified by both the Imperial and British governments, I went to Halle to inspect the place of detention for officers there. Halle is some hours from Berlin and when I had driven out to the camp, I was met by the commander who told me that I might visit the camp but that I could not speak to the prisoners out of hearing. I told him that our arrangement was otherwise, but, as he remained firm, I returned to Berlin. I complained to the Foreign Office and was told there that the matter would be arranged and so I again, some days later, returned to Halle. My experience on the second trip was exactly the same as the first. I spoke to von Jagow who explained the situation to me, and advised me to visit first the corps commander at Magdeburg and try and arrange the matter with him. I did so and was finally permitted to visit this camp and to talk to the officers out of ear-shot.

This camp of Halle was continued during the war, although not at all a fit place for the detention of officers, who were lodged in the old factory buildings surrounded by a sort of courtyard covered with cinders. This building was situated in the industrial part of the town of Halle. There was no opportunity for recreation or games, although several enterprising officers had tried to arrange a place where they could knock a tennis ball against the wall.

It was the policy of the Germans to put some prisoners of each nation in each camp. This was probably so that no claim could be made that the prisoners from one nation among the Allies were treated better or worse than the prisoners from another nation.

In the beginning of the war the Germans were surprised by the great number of prisoners taken and had made no adequate preparations for their reception. Clothing and blankets were woefully wanting, so I immediately bought what I could in the way of underclothes and blankets at the large department stores of Berlin and the wholesalers and sent these to the camps where the British prisoners were confined. I also sent to the Doeberitz camp articles such as sticks for wounded men who were recovering, and crutches, and even eggs and other nourishing delicacies for the sick.

At first the prisoners were not compelled to work to any extent, but at the time I left Germany the two million prisoners of war were materially assisting the carrying on of the agriculture and industries of the Empire.

The League of Mercy of New York having telegraphed me in 1914, asking in what way funds could best be used in the war, I suggested in answer that funds for the prisoners of war were urgently needed. Many newspapers poked fun at me for this suggestion, and one bright editor said that if the Germans did not treat their prisoners properly they should be made to! Of course, unless this particular editor had sailed up the Spree in a canoe and bombarded the royal palace, I know of no other way of "making" the Germans do anything. The idea, however, of doing some work for the prisoners of war was taken up by the Young Men's Christian Association. Dr. John R. Mott was at the head of this work and was most ably and devotedly assisted by the Rev. Archibald C. Harte. I shall give an account of their splendid work in a chapter devoted to the charitable work of the war.

At only one town in Germany was any interest in the fate of the prisoners of war evinced. This was, I am glad to say, in the quaint university town of Göttingen. I visited this camp with Mr. Harte, in April, 1915, to attend the opening of the first Y. M. C. A. camp building in Germany. The camp was commanded by Colonel Bogen, an officer strict in his discipline, but, as all the prisoners admitted, just in his dealings with them. There were, as I recall, about seven thousand prisoners in this camp, Russian, French, Belgian and British. It is a pity that the methods of Colonel Bogen and his arrangements for camp buildings, etc., were not copied in other camps in Germany. Here, as I have said, the civil population took some interest in the fate of the unfortunate prisoners within their gates, led in this by several professors in the University. The most active of these professors was Professor Stange who, working with a French lawyer who had been captured near Arras while in the Red Cross, provided a library for the prisoners and otherwise helped them. Of course, these charitable acts of Professor Stange did not find favor with many of his fellow townsmen of Göttingen, and he was not surprised when he awoke one morning to find that during the night his house had been painted red, white and blue, the colours of France, England and America.

I heard of so many instances of the annoyance of prisoners by the civil population that I was quite pleased one day to read a paragraph in the official newspaper, the *North German Gazette,* which ran somewhat as follows: "The following inhabitants of (naming a small town near the borders of Denmark), having been guilty of improper conduct towards prisoners of war, have been sentenced to the following terms of imprisonment and the following fines and their names are printed here in order that they may be held up to the contempt of all future generations of Germans." And then followed a list of names and terms of imprisonment and fines. I thought that this was splendid, that the German government had at last been aroused to the necessity of protecting their prisoners of war from the annoyances of the civil population, and I wrote to our consul in Kiel and asked him to investigate the case. From him I learned that some unfortunate prisoners passing through the town (in a

part of Germany inhabited by Scandinavians)
had made signs that they were suffering from
hunger and thirst, that some of the kind-hearted
people among the Scandinavian population had
given them something to eat and drink and for
this they were condemned to fines, to prison and
to have their names held up to the contempt of
Germans for all time.

I do not know of any one thing that can give
a better idea of the official hate for the nations
with which Germany was at war than this.

The day after visiting the camp at Göttingen,
I visited the officers' camp situated at the town
of Hanover Münden. Here about eight hundred
officers, of whom only thirteen were British, were
confined in an old factory building situated on
the bank of the river below the town. The Russian officers handed me some arrows tipped with
nails which had been shot at them by the kind-
hearted little town boys, and the British pointed
out to me the filthy conditions of the camp. In
this, as in unfortunately many other officer
camps, the inclination seemed to be to treat the
officers not as captured officers and gentlemen,
but as convicts. I had quite a sharp talk with
the commander of this camp before leaving and
he afterwards took violent exception to the report which I made upon his camp. However, I
am pleased to say that he reformed, as it were,

and I was informed by my inspectors that he had finally made his camp one of the best in Germany.

Much as I should have liked to, I could not spend much time myself in visiting the prison camps; many duties and frequent crises kept me in Berlin, but members of the Embassy were always travelling in this work of camp inspection.

For some time my reports were published in parliamentary "White Papers," but in the end our government found that the publication of these reports irritated the Germans to such a degree that the British Government was requested not to publish them any more. Copies of the reports were always sent by me both to Washington and to London, and handed to the Berlin Foreign Office.

While Winston Churchill was at the head of the British Admiralty, it was stated that the German submarine prisoners would not be treated as ordinary prisoners of war; but would be put in a place by themselves on the ground that they were pirates and murderers, and not entitled to the treatment accorded in general to prisoners of war. Great indignation was excited by this in Germany; the German government immediately seized thirty-seven officers, picking those whom they supposed related to the most prominent families in Great Britain, and placed them

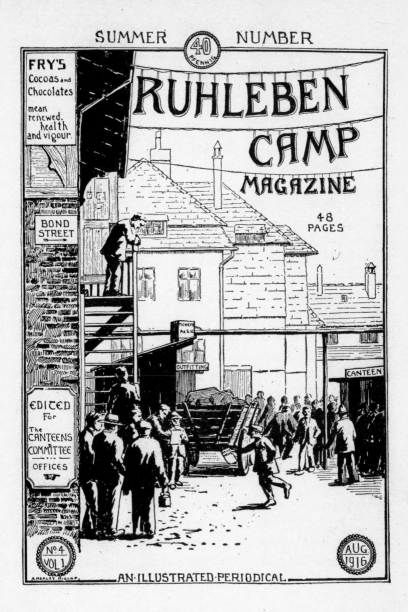

SUMMER NUMBER

40 PFENNIG

RUHLEBEN CAMP MAGAZINE

48 PAGES

FRY'S Cocoas and Chocolates mean renewed health and vigour.

BOND STREET

EDITED For The CANTEENS COMMITTEE and OFFICES

No 4 VOL 1

AUG 1916

AN·ILLUSTRATED·PERIODICAL

A. HEALEY HISLOP

A COVER OF THE MONTHLY ISSUED BY THE RUHLEBEN PRISONERS

in solitary confinement. A few were confined in this way in Cologne, but the majority were put in the ordinary jails of Magdeburg and Burg.

As soon as I heard of this, accompanied by Mr. Charles H. Russell, Jr., of my staff, I went to Magdeburg, using my ordinary pass for the visiting of prisoners. The German authorities told me afterwards that if they had known I was going to make this visit they would not have permitted it, but on this occasion the corps commander system worked for me. Accompanied by an adjutant, in peace times a local lawyer from the corps commander's office in Magdeburg, and other officers, I visited these British officers in their cells in the common jail at Magdeburg. They were in absolutely solitary confinement, each in a small cell about eleven feet long and four feet wide. Some cells were a little larger, and the prisoners were allowed only one hour's exercise a day in the courtyard of the prison. The food given them was not bad, but the close confinement was very trying, especially to Lieutenant Goschen, son of the former Ambassador to Germany, who had been wounded and in the hospital at Douai. Among them I found an old acquaintance, Captain Robin Grey, who had been often in New York. The German authorities agreed to correct several minor matters of which the officers complained and then we went to the neighbouring town of Burg, where other officers were confined in the same manner and under similar conditions in the ordinary jail. After visiting these prisoners and obtaining for them from the authorities some modifications of the rules which had been established we visited the regular officers' camp at Burg.

This was at that time what I should call a bad camp, crowded and with no space for recreation. Later, conditions were improved and more ground allowed to the prisoners for games, etc. At the time of my first visit I found that the commander, a polite but peppery officer, was in civil life a judge of the Supreme Court at Leipzig, the highest court in the Empire. As I had been a judge in the State of New York, we foregathered and adjourned for lunch with his staff to the hotel in Burg.

After Churchill left the British Admiralty, his successor reversed his ruling and the submarine prisoners were placed in the ordinary confinement of prisoners of war. When the Germans were assured of this, the thirty-seven officers who had been in reprisal placed in solitary confinement were sent back to ordinary prison camps. In fact in most cases I managed to get the Germans to send them to what were called "good" camps.

Lieutenant Goschen, however, became quite ill

and was taken to the hospital in Magdeburg. At the time of his capture, the Germans had told me, in answer to my inquiries, that he was suffering from a blow on the head with the butt end of a rifle, but an X-ray examination at Magdeburg showed that fragments of a bullet had penetrated his brain and that he was, therefore, hardly a fit subject to be chosen as one of the reprisal prisoners. I told von Jagow that I thought it in the first place a violation of all diplomatic courtesy to pick out the son of the former Ambassador to Germany as a subject for reprisals and secondly that, in picking him, they had taken a wounded man; that the fact that they did not know that he had fragments of a bullet in his brain made the situation even worse because that ignorance was the result of the want of a proper examination in the German hospitals; and I insisted that, because of this manifestly unfair treatment which had undoubtedly caused the very serious condition of Lieutenant Goschen, he should be returned to England in the exchange of those who were badly wounded. I am pleased to say that von Jagow saw my point of view and finally secured permission for Lieutenant Goschen to leave for England.

Dr. Ohnesorg, one of our assistant Naval Attachés, went with him to England on account of the seriousness of his condition, and I was very glad to hear from his father that he had arrived safely in London.

Undoubtedly the worst camp which I visited in Germany was that of Wittenberg. Wittenberg is the ancient town where Luther lived and nailed his theses to the church door. The camp is situated just outside the city in a very unattractive spot next to the railway. An outbreak of typhus fever prevented us from visiting the camp, although Mr. Jackson conversed with some of the prisoners from outside the barrier of barbed wire. When the typhus was finally driven out, Mr. Lithgow Osborne visited the camp and his report of conditions there was such that I visited it myself, in the meantime holding up his report until I had verified it.

With Mr. Charles H. Russell, Jr., I visited the camp. Typhus fever seems to be continually present in Russia. It is carried by the body louse and it is transmitted from one person to another. Russian soldiers seem to carry this disease with them without apparently suffering much from it themselves. The Russian soldiers arriving at Wittenberg were not properly disinfected and, in consequence, typhus fever broke out in camp. Several British medical officers were there with their prisoners, because, by the provisions of the Hague conventions, captured medical officers may be kept with the troops of their nation, if prisoners have need of their services. These medical officers protested with the camp commander against the herding together of the French and British prisoners with the Russians, who, as I have said, were suffering from typhus fever. But the camp commander said, "You will have to know your Allies;" and kept all of his prisoners together, and thus as surely condemned to death a number of French and British prisoners of war as though he had stood them against the wall and ordered them shot by a firing squad. Conditions in the camp during the period of this epidemic were frightful. The camp was practically deserted by the Germans and I understand that the German doctor did not make as many visits to the camp as the situation required.

At the time I visited the camp the typhus epidemic, of course, had been stamped out. The Germans employed a large number of police dogs in this camp and these dogs not only were used in watching the outside of the camp in order to prevent the escape of prisoners but also were used within the camp. Many complaints were made to me by prisoners concerning these dogs, stating that men had been bitten by them. It seemed undoubtedly true that the prisoners there had been knocked about and beaten in a terrible manner by their guards, and one guard went so far as to strike one of the British medical officers. There were about thirty-seven civilian prisoners in the camp who had been there all through the typhus epidemic. I secured the removal of these civilian prisoners to the general civilian camp at Ruhleben, and the conditions at Wittenberg may be judged by the fact that when it was announced to these civilians that they were to be taken from Wittenberg to another camp one of them was so excited by the news of release that he fell dead upon the spot.

In talking over conditions at Wittenberg with von Jagow I said, "Suppose I go back to Wittenberg and shoot some of these dogs, what can you do to me?" Soon after the dogs disappeared from the camp.

The food in all these camps for civilians and for private soldiers was about the same. It consisted of an allowance of bread of the same weight as that given the civilian population. This was given out in the morning with a cup of something called coffee, but which in reality was an extract of acorns or something of the kind without milk or sugar; in the middle of the day, a bowl of thick soup in which the quantity of meat was gradually diminished as war went on, as well as the amount of potatoes for which at a later period turnips and carrots were, to a large extent, substituted; and in the evening in good camps there was some sort of thick soup given

out or an apple, or an almost infinitesimal piece
of cheese or sausage.

In the war department at Berlin there was a
Prisoners of War Department in charge of
Colonel, later General, Friedrich. This department, however, did not seem to be in a position
to issue orders to the corps commanders commanding the army corps districts of Germany,
who had absolute control of the prison camps
within their districts. Colonel Friedrich, however, and his assistants endeavoured to stand-
ardise the treatment of prisoners of war in the
different corps districts, and were able to exert
a certain amount of pressure on the corps commanders. They determined on the general reprisals to be taken in connection with prisoners
of war. For instance, when some of the Germans, who had been taken prisoners by the British and who were in England, were sent to work
in the harbour of Havre, the Germans retaliated
by sending about four times the number of British prisoners to work at Libau in the part of Russia then occupied by the Germans. But while the
British permitted our Embassy in Paris to inspect
the prisoners of war at Havre, the Germans for
months refused to allow me permission to send
any one to inspect those British prisoners at
Libau.

Cases came to my attention where individual

corps commanders on their own initiative directed punitive measures against the prisoners of war in their districts, on account of the rumours of the bad treatment of German citizens in England. Thus the commander in the district where the camp of Doeberitz was situated issued an order directing reprisals against prisoners under his command on account of what he claimed to be the bad treatment of German women in England. It required constant vigilance to seek out instances of this kind and cause them to be remedied.

I did not find the Germans at all efficient in the handling of prisoners of war. The authority was so divided that it was hard to find who was responsible for any given bad conditions. For instance, for a long period of time I contended with the German authorities for better living conditions at the civilian camp of Ruhleben. I was promised time and again by Colonel Friedrich, by the camp commander and by the Foreign Office that these conditions would be remedied. In that camp men of education, men in delicate health, were compelled to sleep and live six in a box stall or so closely that the beds touched each other in hay-lofts, the outside walls of which were only four feet high.

I finally almost in despair wrote identical personal letters, after having exhausted all ordinary diplomatic steps, to General von Kessel, Commander of the Mark of Brandenburg, to the commander of the corps district in which the Ruhleben camp was situated, and to the Minister of War: and the only result was that each of the officers addressed claimed that he had been personally insulted by me because I had presumed to call his attention to the inhuman conditions under which the prisoners were compelled to live in the Ruhleben camp.

The commander of this civilian camp of Ruhleben was a very handsome old gentleman, named Count Schwerin. His second in command for a long time was a Baron Taube. Both of these officers had been long retired from the army and were given these prison commands at the commencement of the war. Both of them were naturally kind-hearted but curiously sensitive and not always of even temper. On the whole I think that they sympathised with the prisoners and did their best to obtain a bettering of the conditions of their confinement. The prisoners organised themselves in their various barracks, each barrack having a captain of the barrack, the captains electing one of their number as a camp captain or *Obmann*.

The man who finally appeared as head man of the camp was an ex-cinematograph proprietor, named Powell. In my mind he, assisted by Beaumont and other captains, conducted the affairs of the camp as well as possible, given the difficulty of dealing with the prisoners on one hand and the prison authorities on the other hand. Naturally he was always subject to opposition from many prisoners, among whom those of aristocratic tendencies objected to being under the control of one not of the highest caste in Great Britain; and there were others who either envied him his authority or desired his place. The camp authorities allowed Powell to visit the Embassy at least once a week and in that way I was enabled to keep in direct touch with the camp. At two periods during my stay in Berlin I spent enough days at the camp to enable every prisoner who had a complaint of any kind to present it personally to me.

The organisation of this camp was quite extraordinary. I found it impossible to get British prisoners to perform the ordinary work of cleaning up the camp, and so forth, always expected of prisoners themselves; and so, with the funds furnished me from the British Government, the camp captain was compelled to pay a number of the poorer prisoners to perform this work. Secretaries Ruddock and Kirk of our Embassy undertook the uninteresting and arduous work of superintending these payments as well as of our other financial affairs. This work was most trying and they deserve great credit for their self-denial. By arrangement with the British Government, I was also enabled to pay the poorer prisoners an allowance of five marks a week, thus permitting them to buy little luxuries and necessities and extra food at the camp canteen which was early established in the camp. I also furnished the capital to the camp canteen, enabling it to make its purchases and carry on its business. In this establishment everything could be purchased which was purchasable in Germany, and for months after the commencement of the war articles of luxury were sold at a profit and articles of food sold at a loss for the benefit of those who required an addition to the camp diet. There was a street in the camp of little barracks or booths which the prisoners christened Bond Street, and where many stores were in operation such as a tailor shop, shoe-maker's, watch-maker's, etc. Acting with Powell, I succeeded in getting the German authorities to turn over the kitchens to the prisoners. Four of the prisoners who did most excellent self-denying work in these kitchens deserve to be specially mentioned. They were Ernest L. Pyke, Herbert Kastner, Richard H. Carrad and George Fergusson.

The men in this camp subsisted to a great extent upon the packages of food sent to them from

England. Credit must be given to the German authorities for the fairly prompt and efficient delivery of the packages of food sent from England, Denmark and Switzerland to prisoners of war in all camps.

In Ruhleben the educated prisoners volunteered to teach the ignorant: two hundred and ninety-seven different educational courses were offered to those who desired to improve their minds. A splendid orchestra was organised, a dramatic society which gave plays in French and one which gave plays in English and another one which gave operas. On New Year's day, 1916, I attended at Ruhleben a really wonderful performance of the pantomime of "Cinderella"; and, in January, 1917, a performance of "The Mikado" in a theatre under one of the grand stands. In these productions, of course, the female parts were taken by young men and the scenery, costumes and accessories were all made by the prisoners. There was a camp library of over five thousand volumes sent over by the British Government and a reading and meeting hall, erected by the American Y. M. C. A. There was even a system of postal service with special stamps so that a prisoner in one barrack could write to a friend in another and have a letter delivered by the camp postal authorities. The German authorities had not hired the entire race track from the Race Track Association so that I made a special contract with the race track owners and hired from them the in-field and other portions not taken over by German authorities. Here the prisoners had tennis courts and played hockey, foot-ball and cricket and held athletic games. Expert dentists in the camp took care of the poorer prisoners as did an oculist hired by me with British funds, and glasses were given them from the same funds.

The prisoners who needed a little better nourishment than that afforded by the camp diet and their parcels from England, could obtain cards giving them the right to eat in the Casino or camp official restaurant where they were allowed a certain indicated amount of wine or beer with their meals, and finally arrangements were arrived at by which the German guards left the camp, simply guarding it from the outside; and the policing was taken over by the camp police department, under the charge of the prison camp commander and committee. The worst features, of course, were the food and housing. Human nature seems always to be the same. Establishment of clubs seems inherent to the Anglo-Saxon nature. Ten or more persons would combine together and erect a sort of wooden shed against the brick walls of a barrack, hire some poorer person to put on a white jacket and be addressed as "steward," put in the shed a few deck chairs and a table and enjoy the sensation of exclusiveness and club life thereby given.

Owing to the failure of Germany and Great Britain to come to an agreement for a long time as to the release of captured crews of ships, there were in Ruhleben men as old as seventy-five years and boys as young as fifteen. There were in all between fifty and sixty of these ships' boys. They lived in a barrack by themselves and under the supervision of a ship's officer who volunteered to look after them as sort of a monitor. They were taught navigation by the older prisoners and I imagine were rather benefited by their stay in the camp. I finally made arrangements by which these boys were released from England and Germany. With the exception of the officers and crews of the ships, prisoners were not interned who were over fifty-five.

The British Government was generous in the allowance of money for Ruhleben prisoners. The amount allowed by the German Government to the camp commanders for feeding the prisoners was extremely small, only sixty pfennigs a day. At first many of the camp commanders made contracts with caterers for the feeding of the prisoners and as the caterers' profit had to come out of this very small sum the amount of food which the remainder purchased for the prisoners was small indeed. As the war went on the prisoners' department of the war office tried to induce the camp commanders to abandon the contractors' system and purchase supplies themselves. A sort of convention of camp commanders was held in Berlin which I attended. Lectures were there given on food and its purchase, and methods of disinfecting prisoners, on providing against typhus, and on housing and other subjects. A daily lunch was served, supposed to be composed of the exact rations given at the prison camps.

The schedules of food, etc., made out by the camp commanders and furnished to foreign correspondents were often not followed in practice. I know on one occasion when I was at the camp at Doeberitz, the camp commander gave me his schedule of food for the week. This provided that soup with pieces of meat was to be given on the day of my visit, but on visiting the camp kitchen I found that the contractor was serving fish instead of meat. Some of the camp commanders not only treated their prisoners kindly but introduced manufactures of furniture, etc., to help the prisoners to pass their time. The camps of Krossen and Göttingen deserve special mention. At Giessen, the camp commander had permitted the erection of a barrack in which certain prisoners who were electrical experts gave lessons in electrical fitting, etc., to their fellow prisoners. There was also a studio in this camp where prisoners with artistic talent were furnished with paints and allowed to work. As more and more people were called to the front in Germany, greater use was made of the prisoners, and in the summer of 1916 practically all the prisoners were compelled to work outside of the camps. They were paid a small extra sum for this, a few cents a day, and as a rule were benefited by the change of scene and occupation. The Russians especially became very useful to the Germans as agricultural laborers.

Professor Alonzo E. Taylor of the University of Pennsylvania, a food expert, and Dr. D. J. McCarthy, also of Philadelphia, joined my staff in 1916 and proved most efficient and fearless inspectors of prison camps. Dr. Taylor could use the terms calories, proteins, etc., as readily as German experts and at a greater rate of speed. His report showing that the official diet of the prisoners in Ruhleben was a starvation diet incensed the German authorities to such fury that they forbade him to revisit Ruhleben. Professor Buckhaus, the German expert, agreed with him in some of his findings. I do not know what will happen to the Professor, who seemed willing to do his best for the prisoners. He wrote a booklet on the prison camps which he asked permission to dedicate to me, but the War Office, which published the book, refused to allow him to make this dedication. It was a real pleasure to see the way in which Dr. Taylor carried on his work of food inspection; and his work, as well as that of the other doctors sent from America to join my staff, Drs. Furbush, McCarthy, Roler, Harns, Webster and Luginbuhl, did much to better camp conditions.

Dr. Caldwell, the sanitary expert, known for his great work in Serbia, now I believe head of the hospital at Pittsburgh, reported in regard to the prison diet: "While of good quality and perhaps sufficient in quantity by weight, it is lacking in the essential elements which contribute to the making of a well-balanced and satisfactory diet. It is lacking particularly in fat and protein content which is especially desirable during the colder months of the year. * * * There is considerable doubt whether this diet alone without being supplemented by the articles of food received by the prisoners from their homes would in any way be sufficient to maintain the prisoners in health and strength."

Dr. Caldwell also visited Wittenberg and found the commander by temperament, and so on, unfitted for such a position.

The Germans, as Dr. Taylor has pointed out, tried to feed prisoners on schedule like horses.

There is, however, a nervous discrimination in eating so far as man is concerned; and a diet, scientifically fitted to keep him alive, may fail because of its mere monotony.

Think of living as the prisoners of war in Germany have for years, without ever having anything (except black bread) which cannot be eaten with a spoon.

Officer prisoners were, after matters had settled down and after several bitter contests which I had with the German authorities, fairly well treated. There was, as in the case of the camps for the privates, a great difference between camps, and a great difference between camp commanders. Mr. Jackson did most of the visiting of the officers' camps. In many camps the officers were allowed a tennis court and other amusements, as well as light wine or beer at meals, but the length of the war had a bad effect on the mental condition of many of the officers.

A great step forward was made when arrangements were entered into between Germany and Great Britain whereby wounded and sick officers and men, when passed by the Swiss Commission which visited both countries, were sent to Switzerland; sent still as prisoners of war, subject to return to Germany or England respectively, but the opportunity afforded by change of food and scene, as well as reunion of families, saved many a life. By arrangements between the two countries, also, the severely wounded prisoners were set free. I believe that this exchange of the heavily wounded between the Germans and the Russians was the factor which prevented the entrance of Sweden into the war. These wounded men traversed the whole length of Sweden in the railway, and the spectacle afforded to the Swedish population of these poor stumps of humanity, victims of war, has quite effectually kept the Swedish population from an attack of unnecessary war fever.

Officers and men who tried to escape were not very severely punished in Germany unless they had broken or stolen something in their attempt. Officers were usually subjected to a jail confinement for a period and then often sent to a sort of punitive camp. Such a camp was situated in one of the Ring forts surrounding the city of Kustrin which I visited in September, 1916. There the officers had no opportunity for exercise except in a very small courtyard or on the roof, which was covered with grass, of the building in which they were confined. I arranged, however, on my visit for the construction of a tennis court outside. The British officers in Germany practically subsisted on their parcels received from home, and during the end of my stay a much better tea could be had with the prison officers than with the camp commander. The prisoners had real tea and marmalade and white bread to offer, luxuries which had long since disappeared from all German tables. On the whole, the quarters given to the officers' prisons in Germany were not satisfactory, and were not of the kind that should have been offered to officer prisoners of war.

At the time I left Germany there were nearly two million prisoners of war in the Empire, of whom about ten thousand were Russian officers, nine thousand French officers and about one thousand British officers.

As a rule our inspectors found the hospitals, where the prisoners of war were, in as good condition as could be expected.

I think this was largely due to the fact that so many doctors in Germany are Jews. The people who are of the Jewish race are people of gentle instincts. In these hospitals a better diet was given to the prisoners. There were, of course, in addition to the regular hospitals, hospitals where the severely wounded prisoners were sent. Almost uniformly these hospitals were clean and the prisoners were well taken care of.

At Ruhleben there was a hospital which in spite of many representations was never in proper shape. In addition, there was in the camp a special barrack established by the prisoners

25

SOME MEMBERS
OF BAR 2 -

IN RUHLEBEN CAMP. A SPECIMEN BOTH
OF THE PRISONER-ARTIST'S WORK AND OF
THE TYPES ABOUT HIM

themselves for the care of those who were so ill or so weak as to require special attention but who were not ill enough to be sent to the hospital. This barrack was for a long time in charge of a devoted gentleman, a prisoner, whose name I have unfortunately forgotten, but whose self-sacrifice deserves special mention.

I arranged with the camp authorities and the German authorities for permission to enter into a contract with Dr. Weiler. Under this contract Dr. Weiler, who had a sanatorium in the West of Berlin, received patients from Ruhleben. Those who were able paid for themselves, the poorer ones being paid for by the British Government. This sanatorium occupied several villas. I had many disputes with Dr. Weiler, but finally managed to get this sanatorium in such condition that the prisoners who resided there were fairly well taken care of.

An arrangement was made between Great Britain and Germany by which civilians unfit for military service were sent to their respective countries, and just before I left I effected an arrangement by which all civilians over forty-five years old, with the exception of twenty who might be held by each country for military reasons, were to be released. I do not know whether this arrangement was actually carried out in full.

With the lapse of time the mental condition of

the older prisoners in Ruhleben had become quite alarming. Soldier prisoners, when they enter the army, are always in good physical condition and enter with the expectation of either being killed or wounded or taken prisoner, and have made their arrangements accordingly. But these unfortunate civilian prisoners were often men in delicate health, and all were in a constant state of great mental anxiety as to the fate of their business and their enterprises and their families. In 1916, not only Mr. Grafton Minot, who for some time had devoted himself exclusively to the Ruhleben prisoners, but also Mr. Ellis Dresel, a distinguished lawyer of Boston, who had joined the Embassy as a volunteer, took up the work. Mr. Dresel visited Ruhleben almost daily and by listening to the stories and complaints of the prisoners materially helped their mental condition.

The Germans collected all the soldier prisoners of Irish nationality in one camp at Limburg not far from Frankfurt a. M. There efforts were made to induce them to join the German army. The men were well treated and were often visited by Sir Roger Casement who, working with the German authorities, tried to get these Irishmen to desert their flag and join the Germans. A few weaklings were persuaded by Sir Roger who finally discontinued his visits, after obtaining about thirty recruits, because the remaining Irishmen chased him out of the camp.

I received information of the shooting of one prisoner, and although the camp authorities had told Dr. McCarthy that the investigation had been closed and the guard who did the shooting exonerated, nevertheless, when I visited the camp in order to investigate, I was told that I could not do so because the matter of the shooting was still under investigation. Nor was I allowed to speak to those prisoners who had been witnesses at the time of the shooting. I afterwards learned that another Irishman had been shot by a guard on the day before my visit, and the same obstacles to my investigation were drawn about this case.

The Irishmen did not bear confinement well, and at the time of my visit among them many of them were suffering from tuberculosis in the camp hospital. They seemed also peculiarly subject to mental breakdowns. Two devoted Catholic priests, Father Crotty and a Brother Warren from a religious house in Belgium, were doing wonderful work among these prisoners.

The sending out of the prisoners of war to work throughout Germany has had one very evil effect. It has made it to the financial advantage of certain farmers and manufacturers to have the war continued. The Prussian land owners or

Junkers obtain four or five times as much for their agricultural products as they did before the war and have the work on their farms performed by prisoners of war to whom they are required to pay only six cents a day. When the *Tageblatt* called attention to this it was suppressed for several days.

At many of these so-called working camps our inspectors were refused admission on the ground that they might learn trade or war secrets. They succeeded, however, in having the men sent outside in order that they might inspect them and hear their complaints. There were in Germany about one hundred central camps and perhaps ten thousand or more so-called working camps, in summer time, throughout the country. Some of the British prisoners were put to work on the sewage farm of Berlin but we succeeded in getting them sent back to their parent camp.

The prisoners of war were often accused of various breaches of discipline and crimes. Members of the Embassy would attend these trials, and we endeavoured to see that the prisoners were properly represented. But the Germans often refused us an opportunity to see the prisoners before their trial, or even before their execution. The case of Captain Fryatt is in point.

Captain Fryatt who commanded a British merchant ship was captured and taken to the civilian camp at Ruhleben. In searching him the Germans claimed that he wore a watch presented to him for an attempt to ram a German submarine. They, therefore, took Fryatt from the Ruhleben camp and sent him to Bruges for trial. When I heard of this I immediately sent two formal notes to the German Foreign Office demanding the right to see Fryatt and hire counsel to represent him, inquiring what sort of counsel would be permitted to attend the trial and asking for postponement of the trial until these matters could be arranged. The German Foreign Office had informed me that they had backed up these requests and I believe them, but the answer of the German admiralty to my notes was to cause the trial to proceed the morning after the day on which my notes were delivered and to shoot Fryatt before noon of the same day.

As to the evidence regarding the watch, the British Foreign Office learned that, when captured, Captain Fryatt had neither a watch nor any letter to indicate that he had tried to ram a submarine!

This cruel and high-handed outrage caused great indignation in Great Britain, and even in certain circles in Germany; and the manner in which my request was treated was certainly a direct insult to the country which I represented. In conversation with me, Zimmermann and the

Chancellor and von Jagow all expressed the greatest regret over this incident, which shows how little control the civilian branch of the government has over the military in time of war. Later on, when similar charges were made against another British sea captain, the Foreign Office, I think through the influence of the Emperor, was able to prevent a recurrence of the Fryatt outrage.

As I have said, many of the camp commanders in Germany were men, excellent and efficient and kind hearted, who did what they could for the prisoners. It is a pity that these men should bear the odium which attaches to Germany because of the general bad treatment of prisoners of war in the first days of the war, and because certain commanders of prison camps were not fitted for their positions.

The commander at the camp at Wittenberg was replaced, but the Germans have never acknowledged that bad conditions had existed in that camp. Shortly before we left Germany the war department seemed to gain more control of the prisoners of war situation, and on our representations at least one camp commander was permanently relieved. If examples had been made early in the war of the camp commanders who were not fit for their places and of those who had in any way mishandled prisoners of war, the German people as a whole would not have had to bear the burden of this odium. The many prisoners will return to their homes with a deep and bitter hatred of all things German.

The British Government took a great interest in the British prisoners in Germany. Nothing was omitted and every suggestion made by me was immediately acted on; while many most valuable hints were given me from London as to prisoners' affairs. Their Majesties, the King and Queen, showed a deep personal concern in the welfare of the unfortunate British in German hands; and this concern never flagged during the period of my stay in Berlin. Lord Robert Cecil and Lord Newton were continually working for the benefit of British prisoners.

At a time when the British prisoners were without proper clothing, the British Government sent me uniforms, overcoats, etc., and I hired a warehouse in Berlin as a distributing point; but, after some months, the German authorities refused to allow me to continue this method of distribution on the ground that it was the duty of Germany to provide the prisoners with clothes. But Germany was not performing this duty and the British prisoners had to suffer because of this German official woodenheadedness.

In the spring of 1916, quite characteristically, the Germans broke their "treaty" concerning visits to prisoners, and refused to permit us to speak to prisoners out of hearing. Von Jagow told me that this was because of the trouble made among Russian prisoners by the visits of Madam Sazonoff, but this had nothing to do with the arrangement between Great Britain and Germany.

I think that the Germans suspected that I had learned from fellow prisoners of the cruel and unnecessary shooting of two Irish prisoners at Limburg. It was not from prisoners, however, that I obtained this information. but from Germans who wrote to me.

In addition to the British and Japanese, I had the protection of the Serbian and Roumanian subjects and the protection of the interests of a very small country, the Republic of San Marino. Soon after the Serbians and Roumanians appeared in the prison camps of Germany we made reports on the condition and treatment of these prisoners, as well as reports concerning the British.

I was able to converse with some Serbians, in the first days of the war, in their native tongue, which, curiously enough, was Spanish. Immediately after the persecution of the Jews in Spain by Ferdinand and Isabella and other monarchs, a number of Spanish Jews emigrated to Serbia where they have remained ever since, keeping their old customs and speaking the old Spanish of the time of Cervantes.

The German authorities, in the most petty manner, often concealed from me the presence of British prisoners, especially civilians, in prison camps. For a long time I was not informed of the presence of British civilians in Sennelager and it was only by paying a surprise visit by motor to the camp at Brandenburg that I discovered a few British, the crew of a trawler, there. It was on information contained in an anonymous letter, evidently from the wife of some German officer, that I visited Brandenburg where the crew of this trawler, deprived of money, were without any of the little comforts or packages that mitigate life in a German prison camp.

CHAPTER XI

AT the commencement of the war for some days I was cut off from communication with the United States; but we soon established a chain of communication, at first through Italy and later by way of Denmark. At all times cables from Washington to Berlin, or *vice versa,* took, on the average, two days in transmission.

After the fall of Liège, von Jagow sent for me and asked me if I would transmit through the American Legation a proposition offering Belgium peace and indemnity if no further opposition were made to the passage of German troops through Belgium. As the proposition was a proposition for peace, I took the responsibility of forwarding it and sent the note of the German Government to our Minister at the Hague for transmission to our Minister in Belgium.

Dr. Van Dyke, our Minister at the Hague, refused to have anything to do with the transmission of this proposition and turned the German note over to the Holland Minister for Foreign Affairs, and through this channel the proposition reached the Belgian Government.

The State Department cabled me a message from the President to the Emperor which stated that the United States stood ready at any time to mediate between the warring powers, and directed me to present this proposition direct to the Emperor.

I, therefore, asked for an audience with the Emperor and received word from the chief Court Marshal that the Emperor would receive me at the palace in Berlin on the morning of August tenth. I drove in a motor into the courtyard of the palace and was there escorted to the door which opened on a flight of steps leading to a little garden about fifty yards square, directly on the embankment of the River Spree, which flows past the Royal Palace. As I went down the steps, the Empress and her only daughter, the Duchess of Brunswick, came up. Both stopped and shook hands with me, speaking a few words. I found the Emperor seated at a green iron table under a large canvas garden umbrella. Telegraph forms were scattered on the table in front of him and basking in the gravel were two small dachshunds. I explained to the Emperor the object of my visit and we had a general conversation about the war and the state of affairs.

The Emperor took some of the large telegraph blanks and wrote out in pencil his reply to the President's offer.* This reply, of course, I cabled immediately to the State Department.

*For the President of the
United States personally:*

10/VIII 14.

1. H. R. H. Prince Henry was received by his Majesty King George V in London, who empowered him to transmit to me verbally, that England would remain neutral if war broke out on the Continent involving Germany and France, Austria and Russia. This message was telegraphed to me by my brother from London after his conversation with H. M. the King, and repeated verbally on the twenty-ninth of July.

2. My Ambassador in London transmitted a message from Sir E. Grey to Berlin saying that only in case France was likely to be crushed England would interfere.

3. On the thirtieth my Ambassador in London reported that Sir Edward Grey in course of a "private" conversation told him that if the conflict remained localized between *Russia*—not Serbia—and *Austria,* England would not move, but if we "mixed" in the fray she would take quick decisions and grave measures; i. e., if I left my ally Austria in the lurch to fight alone England would not touch me.

4. This communication being directly counter to the King's message to me, I telegraphed to H. M. on the twenty-ninth or thirtieth, thanking him for kind

* See facsimile, page 433.

messages through my brother and begging him to use all his power to keep France and Russia—his Allies—from making any war-like preparations calculated to disturb my work of mediation, stating that I was in constant communication with H. M. the Czar. In the evening the King kindly answered that he had ordered his Government to use every possible influence with his Allies to refrain from taking any provocative military measures. At the same time H. M. asked me if I would transmit to Vienna the British proposal that Austria was to take Belgrade and a few other Serbian towns and a strip of country as a "main-mise" to make sure that the Serbian promises on paper should be fulfilled in reality. This proposal was in the same moment telegraphed to me from Vienna for London, quite in conjunction with the British proposal; besides, I had telegraphed to H. M. the Czar the same as an idea of mine, before I received the two communications from Vienna and London, as both were of the same opinion.

5. I immediately transmitted the telegrams *vice versa* to Vienna and London. I felt that I was able to tide the question over and was happy at the peaceful outlook.

6. While I was preparing a note to H. M. the Czar the next morning, to inform him that Vienna, London and Berlin were agreed about the treatment of affairs, I received the telephones from H. E. the Chancellor that in the night before the Czar had given the order to mobilize the whole of the Russian army, which was, of course, also meant against Germany; whereas up till then the southern armies had been mobilized against Austria.

7. In a telegram from London my Ambassador informed me he understood the British Government would guarantee neutrality of France and wished to know whether Germany would refrain from attack. I telegraphed to H. M. the King personally that mobilization being already carried out could not be stopped, but if H. M. could guarantee with his armed forces the neutrality of France I would refrain *from attacking her, leave her alone* and employ my troops elsewhere. H. M. answered that he thought my offer was based on a misunderstanding; and, as far as I can make out, Sir E. Grey never took my offer into serious consideration. He never answered it. Instead, he declared England had to defend Belgian neutrality, which had to be violated by Germany on strategical grounds, news having been received that France was already preparing to enter Belgium, and the King of Belgians having refused my petition for a free passage under guarantee of his country's freedom. I am most grateful for the President's message.

WILLIAM, H. R.

When the German Emperor in my presence indited his letter to President Wilson of August tenth, 1914, he asked that I cable it immediately to the State Department and that I simultaneously give it to the press. As I have already stated, I cabled the document immediately to the State Department at Washington, but I withheld it from publication.

My interview with the Emperor was in the morning. That afternoon a man holding a high position in Germany sent for me. I do not give his name because I do not wish to involve him in any way with the Emperor, so I shall not even indicate whether he is a royalty or an official. He said:

"You had an interview today with the Emperor. What happened?"

I told of the message given me for the President which was intended for publication by the Emperor. He said:

"I think you ought to show that message to me; you know the Emperor is a constitutional Emperor and there was once a great row about such a message."

I showed him the message, and when he had read it he said: "I think it would be inadvisable for us to have this message published, and in the interest of good feeling between Germany and America. If you cable it ask that publication be withheld."

I complied with his request and it is characteristic of the President's desire to preserve good relations that publication was withheld. Now, when the two countries are at war; when the whole world, and especially our own country, has an interest in knowing how this great calamity of universal war came to the earth, the time has come when this message should be given out and I have published it by permission.

This most interesting document in the first place clears up one issue never really obscure in the eyes of the world—the deliberate violation of the neutrality of Belgium, whose territory "had to be violated by Germany on strategical grounds." The very weak excuse is added that "news had been received that France was already preparing to enter Belgium,"—not even a pretense that there had ever been any actual violation of Belgium's frontier by the French prior to the German invasion of that unfortunate country. Of course the second excuse that the King of the Belgians had refused entrance to the Emperor's troops under guarantee of his country's freedom is even weaker than the first. It would indeed inaugurate a new era in the intercourse of nations if a small nation could only preserve its freedom by at all times, on request, granting free passage to the troops of a powerful neighbour on the march to attack an adjoining country.

And aside from the violation of Belgian neutrality, what would have become of Great Britain and of the world if the Prussian autocracy had been left free to defeat—one by one—the nations of the earth? First, the defeat of Russia and Serbia by Austria and Germany, the incorporation of a large part of Russia in the German Empire, German influence predominant in Russia and all

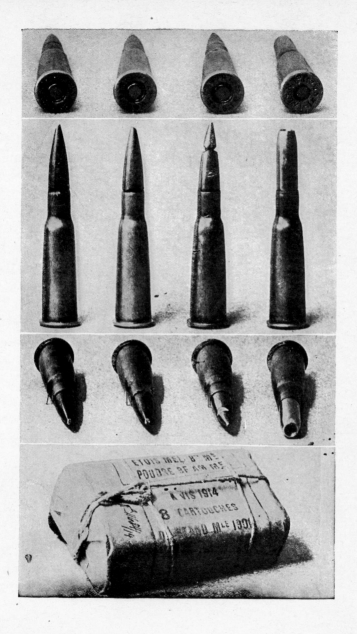

ALLEGED DUM-DUM BULLETS, WHICH THE GERMANS DECLARED
HAD BEEN FOUND IN LONGWY

the vast resources of that great Empire at the command of Germany. All the fleets in the world could uselessly blockade the German coasts if Germany possessed the limitless riches of the Empire of the Romanoffs.

The German army drawing for reserves on the teeming populations of Russia and Siberia would never know defeat. And this is not idle conjecture, mere dreaming in the realm of possibilities, because the Russian revolution has shown us how weak and tottering in reality was the dreaded power of the Czar.

Russia, beaten and half digested, France would have been an easy prey, and Great Britain, even if then joining France in war, would have a far different problem to face if the U-boats were now sailing from Cherbourg and Calais and Brest and Bordeaux on the mission of piracy and murder, and then would come our turn and that of Latin America. The first attack would come not on us, but on South or Central America—at some point to which it would be as difficult for us to send troops to help our neighbor as it would be for Germany to attack.

Remember that in Southern Brazil nearly four hundred thousand Germans are sustained, as I found out, in their devotion to the Fatherland by annual grants of money for educational purposes from the Imperial treasury in Berlin.

It was not without reason that at this inter-view, when the Kaiser wrote this message to the President, he said that the coming in of Great Britain had changed the whole situation and would make the war a long one. The Kaiser talked rather despondently about the war. I tried to cheer him up by saying the German troops would soon enter Paris, but he answered, "The British change the whole situation—an obstinate nation—they will keep up the war. It cannot end soon."

It was the entry of Great Britain into the war, in defence of the rights of small nations, in de-fence of the guaranteed neutrality of Belgium, which saved the world from the harsh dominion of the conquest-hungry Prussians and therefore saved as well the two Americas and their pro-tecting doctrine of President Monroe.

The document, which is dated August tenth, 1914, supersedes the statement made by the Ger-man Chancellor von Bethmann-Hollweg in his speech before the Reichstag on August fourth, 1914, in which he gave the then official account of the entrance into the war of the Central Empires. It will be noted that von Bethmann-Hollweg in-sisted that France began the war in the sentence reading: "There were bomb-throwing fliers, cavalry patrols, invading companies in the Reichs-land (Alsace-Lorraine). Thereby France, although the condition of war had not yet been declared, had attacked our territory." But the Emperor makes no mention of this fact, of supreme importance if true, in his writing to President Wilson six days later.

Quite curiously, at this time there was a belief on the part of the Germans that Japan would declare war on the Allies and range herself on the side of the Central Powers. In fact on one night there was a friendly demonstration in front of the Japanese Embassy, but these hopes were soon dispelled by the ultimatum of Japan sent on the sixteenth of August, and, finally, by the declaration of war on August twenty-third.

During the first days of the war the warring powers indulged in mutual recriminations as to the use of dumdum bullets and I was given several packages of cartridges containing bullets bored out at the top which the Germans said had been found in the French fortress of Longwy, with a request that I send an account of them to President Wilson and ask for his intervention in the matter. Very wisely President Wilson refused to do anything of the kind, as otherwise he would have been deluged with constant complaints from both sides as to the violations of the rules of war.

The cartridges given to me were in packages marked on the outside *"Cartouches de Stand"* and from this I took it that possibly these cartridges had been used on some shooting range near the fort and the bullets bored out in order that they might not go too far, if carelessly fired over the targets.

On August fifth, with our Naval Attaché, Commander Walter Gherardi, I called upon von Tirpitz, to learn from him which ports be considered safest for the ships to be sent from America with gold for stranded Americans. He recommended Rotterdam.

I also had a conversation on this day with Geheimrat Letze of the Foreign Office with reference to the proposition that British and German ships respectively should have a delay of until the fourteenth of August in which to leave the British or German ports in which they chanced to be.

The second week in August, my wife's sister and her husband, Count Sigray, arrived in Berlin. Count Sigray is a reserve officer of the Hungarian Hussars and was in Montana when the first rumours of war came. He and his wife immediately started for New York and sailed on the fourth of August. They landed in England, and as Great Britain had not yet declared war on Austria, they were able to proceed on their journey. With them were Count George Festetics and Count Cziraki, the former from the Austrian

Embassy in London and the latter from that in Washington. They were all naturally very much excited about war and the events of their trip.

The Hungarians as a people are quite like Americans. They have agreeable manners and are able to laugh in a natural way, something which seems to be a lost art in Prussia. Nearly all the members of Hungarian noble families speak English perfectly and model their clothes, sports and country life, as far as possible, after the British.

The thirteenth saw the departure of our first special train containing Americans bound for Holland. I saw the Americans off at the Charlottenburg station. They all departed in great spirits and very glad of an opportunity to leave Germany.

I had some negotiations about the purchase by America or Americans of the ships of the North German Lloyd, but nothing came of these negotiations. Trainloads of Americans continued to leave, but there seemed to be no end to the Americans coming into Berlin from all directions.

On August twenty-ninth, Count Szoegyeny, the Austrian Ambassador, left Berlin. He had been Ambassador there for twenty-two years and I suppose because of his advancing years the Austrian Government thought that he had outlived his usefulness. Quite a crowd of Germans and diplomats were at the station to witness the rather sad farewell. His successor was Prince Hohenlohe, married to a daughter of Archduke Frederick. She expressly waived her right to precedence as a royal highness, and agreed to take only the precedence given to her as the wife of the Ambassador, in order not to cause feeling in Berlin. Prince Hohenlohe, a rather easygoing man, who had been most popular in Russia and Austria, immediately made a favourable impression in Berlin and successfully occupied the difficult position of mediator between the governments of Berlin and Vienna.

On September fourth von Bethmann-Hollweg gave me a statement to give to the reporters in which he attacked Great Britain, claiming that Great Britain did not desire the friendship of Germany but was moved by commercial jealousy and a desire to crush her; that the efforts made for peace had failed because Russia, under all circumstances, was resolved upon war; and that Germany had entered Belgium in order to forestall the planned French advance. He also claimed that Great Britain, regardless of consequences to the white race, had excited Japan to a pillaging expedition, and claimed that Belgian girls and women had gouged out the eyes of the wounded; that officers had been invited to dinner and shot across the table; and that Belgian women had cut the throats of soldiers quartered in their houses while they were asleep. The Chancellor concluded by saying, in this statement, that every one knows that the German people is not capable of unnecessary cruelty or of any brutality.

We were fully occupied with taking care of the British prisoners and interests, the Americans, and negotiations relating to commercial questions, and to getting goods required in the United States out of Germany, when, on October seventh, a most unpleasant incident, and one which for some time caused the members of our Embassy to feel rather bitterly toward the German Foreign Office, took place.

A great number of British civilians, men and women, were stranded in Berlin. To many of these were paid sums of money in the form of small allowances on behalf of the British Government. In order to facilitate this work, we placed the clerks employed in this distribution in the building formerly occupied by the British Consul in Berlin. Of course, the great crowds of Americans resorting to our Embassy, when combined with the crowds of British, made it almost impossible even to enter the Embassy, and establishment of this outlying relief station materially helped this situation. I occupied it, and employed British men and British women in this relief work by the express permission of the Imperial Foreign Office, which I thought it wise to obtain in view of the fact that the Germans seemed daily to become more irritable and suspicious, especially after the Battle of the Marne.

On the night of October second, our Second Secretary, Harvey, went to this relief headquarters at about twelve o'clock at night, and was witness to a raid made by the Berlin police on this establishment of ours. The men and women working were arrested, and all books and papers which the police could get at were seized by them. The next morning I went around to the place and on talking with the criminal detectives in charge, was told by them that they had made the raid by the orders of the Foreign Office. When I spoke to the Foreign Office about this, they denied that they had given directions for the raid and made a sort of half apology. The raid was all the more unjustified because only the day before I had had a conversation with the Adjutant of the Berlin Kommandantur and told him that, although I had permission from the Foreign Office, I thought it would be better to dismiss the British employed and employ only Americans or Germans; and I sent round to my friend, Herr von Gwinner, head of the Deutsche Bank, and asked him to recommend some German accountants to me.

The Kommandantur is the direct office of mili-

tary control. When the Adjutant heard of the
raid he was almost as indignant as I was, and on
the tenth of October informed me that he had
learned that the raid had been made on the joint
orders of the Foreign Office and von Tirpitz's department.

The books and papers of an Embassy, including those relating to the affairs of foreign nations temporarily in the Embassy's care, are uni-
versally recognised in international law as not
subject to seizure, nor did the fact that I was
carrying on this work outside the actual Embassy building have any bearing on this point so
long as the building was directly under my control and, especially, as the only work carried on
was work properly in my hands in my official
capacity. The Foreign Office saw that they had
made a mistake, but at Zimmermann's earnest request I agreed, as it were, to forget the incident.
Later on, this precedent might have been used by
our government had they desired to press the
matter of the seizure of von Igel's papers. Von
Igel, it will be remembered, was carrying on business of a private nature in a private office hired
by him. Nevertheless, as he had been employed
in some capacity in the German Embassy at
Washington, Count von Bernstorff claimed im-
munity from seizure for the papers found in that
office.

On August sixteenth the Kaiser left Berlin for the front. I wrote to his master of the household, saying that I should like an opportunity to be at the railway station to say good-bye to the Emperor, but was put off on various excuses. Thereafter the Emperor practically abandoned Berlin and lived either in Silesia, at Pless, or at some place near the Western front.

At first, following the precedent of the war of 1870, the more important members of the government followed the Kaiser to the front, even the Chancellor and the Minister of Foreign Affairs abandoning their offices in Berlin. Not long afterwards, when it was apparent that the war must be carried on on several fronts and that it was not going to be the matter of a few weeks which the Germans had first supposed, these officials returned to their offices in Berlin. In the meantime, however, much confusion had been caused by this rather ridiculous effort to follow the customs of the war of 1870.

When von Jagow, Minister of Foreign Affairs, was absent at the Great General Headquarters, the diplomats remaining behind conducted their negotiations with Zimmermann, who in turn had to transmit everything to the Great General Headquarters.

In August, there were apparently rumours afloat in countries outside of Germany that prominent Socialists at the outbreak of the war had been shot. The State Department cabled me to find out whether there was any truth in these rumours, with particular reference to Liebknecht and Rosa Luxemburg.

Liebknecht is a lawyer practicing in Berlin and so I telephoned him, asking him to come and see me. He did so, and of course, by his presence verified the fact that he had not been executed. He told me that the rumours as to the treatment of the Socialists were entirely unfounded and said that he had no objection to my cabling a statement that the Socialists were opposed to Czarismus and that he personally had confidence in the German army and the cause of the German people.

Many people confuse Liebknecht with his father, now dead. Liebknecht, the son, is a man of perhaps forty-three years, with dark bushy hair and moustache and wearing eye-glasses, a man of medium height and not at all of strong build. In the numerous interruptions made by him during the debates in the Reichstag, during the first year of the war, his voice sounded high and shrill. Of course, any one who defies the heavy hand of autocracy must suffer from nervousness. We all knew that sooner or later autocracy would "get" Liebknecht, and its opportunity came when he appeared in citizen's clothes at an attempted mass-meeting at the Potsdamer-platz. For the offence of appearing out of uniform after being called and mobilized, and for alleged incitement of the people, he was condemned for a long term of imprisonment. One can but admire his courage. I believe that he earns his living by the practice of law before one of the minor courts. It is hard to say just what *rôle* he will play in the future. It is probable that when the Socialists settle down after the war and think things over, they will consider that the leadership of Scheidemann has been too conservative; that he submitted too readily to the powers of autocracy and too easily abandoned the program of the Socialists. In this case, Liebknecht perhaps will be made leader of the Socialists, and it is within the bounds of probability that Scheidemann and certain of his party may become Liberals rather than Socialists.

CHAPTER XII

DIPLOMATIC NEGOTIATIONS

IN the autumn of 1914, the rush of getting the Americans out of Germany was over. The care of the British civilians was on a business basis and there were comparatively few camps of prisoners of war. Absolutely tired by working every day and until twelve at night, I went to Munich for a two weeks' rest.

On February fourth, 1915, Germany announced that on February eighteenth the blockade of Great Britain through submarines would commence.

Some very peculiar and mysterious negotiations thereafter ensued. About February eighth, an American who was very intimate with the members of the General Staff came to me with a statement that Germany desired peace and was ready to open negotiations to that end. It was, however, to be made a condition of these peace negotiations that this particular American should go to Paris and to Petrograd and inform the governments there of the overwhelming strength of the German armies and of their positions, which knowledge, it was said, he had obtained by personally visiting both the fronts. It was further intimated that von Tirpitz himself was anxious that peace should be concluded, possibly because of his fear that the proposed blockade would not be successful.

Of course, I informed the State Department of these mysterious manœuvres.

I was taken by back stairways to a mysterious meeting with von Tirpitz at night in his rooms in the Navy Department. When I was alone with him, however, he had nothing definite to say or to offer; if there was any opportunity at that time to make peace nothing came of it. It looked somewhat to me as if the whole idea had been to get this American to go to Paris and Petrograd, certify from his personal observation to the strength of the German armies and position, and thereby to assist in enticing one or both of these countries to desert the allied cause. All of this took place about ten days before the eighteenth of February, the time named for the announcement of the blockade of Great Britain.

Medals were struck having the head of von Tirpitz on one side and on the other the words "Gott strafe England," and a picture of a sort of Neptune assisted by a submarine rising from the sea to blockade the distant British coast.

The Ambassador is supposed to have the right to demand an audience with the Kaiser at any time, and as there were matters connected with the treatment of prisoners as well as this coming submarine warfare which I wished to take up with him, I had on various occasions asked for an audience with him; on each occasion my request had been refused on some excuse or other, and I was not even permitted to go to the railway station to bid him good-bye on one occasion when he left for the front.

When our Military Attaché, Major Langhorne, left in March, 1915, he had a farewell audience with the Kaiser and I then asked him to say to the Kaiser that I had not seen him for so long a time that I had forgotten what he looked like. Langhorne reported to me that he had given his message to the Kaiser and that the Kaiser said, "I have nothing against Mr. Gerard personally, but I will not see the Ambassador of a country which furnishes arms and ammunition to the enemies of Germany."

Before the departure of Langhorne, I had succeeded in getting Germany to agree that six American army officers might visit Germany as military observers. When they arrived, I presented them at the Foreign Office, etc., and they were taken on trips to the East and West fronts.

They were not allowed to see much, and their

request to be attached to a particular unit was refused. Nearly everywhere they were subject to insulting remarks or treatment because of the shipment of munitions of war to the Allies from America; and finally after they had been subjected to deliberate insults at the hands of several German generals, Mackensen particularly distinguishing himself, the United States Government withdrew them from Germany.

Colonel (now General) Kuhn, however, who was of these observers, was appointed Military Attaché in place of Major Langhorne. Speaking German fluently and acting with great tact, he managed for a long time to keep sufficiently in the good graces of the Germans to be allowed to see something of the operations of the various fronts. There came a period in 1916 when he was no longer invited to go on the various excursions made by the foreign military attachés and finally Major Nicolai, the general intelligence officer of the Great General Headquarters, sent for him early in the autumn of 1916, and informed him that he could no longer go to any of the fronts. Colonel Kuhn answered that he was aware of this already. Major Nicolai said that he gave him this information by direct order of General Ludendorf, that General Ludendorf had stated that he did not believe America could do more damage to Germany than she had done if the two countries were actually at war, and that he considered that, practically, America and Germany were engaged in hostilities. On this being reported to Washington, Colonel Kuhn was quite naturally recalled.

I cannot praise too highly the patience and tact shown by Colonel Kuhn in dealing with the Germans. Although accused in the German newspapers of being a spy, and otherwise attacked, he kept his temper and observed all that he could for the benefit of his own country. As he had had an opportunity to observe the Russian-Japanese war, his experiences at that time, coupled with his experiences in Germany, make him, perhaps, our greatest American expert on modern war.

It was with the greatest pleasure that I heard from Secretary Baker that he had determined to promote Colonel Kuhn to the rank of General and make him head of our War College, where his teachings will prove of the greatest value to the armies of the United States.

Colonel House and his wife arrived to pay us a visit on March 19, 1915, and remained until the twenty-eighth. During this period the Colonel met all the principal members of the German Government and many men of influence and prominence in the world of affairs, such as Herr von Gwinner, head of the Deutsche Bank, and Dr. Walter Rathenau, who succeeded his father as head of the Allgemeine Elektricitats Gesellschaft and hundreds of other corporations. The Colonel dined at the house of Dr. Solf, the Colonial Minister, and lunched with von Gwinner.

In April, negotiations were continued about the sinking of the *William P. Frye,* an American boat loaded with food and destined for Ireland. The American Government on behalf of the owners of the *William P. Frye* claimed damages for the boat. Nothing was said about the cargo, but in the German answer it was stated that the cargo of the *William P. Frye* consisting of foodstuffs destined for an armed port of the enemy and, therefore, presumed to be destined for the armed forces of the enemy was, because of this, contraband. I spoke to von Jagow about this and told him that I thought that possibly this would seem to amount to a German justification of the British blockade of Germany. He said that this note had been drawn by Director Kriege who was their expert on international law, and that he would not interfere with Kriege's work. Of course, as a matter of fact, all foodstuffs shipped to Germany would have to be landed at some armed port, and, therefore, according to the contentions of Germany, these would be supposed to be destined to the armed forces of the enemy and become contraband of war.

At international law, it had always been recognised that private individuals and corporations have the right to sell arms and ammunitions of war to any belligerent and, in the Hague Convention held in 1907, this right was expressly ratified and confirmed. This same Director Kriege who represented Germany at this Hague Conference in 1907, in the debates on this point said: "The neutral boats which engage in such a trade, commit a violation of the duties of neutrality. However, according to a principle generally recognised, the State of which the boat flies the flag is not responsible for this violation. The neutral States are not called upon to forbid their subjects a commerce which, from the point of view of the belligerents, ought to be considered as unlawful." (Conférence International de la Paix, La Haye, 15 Juin-18 Octobre 1907. Vol. III, p. 859.)

During our trouble with General Huerta, arms and ammunition for Huerta's forces from Germany were landed from German ships in Mexico. During the Boer war the Germans, who openly sympathised with the Boers, nevertheless furnished to Great Britain great quantities of arms and munitions, expressly destined to be used against the Boers; and this, although it was manifest that there was no possibility whatever that the Boers could obtain arms and munitions from German sources during the war. For instance, the firm of Eberhardt in Düsseldorf furnished one hundred and nine cannon, complete, with wagons, caissons and munitions, etc., to the British which were expressly designed for use against the Boers.

At one time the Imperial Foreign Office sent me a formal note making reference to a paragraph in former Ambassador Andrew D. White's autobiography with reference to the alleged stoppage in a German port of a boat laden with arms and ammunition, for use against the Americans in Cuba during the Spanish War. Of course, former Ambassador White wrote without having the Embassy records at hand and those records show that the position he took at the time of this alleged stoppage was eminently correct.

The files show that he wrote the letter to the State Department in which he stated that knowledge came to him of the proposed sailing of this ship, but he did not protest because he had been advised by a Naval Attaché that the United States did not have the right to interfere. The Department of State wrote to him commending his action in not filing any protest and otherwise interfering.

It seemed as if the German Government expressly desired to stir up hatred against America on this issue in order to force the American Government through fear of either the German Government, or the German-American propagandists at home, to put an immediate embargo on the export of these supplies.

In the autumn of 1914 Zimmermann showed me a long list sent him by Bernstorff showing quantities of saddles, automobiles, motor trucks, tires, explosives, foodstuffs and so on, exported from America to the Allies and intimated that this traffic had reached such proportions that it should be stopped.

In February, 1915, in the official *Communiqué* of the day appeared the following statement: "Heavy artillery fire in certain sections of the West front, mostly with American ammunition;" and in April in the official *Communiqué* something to this effect: "Captured French artillery officers say that they have great stores of American ammunition." I obtained through the State Department in Washington a statement from the French Ambassador certifying that up to that time, the end of April, 1915, no shells whatever of the French artillery had been furnished from America.

Nothing, however, would satisfy the Germans. They seemed determined that the export of every article, whether of food or munitions which might prove of use to the Allies in the war, should be stopped. Newspapers were filled with bitter attacks upon America and upon President Wilson, and with caricatures referring to the sale of munitions.

It never seemed to occur to the Germans that we could not violate the Hague Convention in order to change the rules of the game because one party, after the commencement of hostilities, found that the rule worked to his disadvantage. Nor did the Germans consider that America could not vary its international law with the changing fortunes of war and make one ruling when the Germans lost control of the sea and another ruling if they regained it.

From early in 1915 until I left Germany, I do not think I ever had a conversation with a German without his alluding to this question. Shortly before leaving Germany, in January, 1917, and after I had learned of the probability of the resumption of ruthless submarine war, at an evening party at the house of Dr. Solf, the Colonial Minister, a large German who turned out to be one of the Grand Dukes of Mecklenburg-Schwerin, planted himself some distance away from me and addressed me in German saying, "You are the American Ambassador and I want to tell you that the conduct of America in furnishing arms and ammunition to the enemies of Germany is stamped deep on the German heart, that we will never forget it and will some day have our revenge." He spoke in a voice so loud and slapped his chest so hard that every one in the room stopped their conversation in order to hear. He wore on his breast the orders of the Black Eagle, the Red Eagle, the Elephant and the Seraphim, and when he struck all this menagerie the rattle alone was quite loud. I reminded him politely of the Hague Convention, of the fact that we could not change international law from time to time with the change in the situation of the war, and that Germany had furnished arms to England to use against the Boers. But he simply answered, "We care nothing for treaties," and my answer, "That is what they all say," was a retort too obvious to be omitted.

The German press continually published articles to the effect that the war would be finished if it were not for the shipment of supplies from America. All public opinion was with the German Government when the warning was issued on February fourth, 1915, stating that the blockade of Great Britain would commence on the eighteenth and warning neutral ships to keep out of the war zone. From then on we had constant cases and crises with reference to the sinking of American boats by the German submarine. There were the cases of the *Gulfflight* and the *Cushing* and the *Falaba,* a British boat sunk without warning on which Americans were killed.

On May sixth, 1915, Director Kriege of the

Foreign Office asked Mr. Jackson to call and see him, and told him that he would like to have the following three points brought to the attention of the American public:

"1. As the result of the English effort to stop all foreign commerce with Germany, Germany would do everything in her power to destroy English commerce and merchant shipping. There was, however, never at any time an intention to destroy or interfere with neutral commerce or to attack neutral shipping unless engaged in contraband trade. In view of the action of the British Government in arming merchant vessels and causing them to disguise their national character, the occasional destruction of a neutral ship was unavoidable. Naval officers in command of submarines had been instructed originally, and new and more stringent instructions had been issued repeatedly, to use the utmost care, consistent with their own safety, to avoid attacks on neutral vessels.

"2. In case a neutral ship should be destroyed by a submarine the German Government is prepared to make an immediate and formal expression of its regret and to pay an indemnity, without having recourse to a prize court.

"3. All reports with regard to the destruction of a neutral vessel by a German submarine are investigated at once by both the German Foreign Office and Admiralty, and the result is communicated to the Government concerned, which is requested in return to communicate to the German Government the result of its own independent investigation. Where there is any material divergence in the two reports as to the presumed cause of destruction (torpedo or mine), the question is to be submitted to investigation by a commission composed of representatives of the two nations concerned, with a neutral arbiter whose decision will be final. This course has already been adopted in two cases, in which a Dutch and a Norwegian vessel, respectively, were concerned. The German Government reserves its right to refuse this international arbitration in exceptional cases where for military reasons the German Admiralty are opposed to its taking place."

Director Kriege told Mr. Jackson that a written communication in which the substance of the foregoing would be contained, would soon to be made to the Embassy.

Mr. Jackson put this conversation down in the form above given and showed Director Kriege a copy of it. Later in the day Geheimrat Simon called on Mr. Jackson at the Embassy and said that Dr. Kriege would like to have point two read as follows:

"In case *through any unfortunate mistake a neutral ship,*" and continuing to the end; and that Dr. Kriege would like to change what was written on point three beginning with "Where there is" so that it should read, as follows:—"Where there is any material divergence in the two reports as to the presumed cause of destruction (torpedo or mine), the German Government has already in several instances declared its readiness to submit the question to the decision of an international commission in accordance with the Hague Convention for the friendly settlement of international disputes."

This had been suggested by Director Kriege in case it should be decided to make a communication to the American Press. Mr. Jackson told Geheimrat Simon that he would report the subject of his conversation to me, but that it would depend upon me whether any communication should be made to the American Government or to the press upon the subject.

Of course, the news of the torpedoing of the *Lusitania* on May seventh and of the great loss of American lives brought about a very critical situation, and naturally nothing was done with Kriege's propositions.

It is unnecessary here for me to go into the notes which were exchanged between the two governments because all that is already public property.

Sometime after I had delivered our first *Lusitania* Note of May 11th, 1915, Zimmermann was lunching with us. A good looking American woman, married to a German, was also of the party and after lunch although I was talking to some one else I overheard part of her conversation with Zimmermann. When Zimmermann left I asked her what it was that he had said about America, Germany, Mr. Bryan and the *Lusitania*. She then told me that she had said to Zimmermann that it was a great pity that we were to leave Berlin as it looked as if diplomatic relations between the two countries would be broken, and that Zimmermann told her not to worry about that because they had just received word from the Austrian Government that Dr. Dumba, the Austrian Ambassador in Washington, had cabled that the *Lusitania* Note from America to Germany was only sent as a sop to public opinion in America and that the government did not really mean what was said in that note. I then called on Zimmermann at the Foreign Office and he showed me Dumba's telegram which was substantially as stated above. Of course, I immediately cabled to the State Department and also got word to President Wilson. The rest of the incident is public property. I, of course, did not know what actually occurred between Mr. Bryan and Dr. Dumba, but I am sure that Dr. Dumba must have misunderstood friendly statements made by Mr. Bryan.

It was very lucky that I discovered the existence of this Dumba cablegram in this manner which savours almost of diplomacy as represented on the stage. If the Germans had gone on in the belief that the *Lusitania* Note was not really meant, war would have inevitably resulted at that time between Germany and America, and it shows how great events may be shaped by heavy luncheons and a pretty woman.

Before this time much indignation had been caused in Germany by the fact that the *Lusitania* on her eastward voyage from New York early in February, 1915, had raised the American flag when nearing British waters.

Shortly after this incident had become known,

I was at the Wintergarten, a large concert hall in Berlin, with Grant Smith, First Secretary of the Embassy at Vienna and other members of my staff. We naturally spoke English among ourselves, a fact which aroused the ire of a German who had been drinking heavily and who was seated in the next box. He immediately began to call out that some one was speaking English and when told by one of the attendants that it was the American Ambassador, he immediately cried in a loud voice that Americans were even worse than English and that the *Lusitania* had been flying the American flag as protection in British waters.

The audience, however, took sides against him and told him to shut up and as I left the house at the close of the performance, some Germans spoke to me and apologised for his conduct. The next day the manager of the Wintergarten called on me also to express his regret for the occurrence.

About a year afterwards I was at the races one day and saw this man and asked him what he meant by making such a noise at the Wintergarten. He immediately apologised and said that he had been drinking and hoped that I would forget the incident. This was the only incident of the kind which occurred to me during all the time that I was in Germany.

Both before and after the sinking of the *Lusi-*

tania, the German Foreign Office put forward all kinds of proposals with reference to American ships in the war zone. On one afternoon, Zimmermann, who had a number of these proposals drafted in German, showed them to me and I wrote down the English translation for him to see how it would look in English. These proposals were about the sailing from America of what might be called certified ships, the ships to be painted and striped in a distinctive way, to come from certified ports at certain certified times, America to agree that these ships should carry no contraband whatever. All these proposals were sternly rejected by the President.

On February sixteenth, the German answer to our note of February tenth had announced that Germany declined all responsibility for what might happen to neutral ships and, in addition, announced that mines would be allowed in waters surrounding Great Britain and Ireland. This note also contained one of Zimmermann's proposed solutions, namely, that American warships should convoy American merchantmen.

The German note of the sixteenth also spoke about the great traffic in munitions from the United States to the Allies, and contained a suggestion that the United States should induce the Allies to adopt the Declaration of London and admit the importation not only of food but also of all raw materials into Germany.

February twentieth was the date of the conciliatory note addressed by President Wilson to both Great Britain and Germany; and contained the suggestion that submarines should not be employed against merchant vessels of any nationality and that food should be allowed to go through for the civil population of Germany consigned to the agencies named by the United States in Germany, which were to see that the food was received and distributed to the civil population.

In the meantime the mines on the German coast had destroyed two American ships, both loaded with cotton for Germany; one called the *Carib* and the other the *Evelyn*.

In America, Congress refused to pass a law to put it in the power of the President to place an embargo on the export of munitions of war.

In April, Count Bernstorff delivered his note concerning the alleged want of neutrality of the United States, referring to the numerous new industries in war materials being built up in the United States, stating, "In reality the United States is supplying only Germany's enemies, a fact which is not in any way modified by the theoretical willingness to furnish Germany as well."

To this note, Secretary Bryan in a note replied that it was impossible, in view of the indisputable doctrines of accepted international law, to make any change in our own laws of neutrality which meant unequally affecting, during the progress of the war, the relations of the United States with the various nations at war; and that the placing of embargoes on the trade in arms which constituted such a change would be a direct violation of the neutrality of the United States.

But all these negotiations, reproaches and recriminations were put an end to by the torpedoing of the *Lusitania,* with the killing of American women and civilians who were passengers on that vessel.

I believed myself that we would immediately break diplomatic relations, and prepared to leave Germany. On May eleventh, I delivered to von Jagow the *Lusitania* Note, which after calling attention to the cases of the sinking of American boats, ending with the *Lusitania,* contained the statement, "The Imperial German Government will not expect the Government of the United States to omit any word or any act necessary to the sacred duty of maintaining the rights of the United States and its citizens and of safeguarding their free exercises and enjoyments."

During this period I had constant conversations with von Jagow and Zimmermann, and it was during the conversations about this submarine warfare that Zimmermann on one occasion said to me: "The United States does not dare to do anything against Germany because we have five hundred thousand German reservists in America who will rise in arms against your government if your government should dare to take any action against Germany." As he said this, he worked himself up to a passion and repeatedly struck the table with his fist. I told him that we had five hundred and one thousand lamp posts in America, and that was where the German reservists would find themselves if they tried any uprising; and I also called his attention to the fact that no German-Americans making use of the American passports which they could easily obtain, were sailing for Germany by way of Scandinavian countries in order to enlist in the German army. I told him that if he could show me one person with an American passport who had come to fight in the German army I might more readily believe what he said about the Germans in America rising in revolution.

As a matter of fact, during the whole course of the war, I knew of only one man with American citizenship who enlisted in the German army. This was an American student then in Germany who enlisted in a German regiment. His father, a business man in New York, cabled me asking me to have his son released from the

German army; so I procured the discharge of the young man who immediately wrote to me and informed me that he was over twenty-one, and that he could not see what business his father had to interfere with his military ambitions. I thereupon withdrew my request with reference to him, but he had already been discharged from the army. When his regiment went to the West front he stowed away on the cars with it, was present at the attack on Ypres, and was shot through the body. He recovered in a German hospital, received the Iron Cross, was discharged and sailed for America. What has since become of him I do not know.

I do not intend to go in great detail into this exchange of notes and the public history of the submarine controversy, as all that properly belongs to the history of the war rather than to an account of my personal experiences; and besides, as Victor Hugo said, "History is not written with a microscope." All will remember the answer of Germany to the American *Lusitania* Note, which answer, delivered on May twenty-ninth, contained the charge that the *Lusitania* was armed and carried munitions, and had been used in the transport of Canadian troops. In the meantime, however, the American ship, *Nebraskan,* had been torpedoed off the coast of Ireland on the twenty-sixth; and, on May twenty-

THE MEDAL TO COMMEMORATE THE SINKING OF THE LUSITANIA
ON MAY SEVENTH, 1915. NOTE THAT IT IS DATED MAY FIFTH
(PAGE 318)

eighth, Germany stated that the American steamer, *Gulfflight,* had been torpedoed by mistake, and apologised for this act.

Von Jagow gave me, about the same time, a Note requesting that American vessels should be more plainly marked and should illuminate their marking at night.

The second American *Lusitania* Note was published on June eleventh, 1915; and its delivery was coincident with the resignation of Mr. Bryan as Secretary of State. In this last Note President Wilson (for, of course, it is an open secret that he was the author of these Notes) made the issue perfectly plain, referring to the torpedoing of enemy passenger ships. "Only her actual resistance to capture or refusal to stop when ordered to do so for the purpose of visit could have afforded the commander of the submarine any justification for so much as putting the lives of those on board the ship in jeopardy." On July eighth the German answer to this American *Lusitania* Note was delivered, and again stated that "we have been obliged to adopt a submarine war to meet the declared intentions of our enemies and the method of warfare adopted by them in contravention of international law". Again referring to the alleged fact of the *Lusitania's* carrying munitions they said: "If the *Lusitania* had been spared, thousands of cases of munitions would have been sent to Germany's enemies and thereby thousands of German mothers and children robbed of breadwinners." The Note then contained some of Zimmermann's favourite proposals, to the effect that German submarine commanders would be instructed to permit the passage of American steamers marked in a special way and of whose sailing they had been notified in advance, provided that the American Government guaranteed that these vessels did not carry contraband of war. It was also suggested that a number of neutral vessels should be added to those sailing under the American flag, to give greater opportunity for those Americans who were compelled to travel abroad, and the Note's most important part continued: "In particular the Imperial Government is unable to admit that the American citizens can protect an enemy ship by mere fact of their presence on board."

July twenty-first, the American Government rejected the proposals of Germany saying, "The lives of noncombatants may in no case be put in jeopardy unless the vessel resists or seeks to escape after being summoned to submit to examination," and disposed of the claim that the acts of Great Britain gave Germany the right to retaliate, even though American citizens should be deprived of their lives in the course of retaliation by stating: "For a belligerent act of retaliation as *per se* an act beyond the law, and the defense, of an act as retaliatory, is an admission that it is illegal." Continuing it said: "If a belligerent cannot retaliate against an enemy without injuring the lives of neutrals, as well as their property, humanity, as well as justice and a due regard for the dignity of neutral powers, should dictate that the practice be discontinued."

It was also said: "The United States cannot believe that the Imperial Government will longer refrain from disavowing the wanton act of its naval commander in sinking the *Lusitania* or from offering reparation for the American lives lost, so far as reparation can be made for the needless destruction of human life by an illegal act." And the meat of the Note was contained in the following sentence: "Friendship itself prompts it (the United States) to say to the Imperial Government that repetition by the commanders of German naval vessels of acts in contravention of those rights must be regarded by the Government of the United States, when they affect American citizens, as being deliberately unfriendly."

There the matter has remained so far as the *Lusitania* was concerned until now. In the meantime, the attack of the American ship, *Nebraskan*, was disavowed; the German Note stating that "the torpedo was not meant for the American flag and is to be considered an unfortunate accident."

The diplomatic situation with regard to the use of the submarine and the attack on many merchant ships without notice and without putting the passengers in safety was still unsettled when on August nineteenth, 1915, the British ship *Arabic,* was torpedoed, without warning, not far from the place where the *Lusitania* had gone down.   Two Americans were among the passengers killed.

The German Government, after the usual quibbling, at length, in its Note of September seventh, claimed that the Captain of the German submarine, while engaged in preparing to sink the *Dunsley,* became convinced that the approaching *Arabic* was trying to ram him and, therefore, fired his torpedo.   The Imperial Government refused to admit any liability but offered to arbitrate.

There followed almost immediately the case of the *Ancona,* sunk by a submarine flying the Austrian flag.   This case was naturally out of my jurisdiction, but formed a link in the chain, and then came the sinking of the *Persia* in the Mediterranean.   On this boat our consul to Aden lost his life.

In the Note of Count Bernstorff to Secretary Lansing, dated September first, 1915, Count

Bernstorff said that liners would not be sunk by German submarines without warning, and without putting the passengers in safety, provided that the liners did not try to escape or offer resistance; and it was further stated that this policy was in effect before the sinking of the *Arabic*.

There were long negotiations during this period concerning the *Arabic*. At one time it looked as if diplomatic relations would be broken; but finally the Imperial Government consented to acknowledge that the submarine commander had been wrong in assuming that the *Arabic* intended to ram his boat, offered to pay an indemnity and disavowed the act of the commander. It was stated that orders so precise had been given to the submarine commanders that a "recurrence of incidents similar to the *Arabic* is considered out of the question."

In the same way the Austrian Government gave way to the demands of America in the *Ancona* case at the end of December, 1915. Ambassador Penfield, in Austria, won great praise by his admirable handling of this case.

The negotiations as to the still pending *Lusitania* case were carried on in Washington by Count Bernstorff and Secretary Lansing, and finally Germany offered to pay an indemnity for the death of the Americans on the *Lusitania* whose deaths Germany "greatly regretted," but refused to disavow the act of the submarine commander in sinking the *Lusitania* or to admit that such act was illegal.

About this time our State Department sent out a Note proposing in effect that submarines should conform to "cruiser" warfare, only sinking a vessel which defended itself or tried to escape, and that before sinking a vessel its passengers and crew should be placed in safety; and that, on the other hand, merchant vessels of belligerent nationality should be prohibited from carrying any armaments whatever. This suggestion was not followed up.

Zimmermann (not the one in the Foreign Office) wrote an article in the *Lokal Anzeiger* of which he is an editor, saying that the United States had something on their side in the question of the export of munitions. I heard that von Kessel, commander of the *Mark of Brandenburg* said that he, Zimmermann, ought to be shot as a traitor. Zimmermann hearing of this made von Kessel apologise, but was shortly afterwards mobilised.

Colonel House had arrived in Germany at the end of January, 1916, and remained only three days. He was quite worried by the situation and by an interview he had had with Zimmermann in which Zimmermann expressed the readiness of Germany to go to war with the United States.

In February, 1916, the Junkers in the Prussian Lower House started a fight against von Bethmann-Hollweg and discussed submarine war, a matter out of their province. The Chancellor hit back at them hard and had the best of the exchange. At this period it was reported that the Emperor went to Wilhelmshafen to warn the submarine commanders to be careful.

About March first it was reported that a grand council of war was held at Charleville and that in spite of the support of von Tirpitz by Falkenhayn, the Chief of Staff, von Bethmann-Hollweg was supported by the Emperor, and once more beat the propositions to recommence ruthless submarine war.

In March too, the "illness" of von Tirpitz was announced, followed shortly by his resignation. On March nineteenth, his birthday, a demonstration was looked for and I saw many police near his dwelling, but nothing unusual occurred.

I contemplated a trip to America, but both von Bethmann-Hollweg and von Jagow begged me not to go.

From the time of the *Lusitania* sinking to that of the *Sussex* all Germany was divided into two camps. The party of the Chancellor tried to keep peace with America and did not want to have Germany branded as an outlaw among nations. Von Tirpitz and his party of naval and military officers called for ruthless submarine war, and the Conservatives, angry with Bethmann-Hollweg because of his proposed concession as to the extension of the suffrage, joined the opposition. The reception of our last *Lusitania* Note in July, 1915, was hostile and I was accused of being against Germany, although, of course, I had nothing to do with the preparation of this Note.

In August, 1915, the deputies representing the great industrials of Germany joined in the attack on the Chancellor. These men wished to keep Northern France and Belgium, because they hoped to get possession of the coal and iron deposits there and so obtain a monopoly of the iron and steel trade of the continent. Accelerators of public opinion, undoubtedly hired by the Krupp firm, were hard at work. These Annexationists were opposed by the more reasonable men who signed a petition against the annexation of Belgium. Among the signers of this reasonable men's petition were Prince Hatzfeld (Duke of Trachenberg) head of the Red Cross, Dernburg, Prince Henkel Donnersmarck, Professor Delbrück, von Harnack and many others.

The rage of the Conservatives at the *Arabic* settlement knew no bounds, and after a bitter article had appeared in the *Tageszeitung* about the *Arabic* affair, that newspaper was suppressed for some days,—a rather unexpected showing of backbone on the part of von Bethmann-Hollweg. Reventlow who wrote for this newspaper is one of the ablest editorial writers in Germany. An ex-naval officer, he is bitter in his hatred of America. It was said that he once lived in America and lost a small fortune in a Florida orange grove, but I never succeeded in having this verified.

In November, 1915, after the *Arabic* settlement there followed a moment for us of comparative calm. Mrs. Gerard was given the Red Cross Orders of the first and third classes, and Jackson and Rives of the Embassy Staff the second and third class. The third class is always given because one cannot have the first and second unless one has the third or lowest.

There were rumours at this time of the formation of a new party; really the Socialists and Liberals, as the Socialists as such were too unfashionable, in too bad odour, to open a campaign against the military under their own name. This talk came to nothing.

Von Bethmann-Hollweg always complained bitterly that he could not communicate in cipher *via* wireless with von Bernstorff. On one occasion he said to me, "How can I arrange as I wish to in a friendly way the *Ancona* and *Lusitania* cases if I cannot communicate with my Ambassador? Why does the United States Government not allow me to communicate in cipher?" I said, "The Foreign

Office tried to get me to procure a safe-conduct for the notorious von Rintelen on the pretense that he was going to do charitable work for Belgium in America; perhaps Washington thinks you want to communicate with people like that." The Chancellor then changed the subject and said that there would be bad feeling in Germany against America after the war. I answered that that idea had been expressed by a great many Germans and German newspapers, and that I had had private letters from a great many Americans who wrote that if Germany intended to make war on America, after this war, perhaps we had better go in now. He then very amiably said that war with America would be ridiculous. He asked me why public opinion in America was against Germany, and I answered that matters like the Cavell case had made a bad impression in America and that I knew personally that even the Kaiser did not approve of the torpedoing of the *Lusitania.* Von Bethmann-Hollweg said, "How about the *Baralong?*" I replied that I did not know the details and that there seemed much doubt and confusion about that affair, but that there was no doubt about the fact that Miss Cavell was shot and that she was a woman. I then took up in detail with him the treatment of British prisoners and said that this bad treatment could not go on. This was only one of the many times when I complained to the Chancellor about the condition of prisoners. I am sure that he did not approve of the manner in which prisoners of war in Germany were treated; but he always complained that he was powerless where the military were concerned, and always referred me to Bismarck's memoirs.

During this winter of submarine controversy an interview with von Tirpitz, thinly veiled as an interview with a "high naval authority," was published in that usually most conservative of newspapers, the *Frankfurter Zeitung*. In this interview the "high naval authority" advocated ruthless submarine war with England, and promised to bring about thereby the speedy surrender of that country. After the surrender, which was to include the whole British fleet, the German fleet with the surrendered British fleet added to its force, was to sail for America, and exact from that country indemnities enough to pay the whole cost of the war.

After his fall, von Tirpitz, in a letter to some admirers who had sent him verses and a wreath, advocated holding the coast of Flanders as a necessity for the war against England and America.

The successor of von Tirpitz was Admiral von Holtzendorff, whose brother is Ballin's right hand man in the management of the Hamburg American Line. Because of the more reasonable influence and surroundings of von Holtzendorff, I regarded his appointment as a help towards peaceful relations between Germany and America.

I have told in another chapter how the Emperor had refused to receive me as Ambassador of a country which was supplying munitions to the Allies.

From time to time since I learned of this in March, 1915, I kept insisting upon my right as Ambassador to be received by the Emperor; and finally early in October, 1915, wrote the following letter to the Chancellor:

"Your Excellency:

Some time ago I requested you to arrange an audience for me with his majesty.

Please take no further trouble about this matter.

Sincerely yours,
JAMES W. GERARD."

This seemed to have the desired effect. I was informed that I would be received by the Emperor in the new palace at Potsdam on October twenty-second. He was then to pay a flying visit to Berlin to receive the new Peruvian Minister and one or two others. We went down in the train to Potsdam, von Jagow accompanying us, in the morning; and it was arranged that we should return on the train leaving Potsdam a little after one o'clock. I think that the authorities of the palace expected that I would be with the Emperor for a few minutes only, as when I was shown into the room where he was, a large room opening from the famous shell hall of the palace, the Peruvian Minister and the others to be received were standing waiting in that hall.

The Emperor was alone in the room and no one was present at our interview. He was dressed in a Hussar uniform of the new field grey, the parade uniform of which the frogs and trimmings were of gold. A large table in the corner of the room was covered with maps, compasses, scales and rulers; and looked as if the Emperor there, in company with some of his aides, or possibly the chief of staff, had been working out the plan of campaign of the German armies.

The Emperor was standing; so, naturally, I stood also; and, according to his habit, which is quite Rooseveltian, he stood very close to me and talked very earnestly. I was fortunately able to clear up two distinct points which he had against America.

The Emperor said that he had read in a German paper that a number of submarines built in America for Great Britain had crossed the Atlantic to England, escorted by ships of the American Navy. I was, of course, able to deny this ridiculous story at the time and furnish definite proofs later. The Emperor complained because a loan to Great Britain and France had been floated in America. I said that the first loan to a belligerent floated in America was a loan to Germany. The Emperor sent for some of his staff and immediately inquired into the matter. The members of the staff confirmed my statement. The Emperor said that he would not have permitted the torpedoing of the *Lusitania* if he had known, and that no gentleman would kill so many women and children. He showed, however, great bitterness against the United States and repeatedly said, "America had better look out after this war:" and "I shall stand no nonsense from America after the war."

The interview lasted about an hour and a quarter, and when I finally emerged from the room the officers of the Emperor's household were in such a state of agitation that I feel sure they must have thought that something fearful had occurred. As I walked rapidly towards the door of the palace in order to take the carriage which was to drive me to the train, one of them walked along beside me saying, "Is it all right? Is it all right?"

The unfortunate diplomats who were to have

been received and who had been standing all this time outside the door waiting for an audience missed their train and their luncheon.

At this interview, the Emperor looked very careworn and seemed nervous. When I next saw him, however, which was not until the end of April, 1916, he was in much better condition.

I was so fearful in reporting the dangerous part of this interview, on account of the many spies not only in my own Embassy but also in the State Department, that I sent but a very few words in a roundabout way by courier direct to the President.

The year, 1916, opened with this great question still unsettled and, in effect, Germany gave notice that after March first, 1916, the German submarines would sink all armed merchantmen of the enemies of Germany without warning. It is not my place here to go into the agitation of this question in America or into the history of the votes in Congress, which in fact upheld the policy of the President. A proposal as to armed merchantmen was issued by our State Department and the position taken in this was apparently abandoned at the time of the settlement of the *Sussex* case to which I now refer.

In the latter half of March, 1916, a number of boats having Americans on board were torpedoed without warning. These boats were the *Eagle-*

point, the *Englishman,* the *Manchester Engineer* and the *Sussex.* One American was killed or drowned on the *Englishman,* but the issue finally came to a head over the torpedoing of the channel passenger boat, *Sussex,* which carried passengers between Folkstone and Dieppe, France.

On March twenty-fourth the *Sussex* was torpedoed near the coast of France. Four hundred and thirty-six persons, of whom seventy-five were Americans, were on board. The captain and a number of the passengers saw the torpedo and an endeavour was made to avoid it. After the boat was struck the many passengers took to the boats. Three Americans were injured and over forty persons lost their lives, although the boat was not sunk but was towed to Boulogne.

I was instructed to inquire from the German Government as to whether a German submarine had sunk the *Sussex.* The Foreign Office finally, at my repeated request, called on the Admiralty for a report of the torpedoing of the *Sussex;* and at last on the tenth of April the German Note was delivered to me. In the meantime, and before the delivery of this Note I had been assured again and again that the *Sussex* had not been torpedoed by a German submarine. In this Note a rough sketch was enclosed, said to have been made by the officer commanding the submarine, of a vessel which he admitted he had torpedoed, in the same locality where the *Sussex* had been attacked and at about the same time of day. It was said that this boat which was torpedoed was a mine layer of the recently built *Arabic* class and that a great explosion which was observed to occur in the torpedoed ship warranted the certain conclusion that great amounts of munitions were on board. The Note concluded: "The German Government must therefore assume that injury to the *Sussex* was attributable to another cause than attack by a German submarine." The Note contained an offer to submit any difference of opinion that might develop to be investigated by a mixed commission in accordance with the Hague Convention of 1907. The *Englishman* and the *Eaglepoint*, it was claimed, were attacked by German submarines only after they had attempted to escape, and an explanation was given as to the *Manchester Engineer*. With reference to the *Sussex*, the note continued: "Should the American Government have at its disposal other material at the conclusion of the case of the *Sussex*, the German Government would ask that it be communicated, in order to subject this material also to investigation."

In the meantime, American naval officers, etc., had been engaged in collecting facts as to the sinking of the *Sussex*, and this evidence, which seemed overwhelming and, in connection with the admissions in the German note, absolutely conclusive, was incorporated in the note sent to Germany in which Germany was notified: "Unless the Imperial Government should now immediately declare and effect abandonment of this present method of submarine warfare against passenger and freight carrying vessels, the Government of the United States can have no choice but to sever diplomatic relations with the German Empire altogether."

The issue was now clearly defined.

I have already spoken of the fact that for a long time there had been growing up two parties in Germany. One party headed by von Tirpitz in favour of what the Germans called *rücksichtloser,* or ruthless submarine war, in which all enemy merchant ships were to be sunk without warning, and the party then headed by the Chancellor which desired to avoid a conflict with America on this issue.

As I have explained in a former chapter, the military have always claimed to take a hand in shaping the destinies and foreign policies of Germany. When the Germans began to turn their attention to the creation of a fleet, von Tirpitz was the man who, in a sense, became the leader of the movement and, therefore, the creator of the modern navy of Germany. A skilful politician, he for years dominated the Reichstag and on the question of submarine warfare was most efficiently seconded by the efforts of the Navy League, an organization having perhaps one million members throughout Germany. Although only one of the three heads of the navy (he was Secretary of the Navy), by the force of his personality, by the political position which he had created for himself, and by the backing of his friends in the Navy League he really dominated the other two departments of the navy, the Marine Staff and the Marine Cabinet.

Like most Germans of the ruling class, ambition is his only passion. These Spartans do not care either for money or for the luxury which it brings. Their life is on very simple lines, both in the Army and Navy, in order that the officers shall not vie with one another in expenditure, and in order that the poorer officers and their wives shall not be subject to the humiliation which would be caused if they had to live in constant contact with brother officers living on a more luxurious footing.

Von Tirpitz' ambition undoubtedly led him to consider himself as a promising candidate for Bethmann-Hollweg's shoes. The whole submarine issue, therefore, became not only a question of military expediency and a question for the Foreign Office to decide in connection with the relations of America to Germany, but also a question of internal politics, a means of forcing the Chancellor out of office. The advocates for the ruthless war were drawn from the Navy and from the Army, and those who believed in the use of any means of offence against their enemies and particularly in the use of any means that would stop the shipment of munitions of war to the Allies. The Army and the Navy were joined by the Conservatives and by all those who hoped for the fall of the Chancellor. The conservative newspapers, and even the Roman Catholic newspapers were violent in their call for ruthless submarine war as well as violent in their denunciations of the United States of America.

American passengers on merchant ships of the enemy were called *Schutzengel* (guardian angels), and caricatures were published, such as one which showed the mate reporting to the Captain of a British boat that everything was in readiness for sailing and the Captain's inquiry, "Are you sure that the American *Schutzengel* is on board?" The numerous notes sent by America to Germany also formed a frequent subject of caricature and I remember particularly one quite clever one in the paper called *Brummer,* representing the celebrations in a German port on the arrival of the one hundredth note from America when the Mayor of the

town and the military, flower girls and singing
societies and *Turnverein* were drawn up in wel-
coming array. The liberal papers were inclined
to support von Bethmann-Hollweg in his apparent
intention to avoid an open break with America.
But even the liberal papers were not very strong
in their stand.

The military, of course, absolutely despised
America and claimed that America could do no
more harm by declaring war than it was doing
then to Germany; and that possibly the war
preparations of America might cut down the
amount of the munitions available for export
to the enemies of the Empire. As to anything
that America could do in a military way, the
Navy and the Army were unanimous in saying
that as a military or naval factor the United
States might be considered as less than nothing.
This was the situation when the last *Sussex*
Note of America brought matters to a crisis, and
even the crisis itself was considered a farce as it
had been simmering for so long a period.

I arranged that Colonel House should have an
interview with von Bethmann-Hollweg at this
time, and after dinner one night he had a long
talk with the Chancellor in which the dangers of
the situation were pointed out.

With this arrival of the last American *Sussex*
Note, I felt that the situation was almost hope-

less; that this question which had dragged along for so long must now inevitably lead to a break of relations and possibly to war. Von Jagow had the same idea and said that it was "fate," and that there was nothing more to be done. I myself felt that nothing could alter public opinion in Germany; that in spite of von Tirpitz' fall, which had taken place some time before, the advocates of ruthless submarine warfare would win, and that to satisfy them Germany would risk a break with America.

I was sitting in my office in a rather dazed and despairing state when Professor Ludwig Stein, proprietor of a magazine called *North and South* and a writer of special articles on Germany's foreign relations for the *Vossische Zeitung*, under the name of "Diplomaticus," called to see me.

He informed me that he thought the situation was not yet hopeless, that there was still a large party of reasonable men in Germany and that he thought much good could be done if I should go to the Great General Headquarters and have a talk with the Kaiser, who, he informed me, was reported to be against a break.

I told Dr. Stein that, of course, I was perfectly willing to go if there was the slightest chance of preventing war; and I also told the Chancellor that if he was going to decide this question in favor of peace it would be possibly easier for him if the decision was arrived at under the protection, as it were, of the Emperor; or that, if the decision lay with the Emperor, I might possibly be able to help in convincing him if I had an opportunity to lay the American side of the case before him. I said, moreover, that I was ready at any time on short notice to proceed to the Emperor's headquarters.

Dr. Hecksher, a member of the Reichstag, who must be classed among the reasonable men of Germany, also advocated my speaking directly to the Kaiser.

CHAPTER XIII

NOTHING surprised me more, as the war developed, than the discovery of the great variety and amount of goods exported from Germany to the United States.

Goods sent from the United States to Germany are mainly prime materials: approximately one hundred and sixty million dollars a year of cotton; seventy-five million dollars of copper; fifteen millions of wheat; twenty millions of animal fats; ten millions of mineral oil and a large amount of vegetable oil. Of course, the amount of wheat is especially variable. Some manufactured goods from America also find their way to Germany to the extent of perhaps seventy millions a year, comprising machinery such as typewriters and a miscellaneous line of machinery and manufactures. The principal exports from Germany to America consist of dye stuffs and chemical dyes, toys, underwear, surgical instruments, cutlery, stockings, knit goods, etc., and a raw material called potash, also known as kali. The last is a

262

mineral found nowhere in the world except in Germany and in a few places in Austria. Potash is essential to the manufacture of many fertilizers, fertilizer being composed as a rule of potash, phosphates and nitrates. The nitrates in past years have been exported to all countries from Chile. Phosphate rock is mined in South Carolina and Florida and several other places in the world. Curiously enough, both nitrates and potash are essential ingredients also of explosives used in war. Since the war, the German supply from Chile was cut off; but the Germans, following a system used in Norway for many years before the war, established great electrical plants for the extraction of nitrates from the atmosphere. Since the war, American agriculture has suffered for want of potash and German agriculture has suffered for want of phosphates, possibly of nitrates also; because I doubt whether sufficient nitrogen is extracted from the air in Germany to provide for more than the needs of the explosive industry.

The dyestuff industry had been developed to such a point in Germany that Germany supplied the whole world. In the first months of the war some enterprising Americans, headed by Herman Metz, chartered a boat, called *The Matanzas,* and sent it to Rotterdam where it was loaded with a cargo of German dyestuffs. The boat sailed under the American flag and was not interfered with by the British. Later on the German Department of the Interior, at whose head was Delbrück, refused to allow dyestuffs to leave Germany except in exchange for cotton, and, finally, the export of dyestuffs from Germany ceased and other countries were compelled to take up the question of manufacture. This state of affairs may lead to the establishment of the industry permanently in the United States, although that industry will require protection for some years, as, undoubtedly, Germany in her desperate effort to regain a monopoly of this trade will be ready to spend enormous sums in order to undersell the American manufacturers and drive them out of business.

The commercial submarines, *Deutschland* and *Bremen,* were to a great extent built with money furnished by the dyestuff manufacturers, who hoped that by sending dyestuffs in this way to America they could prevent the development of the industry there. I had many negotiations with the Foreign Office with reference to this question of dyestuffs.

The export of toys from Germany to the United States forms a large item in the bill which we pay annually to Germany. Many of these toys are manufactured by the people in their own homes in the picturesque district known as the

Black Forest. Of course, the war cut off, after a time, the export of toys from Germany; and the American child, having in the meantime learned to be satisfied with some other article, his little brother will demand this very article next Christmas, and thus, after the war, Germany will find that much of this trade has been permanently lost.

Just as the textile trade of the United States was dependent upon the German dyestuffs for colours, so the sugar beet growers of America were dependent upon Germany for their seed. I succeeded, with the able assistance of the consul at Magdeburg and Mr. Winslow of my staff, in getting shipments of beet seed out of Germany. I have heard since that these industries too, are being developed in America, and seed obtained from other countries, such as Russia.

Another commodity upon which a great industry in the United States and Mexico depends is cyanide. The discovery of the cyanide process of treating gold and silver ores permitted the exploitation of many mines which could not be worked under the older methods. At the beginning of the war there was a small manufactory of cyanide owned by Germans at Perth Amboy and Niagara Falls, but most of the cyanide used was imported from Germany. The American German Company and the companies manufacturing in Germany and in Great Britain all operated under the same patents, the British and German companies having working agreements as to the distribution of business throughout the world.

The German Vice-Chancellor and head of the Department of the Interior, Delbrück, put an export prohibition on cyanide early in the war; and most pigheadedly and obstinately claimed that cyanide was manufactured nowhere but in Germany, and that, therefore, if he allowed cyanide to leave Germany for the United States or Mexico the English would capture it and would use it to work South African mines, thus adding to the stock of gold and power in war of the British Empire. It was a long time before the German manufacturers and I could convince this gentleman that cyanide sufficient to supply all the British mines was manufactured near Glasgow, Scotland. He then reluctantly gave a permit for the export of a thousand tons of cyanide; and its arrival in the United States permitted many mines there and in Mexico to continue operations, and saved many persons from being thrown out of employment. When Delbrück finally gave a permit for the export of four thousand tons more of cyanide, the psychological moment had passed and we could not obtain through our State Department a pass from the British.

266

I am convinced that Delbrück made a great tactical mistake on behalf of the German Government when he imposed this prohibition against export of goods to America. Many manufacturers of textiles, the users of dyestuffs, medicines, seeds and chemicals in all forms, were clamouring for certain goods and chemicals from Germany. But it was the prohibition against export by the Germans which prevented their receiving these goods. If it had been the British blockade alone a cry might have arisen in the United States against this blockade which might have materially changed the international situation.

The Germans also refused permission for the export of potash from Germany. They hoped thereby to induce the United States to break the British blockade, and offered cargoes of potash in exchange for cargoes of cotton or cargoes of foodstuffs. The Germans claimed that potash was used in the manufacture of munitions and that, therefore, in no event would they permit the export unless the potash was consigned to the American Government, with guarantees against its use except in the manufacture of fertilizer, this to be checked up by Germans appointed as inspectors. All these negotiations, however, fell through and no potash has been exported from Germany to the United States since the commencement of the war. Enough potash, however, is obtained in the United States for munition purposes from the burning of seaweed on the Pacific Coast, from the brines in a lake in Southern California and from a rock called alunite in Utah. Potash is also obtainable from feldspar, but I do not know whether any plant has been established for its production from this rock. I recently heard of the arrival of some potash from a newly discovered field in Brazil, and there have been rumours of its discovery in Spain. I do not know how good this Spanish and Brazilian potash is, and I suppose the German potash syndicate will immediately endeavour to control these fields in order to hold the potash trade of the world in its grip.

It was a long time after the commencement of the war before Great Britain declared cotton a contraband. I think this was because of the fear of irritating the United States; but, in the meantime, Germany secured a great quantity of cotton, which, of course, was used or stored for the manufacture of powder. Since the cotton imports have been cut off the Germans claim that they are manufacturing a powder equally good by using wood pulp. Of course, I have not been able to verify this, absolutely.

Germany had endeavoured before the war in every way to keep American goods out of the

German markets, and even the Prussian state railways are used, as I have shown in the chapter where I speak of the attempt to establish an oil monopoly in Germany, in order to discriminate against American mineral oils. This same method has been applied to other articles such as wood, which otherwise might be imported from America and in some cases regulations as to the inspection of meat, etc., have proved more effective in keeping American goods out of the market than a prohibitive tariff.

The meat regulation is that each individual package of meat must be opened and inspected; and, of course, when a sausage has been individually made to sit up and bark no one desires it as an article of food thereafter. American apples were also discriminated against in the custom regulations of Germany. Nor could I induce the German Government to change their tariff on canned salmon, an article which would prove a welcome addition to the German diet.

The German workingman, undoubtedly the most exploited and fooled workingman in the world, is compelled not only to work for low wages and for long hours, but to purchase his food at rates fixed by the German tariff made for the benefit of the Prussian Junkers and land-owners.

Of course, the Prussian Junkers excuse the imposition of the tariff on food and the regulations made to prevent the entry of foodstuffs on the ground that German agriculture must be encouraged, first, in order to enable the population to subsist in time of war and blockade; and, secondly, in order to encourage the peasant class which furnishes the most solid soldiers to the Imperial armies.

The nations and business men of the world will have to face after the war a new condition which we may call socialized buying and socialized selling.

Not long after the commencement of the war the Germans placed a prohibitive tariff upon the import of certain articles of luxury such as perfumes; their object, of course, being to keep the German people from sending money out of the country and wasting their money in useless expenditures. At the same time a great institution was formed called the Central Einkauf Gesellschaft. This body, formed under government auspices of men appointed from civil life, is somewhat similar to one of our national defence boards. Every import of raw material into Germany falls into the hands of this central buying company, and if a German desires to buy any raw material for use in his factory he must buy it through this central board.

I have talked with members of this board and

they all unite in the belief that this system will be continued after the war.

For instance, if a man in Germany wishes to buy an automobile or a pearl necklace or a case of perfumery, he will be told, "You can buy this if you can buy it in Germany. But if you have to send to America for the automobile, if you have to send to Paris for the pearls or the perfumery, you cannot buy them." In this way the gold supply of Germany will be husbanded and the people will either be prevented from making comparatively useless expenditures or compelled to spend money to benefit home industry.

On the other hand, when a man desires to buy some raw material, for example, copper, cotton, leather, wheat or something of that kind, he will not be allowed to buy abroad on his own hook. The Central Einkauf Gesellschaft will see that all those desiring to buy cotton or copper put in their orders on or before a certain date. When the orders are all in, the quantities called for will be added up by this central board; and then one man, representing the board, will be in a position to go to America to purchase the four million bales of cotton or two hundred million pounds of copper.

The German idea is that this one board will be able to force the sellers abroad to compete against each other in their eagerness to sell. The one German buyer will know about the lowest price at which the sellers can sell their product. By the buyer's standing out alone with this great order the Germans believe that the sellers, one by one, will fall into his hands and sell their product at a price below that which they could obtain if the individual sellers of America were meeting the individual buyers of Germany in the open market.

When the total amount of the commodity ordered has been purchased, it will be divided up among the German buyers who put in their orders with the central company, each order being charged with its proportionate share of the expenses of the commission and, possibly, an additional sum for the benefit of the treasury of the Empire.

Before the war a German manufacturer took me over his great factory where fifteen thousand men and women were employed, showed me great quantities of articles made from copper, and said: "We buy this copper in America and we get it a cent and a half a pound less than we should pay for it because our government permits us to combine for the purpose of buying, but your government does not allow your people to combine for the purpose of selling. You have got lots of silly people who become envious of the rich and pass laws to prevent combination, which is the logical development of all industry."

The government handling of exchange during the war was another example of the use of the centralised power of the Government for the benefit of the whole nation.

In the first year of the war, when I desired money to spend in Germany, I drew a check on my bank in New York in triplicate and sent a clerk with it to the different banks in Berlin, to obtain bids in marks, selling it then, naturally, to the highest bidder. But soon the Government stepped in. The Imperial Bank was to fix a daily rate of exchange, and banks and individuals were forbidden to buy or sell at a different rate. That this fixed rate was a false one, fixed to the advantage of Germany, I proved at the time when the German official rate was 5.52 marks for a dollar, by sending my American checks to Holland, buying Holland money with them and German money with the Holland money, in this manner obtaining 5.74 marks for each dollar. And just before leaving Germany I sold a lot of American gold to a German bank at the rate of 6.42 marks per dollar, although on that day the official rate was 5.52 and although the buyer of the gold, because the export of gold was forbidden, would have to lose interest on the money paid me or on the gold purchased, until the end of the war.

What the Germans thought of the value of the mark is shown by this transaction.

The only thing that can maintain a fair price after the war for the products of American firms, miners and manufacturers is permission to combine for selling abroad. There is before Congress a bill called the Webb Bill permitting those engaged in export trade to combine, and this bill, which is manifestly for the benefit of the American producer of raw materials and foods and manufactured articles, should be passed.

It was also part of our commercial work to secure permits for the exportation from Belgium of American owned goods seized by Germany. We succeeded in a number of cases in getting these goods released. In other cases, the American owned property was taken over by the government, but the American owners were compensated for the loss.

Germany took over belligerent property and put it in the hands of receivers. In all cases where the majority of the stock of a German corporation was owned by another corporation or individuals of belligerent nationality, the German corporation was placed in the hands of a receiver. The German Government, however, would not allow the inquiry into the stock ownership to go further than the first holding corporation. There were many cases where the majority of the stock of a German corporation was owned by a British corporation and the majority of the stock of the British corporation, in turn, owned by an American corporation or by Americans. In this case the German Government refused to consider the American ownership of the British stock, and put the German company under government control.

With the low wages paid to very efficient workingmen who worked for long hours and with no laws against combination, it was always a matter of surprise to me that the Germans who were in the process of getting all the money in the world should have allowed their military autocracy to drive them into war.

I am afraid that, after this war, if we expect to keep a place for our trade in the world, we may have to revise some of our ideas as to so-called trusts and the Sherman Law. Trusts or combinations are not only permitted, but even encouraged in Germany. They are known there as "cartels" and the difference between the American trust and the German cartel is that the American trust has, as it were, a centralised government permanently taking over and combining the competing elements in any given business, while in Germany the competing elements form a combination by contract for a limited number of years. This combination is called a cartel and during these years each member of the cartel is assigned a given amount of the total production and given a definite share of the profits of the combination. The German cartel, therefore, as Consul General Skinner aptly said, may be likened to a confederation existing by contract for a limited period of time and subject to renewal only at the will of its members.

It may be that competition is a relic of barbarism and that one of the first signs of a higher civilisation is an effort to modify the stress of competition. The debates of Congress tend to show that, in enacting the Sherman Law, Congress did not intend to forbid the restraint of competition among those in the same business but only intended to prohibit the forming of a combination by those who, combined, would have a monopoly of a particular business or product. It is easy to see why all the coal mines in the country should be prohibited from combining; but it is not easy to see why certain people engaged in the tobacco business should be prohibited from taking their competitors into their combination, because tobacco is a product which could be raised upon millions of acres of our land and cannot be made the subject of a monopoly.

The German courts have expressly said that if prices are so low that the manufacturers of a particular article see financial ruin ahead, a formation of a cartel by them must be looked upon as a justified means of self-preservation. The German laws are directed to the end to which it seems to be such laws should logically be directed; namely, to the prevention of unfair competition.

So long as the question of monopoly is not involved, competition can always be looked for when a combination is making too great profits; and the new and competing corporation and individuals should be protected by law against the danger of price cutting for the express purpose of driving the new competitior out of business. However, it must be remembered that a combination acting unfairly in competition may be more oppressive than a monopoly. I myself am not convinced by the arguments of either side. It is a matter for the most serious study.

The object of the American trust has been to destroy its competitors. The object of the German cartel to force its competitors to join the cartel.

In fact the government in Germany becomes part of these cartels and takes an active hand in them, as witness the participation of the German Government in the potash syndicate, when contracts made by certain American buyers with German mines were cancelled and all the potash producing mines of Germany and Austria forced into one confederation; and witness the attempt by the government, which I have described in another chapter, to take over and make a monopoly of the wholesale and retail oil business of the country.

The recent closer combination of dyestuff industries of Germany, with the express purpose of meeting and destroying American competition after the war, is interesting as showing German methods. For a number of years the dyestuff industry of Germany was practically controlled by six great companies, some of these companies employing as high as five hundred chemists in research work. In 1916 these six companies made an agreement looking to a still closer alliance not only for the distribution of the product but also for the distribution of ideas and trade secrets. For years, these great commercial companies supplied all the countries of the world not only with dyestuffs and other chemical products but also with medicines discovered by their chemists and made from coal tar; which, although really nothing more than patent medicines, were put upon the market as new and great and beneficial discoveries in medicine. The Badische Anilin and Soda Fabrik, with a capital of fifty-four million marks has paid dividends in the ten years from 1903 to 1913, averaging over twenty-six per cent.

The Farbwerke Meister Lucius und Bruning at Hoeckst, near Frankfort, during the same period, with a capital of fifty million marks, has paid dividends averaging over twenty-seven per cent; and the chemical works of Bayer and Company, near Cologne, during the same period with a capital of fifty-four millions of marks has paid dividends averaging over thirty per cent.

Much of the commercial success of the Germans during the last forty years is due to the fact that each manufacturer, each discoverer in Germany, each exporter knew that the whole weight and power of the Government was behind him in his efforts to increase his business. On the other hand, in America, business men have been terrorized, almost into inaction, by constant prosecutions. What was a crime in one part of the United States, under one Circuit Court of Appeals, was a perfectly legitimate act in another.

If we have to meet the intense competition of Germany after the war, we have got to view all these problems from new angles. For instance, there is the question of free ports. Representative Murray Hulbert has introduced, in the House of Representatives, a resolution directing the Secretary of the Treasury, the Secretary of War and the Secretary of Commerce to report to Congress as to the advisability of the establishment of free ports within the limits of the established customs of the United States. Free ports exist in Germany and have existed for a long time, although Germany is a country with a protective tariff. In a free port raw goods are manufactured and then exported, of course to the advantage of the country permitting the establishment of free ports, because by this manufacture of raw materials and their re-export, without being subject to duty, money is earned by the manufacturers to the benefit of their own country and employment is given to many workingmen. This, of course, improves the condition of these workingmen and of all others in the country; as it is self-evident that the employment of each workingman in an industry, which would not exist except for the existence of the free port, withdraws that workingman from the general labour market and, therefore, benefits the position of his remaining fellow labourers.

Although free ports do not exist in the United States, an attempt has been made to give certain industries, by means of what are known as "drawbacks," the same benefit that they would enjoy were free ports existant in our country.

Thus the refiners of raw sugar from Cuba pay a duty on this sugar when it enters the United States, but receive this duty back when a corresponding amount of refined sugar is exported to other countries.

There has lately been an attack made upon this system in the case, however, of the sugar refiners only, and the question has been treated in some newspapers as if these refiners were obtaining some unfair advantage from the government, whereas, as a matter of fact, the allowance of these "drawbacks" enables the sugar refiners to carry on the refining of the sugar for export much as they would if their refineries existed in free ports modelled on the German system.

The repeal of the provision of allowing "drawbacks" in this and other industries will probably send the industries to Canada or some other territory where this system, equivalent to the free port, is permitted to exist.

A few days before I left Germany I had a conversation with a manufacturer of munitions who employs about eighteen thousand people in his factories, which, before the war, manufactured articles other than munitions. I asked him how the government treated the manufacturers of munitions, and he said that they were allowed to make good profits, although they had to pay out a great proportion of these profits in the form of taxes on their excess or war profits; that the government desired to encourage manufacturers to turn their factories into factories for the manufacture of all articles in the war and required by the nation in sustaining war; and that the manufacturers would do this provided that it were only a question as to how much of their profits they would be allowed to keep, but that if the Government had attempted to fix prices so low that there would have been a doubt as to whether the manufacturer could make a profit or not, the production of articles required for war would never have reached the high mark that it had in Germany.

As a matter of fact, about the only tax imposed in Germany since the outbreak of the war has been the tax upon cost or war profits. It has been the policy of Germany to pay for the war by great loans raised by popular subscription, after authorisation by the Reichstag. I calculate that the amounts thus raised, together with the floating indebtedness, amount to date to about eighty billions of marks.

For a long time the Germans expected that the expenses of the war would be paid from the indemnities to be recovered by Germany from the nations at war with it.

Helfferich shadowed this forth in his speech in the Reichstag, on August 20, 1915, when he said: "If we wish to have the power to settle the terms of peace according to our interests and our requirements, then we must not forget the question of cost. We must have in view that the whole future activity of our people, so far as this is at all possible, shall be free from burdens. The leaden weight of billions has been earned by the instigators of this war, and in the future they, rather than we, will drag it about after them."

Of course, by "instigators of the war" Helfferich meant the opponents of Germany, but I think that unconsciously he was a true prophet and that the "leaden weight of the billions" which this war has cost Germany will be dragged about after the war by Germany, the real instigator of this world calamity.

In December, 1915, Helfferich voiced the comfortable plea that, because the Germans were spending their money raised by the war loans in Germany, the weight of these loans was not a real weight upon the German people. He said: "We are paying the money almost exclusively to ourselves; while the enemy is paying its loans abroad —a guarantee that in the future we shall maintain the advantage."

This belief of the Germans and Helfferich is one of the notable fallacies of the war. The German war loans have been subscribed mainly by the great companies of Germany; by the Savings Banks, the Banks, the Life and Fire Insurance and Accident Insurance Companies, etc.

Furthermore, these loans have been pyramided; that is to say, a man who subscribed and paid for one hundred thousand marks of loan number one could, when loan number two was called for, take the bonds he had bought of loan number one to his bank and on his agreement to spend the proceeds in subscribing to loan number two, borrow from the bank eighty thousand marks on the security of his first loan bonds, and so on.

There is an annual increment, not easily ascertainable with exactness, but approximately ascertainable to the wealth of every country in the world. Just as when a man is working a farm there is in normal years an increment or accretion of wealth or income to him above the cost of the production of the products of the soil which he sells, there is such an annual increment to the wealth of each country taken as a whole. Some experts have told me they calculated that, at the outside, in prosperous peace times the annual increment of German wealth is ten billion marks.

Now when we have the annual interest to be paid by Germany exceeding the annual increment of the country, the social and even moral bankruptcy of the country must ensue. If repudiation of the loan or any part of it is then forced, the loss naturally falls upon those who have taken the loan. The working-man or small capitalist, who put all his savings in the war loan, is without support for his old age, and so with the man who took insurance in the Insurance Companies or put his savings in a bank. If that bank becomes bankrupt through repudiation of the war loan, you then have the country in a position where the able-bodied are all working to pay what they can towards the interest of the government loan, after earning enough to keep themselves and their families alive; and the old and the young, without support and deprived of their savings, become mere poor-house burdens on the community.

Already the mere interest of the war loan of Germany amounts to four billions of marks a year; to this must be added, of course, the interest of the previous indebtedness of the country and of each political subdivision thereof, including cities, all of which have added to their before-the-war debt, by incurring great debts to help the destitute in this war; and, of course, to all this must be added the expenses of the administration of the government and the maintenance of the army and navy.

It is the contemplation of this state of affairs, when he is convinced that indemnities are not to be exacted from other countries, that will do most to persuade the average intelligent German business man that peace must be had at any cost.

CHAPTER XIV

WORK FOR THE GERMANS

THE interests of Germany in France, Great Britain and Russia were placed with our American Ambassadors in these countries. This, of course, entailed much work upon our Embassy, because we were the medium of communication between the German Government and these Ambassadors. I found it necessary to establish a special department to look after these matters. At its head was Barclay Rives who had been for many years in our diplomatic service and who joined my Embassy at the beginning of the war. First Secretary of our Embassy in Vienna for ten or twelve years, he spoke German perfectly and was acquainted with many Germans and Austrians. Inquiries about Germans who were prisoners, negotiations relative to the treatment of German prisoners, and so on, came under this department.

One example will show the nature of this work. When the Germans invaded France, a German cavalry patrol with two officers, von Schierstaedt and Count Schwerin, and several men penetrated as far as the forest of Fontainebleau, south of Paris. There they got out of touch with the German forces and wandered about for days in the forest. In the course of their wanderings they requisitioned some food from the inhabitants, and took, I believe, an old coat for one of the officers who had lost his, and requisitioned a wagon to carry a wounded man. After their surrender to the French, the two officers were tried by a French court martial, charged with pillaging and sentenced to be degraded from their rank and transported to Cayenne (the Devil's Island of the Dreyfus case). The Germans made strong representations, and our very skilled Ambassador in Paris, the Honourable William C. Sharp, took up the matter with the Foreign Office and succeeded in preventing the transportation of the officers. The sending of the officers and men, however, into a military prison where they were treated as convicts caused great indignation throughout Germany. The officers had many and powerful connections in their own country who took up their cause. There were bitter articles in the German press and caricatures and cartoons were published.

I sent Mr. Rives to Paris and told him not to leave until he had seen these officers. He remained in Paris some weeks and finally through

Mr. Sharp obtained permission to visit the officers in the military prison. Later the French showed a tendency to be lenient in this case, but it was hard to find a way for the French Government to back down gracefully. Schierstaedt having become insane in the meantime, a very clever way out of the difficulty was suggested, I believe by Mr. Sharp. Schierstaedt having been found to be insane was presumably insane at the time of the patrol's wandering in the forest of Fontainebleau. As he was the senior officer, the other officer and the men under him were not responsible for obeying his commands. The result was that Schwerin and the men of the patrol were put in a regular prison camp and Schierstaedt was very kindly sent by the French back to Germany, where he recovered his reason sufficiently to be able to come and thank me for the efforts made on his behalf.

I made every endeavour so far as it lay in my power to oblige the Germans. We helped them in the exchange of prisoners and the care of German property in enemy countries.

There were rumours in Berlin that Germans taken as prisoners in German African Colonies were forced to work in the sun, watched and beaten by coloured guards. This was taken up by one of the Grand Dukes of Mecklenburg who had been Governor of Togoland and who also took great interest in sending clothes, etc., to these prisoners. Germany demanded that the prisoners in Africa be sent to a more temperate climate.

Another royalty who was busied with prisoners' affairs was Prince Max of Baden. He is heir to the throne of Baden, although not a son of the reigning Duke. He is very popular and, for my part, I admire him greatly. He travels with Emerson's essays in his pocket and keeps up with the thought and progress of all countries. Baden will be indeed happy in having such a ruler. Prince Max was a man so reasonable, so human, that I understand that von Jagow was in favour of putting him at the head of a central department for prisoners of war. I agreed with von Jagow that in such case all would go smoothly and humanely. Naturally, von Jagow could only mildly hint at the desirability of this appointment. A prince, heir to one of the thrones of Germany, with the rank of General in the army, he seemed ideally fitted for such a position, but unfortunately the opposition of the army and, particularly, of the representative corps commanders was so great that von Jagow told me the plan was impossible of realisation. I am sure if Prince Max had been at the head of such a department, Germany would not now be suffering from the odium of mistreating its prisoners, and that the two million prisoners of war in Germany would not return to their homes imbued with an undying hate.

Prince Max was very helpful in connection with the American mission to Russia for German prisoners which I had organised and which I have described in the chapter on war charities.

All complaints made by the Imperial Government with reference to the treatment of German prisoners, and so forth, in enemy countries were first given to me and transmitted by our Embassy to the American Ambassadors having charge of German interests in enemy countries. All this, with the correspondence ensuing, made a great amount of clerical work.

I think that every day I received one or more Germans, who were anxious about prisoner friends, making inquiries, and wishing to consult me on business matters in the United States, etc. All of these people showed gratitude for what we were able to do for them, but their gratitude was only a drop in the ocean of officially inspired hatred of America.

CHAPTER XV

WAR CHARITIES

A S soon as the war was declared and millions of men marched forward intent upon killing, hundreds of men and women immediately took up the problem of helping the soldiers, the wounded and the prisoners and of caring for those left behind by the men who had gone to the front.

The first war charity to come under my observation was the American Red Cross. Two units containing three doctors and about twelve nurses, each, were sent to Germany by the American National Red Cross. Before their arrival I took up with the German authorities the questions as to whether these would be accepted and where they would be placed. The German authorities accepted the units and at first decided to send one to each front. The young man assigned to the West front was Goldschmidt Rothschild, one of the last descendants of the great Frankfort family of Rothschild. He had been attached to the German Embassy in London before the war.

The one assigned to the unit for the East front was Count Hélie de Talleyrand. Both of these young men spoke English perfectly and were chosen for that reason, and both have many friends in England and America.

Talleyrand was of a branch of the celebrated Talleyrand family and possessed German citizenship. During the Napoleonic era the great Talleyrand married one of his nephews to a Princess of Courland who, with her sister, was joint heiress of the principality of Sagan in Germany. The share of the other sister was bought by the sister who married young Talleyrand, and the descendants of that union became princes of Sagan and held the Italian title of Duke de Dino and the French title of Duke de Valençay.

Some of the descendants of this nephew of the great Talleyrand remained in Germany, and this young Talleyrand, assigned to the Red Cross unit, belonged to that branch. Others settled in France, and among these was the last holder of the title and the Duke de Dino, who married, successively, two Americans, Miss Curtis and Mrs. Sampson. It was a custom in this family that the holder of the principal title, that of the Prince of Sagan, allowed the next two members in succession to bear the titles of Duke de Dino and Duke de Valançay. Before the last Prince of Sagan died in France, his son Hélie married the American, Anna Gould, who had divorced the Count Castellane. On the death of his father and in accordance with the statutes of the House of Sagan the members of the family who were German citizens held a family council and, with the approval of the Emperor of Germany, passed over the succession from Anna Gould's husband to her son, so that her son has now the right to the title and not his father, but the son must become a German citizen at his majority.

The younger brother of the husband of Anna Gould bears the title of Duke de Valençay and is the divorced husband of the daughter of Levi P. Morton, formerly Vice-President of the United States. This young Talleyrand to whom I have referred and who was assigned to the American Red Cross unit, although he was a German by nationality, did not wish to fight in this war against France in which country he had so many friends and relations and, therefore, this assignment to the American Red Cross was most welcome to him.

On the arrival of the American doctors and nurses in Berlin, it was decided to send both units to the East front and to put one in the small Silesian town of Gleiwitz and the other in the neighbouring town of Kosel. Count Talleyrand went with these two units, Goldschmidt

Rothschild being attached to the Prussian Legation in Munich.

We had a reception in the Embassy for these doctors and nurses which was attended by Prince Hatzfeld, Duke of Trachenberg, who was head of the German Red Cross, and other Germans interested in this line of work. The Gleiwitz and Kosel units remained in these towns for about a year until the American Red Cross withdrew its units from Europe.

At about the time of the withdrawal of these units, I had heard much of the sufferings of German prisoners in Russia. I had many conversations with Zimmermann of the German Foreign Office and Prince Hatzfeld on this question, as well as with Prince Max of Baden, the heir presumptive to the throne of that country; and I finally arranged that such of these American doctors and nurses as volunteered should be sent to Russia to do what they could for the German prisoners of war there. Nine doctors and thirty-eight nurses volunteered. They were given a great reception in Berlin, the German authorities placed a large credit in the hands of this mission, and, after I had obtained through our State Department the consent of the Russian Government for the admission of the mission, it started from Berlin for Petrograd. The German authorities and the Germans, as a whole, were very much pleased with this arrangement. Officers of the Prussian army were present at the departure of the trains and gave flowers to all the nurses. It is very unfortunate that after their arrival in Russia this mission was hampered in every way, and had the greatest difficulty in obtaining permission to do any work at all. Many of them, however, managed to get in positions where they assisted the German prisoners. For instance, in one town where there were about five thousand Germans who had been sent there to live one of our doctors managed to get appointed as city physician and, aided by several of the American nurses, was able to do a great work for the German population. Others of our nurses managed to get as far as Tomsk in Siberia and others were scattered through the Russian Empire.

Had this mission under Dr. Snoddy been able to carry out its work as originally planned, it would not only have done much good to the German prisoners of war, but would have helped a great deal to do away with the bitter feeling entertained by Germans towards Americans. Even with the limited opportunity given this mission, it undoubtedly materially helped the prisoners.

On arriving in Berlin on their way home to America from Gleiwitz and Kosel, the doctors

295

and nurses of these American units were all awarded the German Red Cross Order of the second class and those who had been in Austria were similarly decorated by the Austro-Hungarian Government.

Among those who devoted themselves to works of charity during this war no one stands higher than Herbert C. Hoover.

I cannot find words to express my admiration for this man whose great talents for organisation were placed at the service of humanity. Every one knows of what he accomplished in feeding the inhabitants of Belgium and Northern France. Mr. Hoover asked me to become one of the chairmen of the International Commission for the Relief of Belgium and I was happy to have the opportunity in Berlin to second his efforts. There was considerable business in connection with the work of the commission. I had many interviews with those in authority with reference to getting their ships through, etc. Mr. Hoover and I called on the Chancellor and endeavoured to get him to remit the fine of forty million francs a month which the Germans had imposed upon Belgium. This, however, the Chancellor refused to do. Later on in April, 1915, I was able as an eye-witness to see how efficiently Mr. Hoover's organisation fed, in addition to the people of Belgium, the French population in that part of

Northern France in the occupation of the Germans.

Mr. Hoover surrounded himself with an able staff, Mr. Vernon Kellogg and others, and in America men like Mr. A. J. Hemphill were his devoted supporters.

Early in 1915, Mr. Ernest P. Bicknell, who had first come to Germany representing the American Red Cross, returned representing not only that organisation but also the Rockefeller Foundation. With him was Mr. Wickliffe Rose, also of the Rockefeller Foundation; and with these two gentlemen I took up the question of the relief of Poland. Mr. Rose and Mr. Bicknell together visited Poland and saw with their own eyes the necessity for relief. A meeting was held in the Reichstag attended by Prince Hatzfeld of the German Red Cross, Director Guttmann, of the Dresdener Bank, Geheimrat Lewald, of the Imperial Ministry of the Interior, representing the German Government, and many others connected with the government, military and financial interests of Germany.

The Commission for the Relief in Poland, of which I was to be chairman, was organised and included the Spanish Ambassador, His Excellency the Bishop of Posen, the Prince Bishop of Cracow, Jacob H. Schiff of New York, and others. Messrs. Warwick, Greene and Wadsworth were to take up the actual executive work.

In conjunction with Messrs. Rose and Bicknell, I drew up a sort of treaty, having particularly in mind certain difficulties encountered by the American Relief Commission in Belgium. The main point in this treaty was that the German Government agreed not to requisition either food or money within the limits of the territory to be relieved, which territory comprised that part of Poland within German occupation up to within, as I recall it, fifty kilometres of the firing line. The one exception was that a fine might be levied on a community where all the inhabitants had made themselves jointly and severally liable according to the provisions of the Hague Convention. The Rockefeller Foundation on its part agreed to pay all the expenses of the executive work of the commission. This treaty, after being submitted to General Hindenburg and approved by him, was signed by Dr. Lewald, representing the German Government, by Mr. Bicknell, representing the Rockefeller Foundation, and by me, representing the new commission for the relief of Poland.

Work was immediately commenced under this arrangement and, so far as possible, food was purchased in Holland and Denmark, but there was little to be had in these countries. The Allies, however, refused to allow food to enter

Germany for the purpose of this commission, and so the matter fell through. Later, when the Allies were willing to permit the food to enter, it was the German Government that refused to reaffirm this treaty and refused to agree that the German army of occupation should not requisition food in occupied Poland. Of course, under these circumstances, no one could expect the Allies to consent to the entry of food; because the obvious result would be that the Germans would immediately, following the precedent established by them in Northern France, take all the food produced in the country for their army and the civil population of Germany, and allow the Poles to be fed with food sent in from outside, while perhaps their labour was utilised in the very fields the products of which were destined for German consumption.

There is no question that the sufferings of the people of Poland have been very great, and when the history of Poland during the war comes to be written the world will stand aghast at the story of her sufferings. It is a great pity that these various schemes for relief did not succeed. The Rockefeller Commission, however, up to the time I left Germany did continue to carry on some measure of relief and succeeded in getting in condensed milk, to some extent, for the children of that unfortunate country. These negotiations brought me in contact with a number of Poles resident in Berlin, whom I found most eager to do what they could to relieve the situation. I wish here to express my admiration for the work of the Rockefeller Commission in Europe. Not only were the ideas of the Commission excellent and businesslike but the men selected to carry them into effect were without exception men of high character and possessed of rare executive ability.

As I have said in a previous chapter, I was ridiculed in the American newspapers because I had suggested, in answer to a cable of the League of Mercy, that some work should be done for the prisoners of war. I do not know whether the great work undertaken by Dr. John R. Mott and his associates was suggested by my answer or not; that does not matter. But this work undertaken by the American Y. M. C. A. certainly mattered a great deal to the prisoners of war in Europe. Dr. Mott after serving on the Mexican Commission, has gone to Russia as a member of the Commission to that country.

The Y. M. C. A. organisation headed by Dr. Mott, who was most ably assisted by the Reverend Archibald C. Harte, took up this work, which was financed, I have been told, by the McCormick family of Chicago, Cleveland H. Dodge, John D. Rockefeller and others. Mr.

Harte obtained permission from the German authorities for the erection of meeting halls and for work in German camps. When he had obtained this authorisation from Germany he went to Russia, where he was able to get a similar authorisation.

At first in Russia, I have heard, the prisoners of war were allowed great liberty and lived unguarded in Siberian villages where they obtained milk, bread, butter, eggs and honey at very reasonable rates. As the war went on they were more and more confined to barracks and there their situation was sad indeed. In the winter season, it is dark at three in the afternoon and remains dark until ten the following morning. Of course, I did not see the Russian prison camps. The work carried on there was similar to that carried on in the German camps by Mr. Harte and his band of devoted assistants.

I was particularly interested in this work because I hoped that the aid given to the German prisoners of war in Russia would help to do away with the great hate and prejudice against Americans in Germany. So I did all I could, not only to forward Mr. Harte's work, but to suggest and organise the sending of the expedition of nurses and doctors, which I have already described, to the Russian camps.

Of course, Mr. Harte in this work did not attempt to cover all the prison camps in Germany. He did much to help the mental and physical conditions of the prisoners in Ruhleben, the English civilian camp near Berlin. The American Y. M. C. A. built a great hall where religious exercises were held, plays and lectures given, and where prisoners had a good place to read and write in during the day. A library was established in this building.

The work carried on by the Y. M. C. A. may be briefly described as coming under the following heads: religious activities; educational activities; work shops, and gardens; physical exercises and out-door sports; diet kitchens for convalescents; libraries and music, including orchestra, choruses, and so on.

When I left Germany on the breaking of diplomatic relations, a number of these Y. M. C. A. workers left with me.

The German women exhibited notable qualities in war. They engaged in the Red Cross work, including the preparation of supplies and bandages for the hospitals, and the first day of mobilisation saw a number of young girls at every railway station in the country with food and drink for the passing soldiers. At railway junctions and terminals in the large cities, stations were established where these Red Cross workers gave a warm meal to the soldiers passing

302

through. In these terminal stations there were also women workers possessed of sufficient skill to change the dressings of the lightly wounded.

On the Bellevuestrasse, Frau von Ihne, wife of the great architect, founded a home for blinded soldiers. In this home soldiers were taught to make brooms, brushes, baskets, etc.

German women who had country places turned these into homes for the convalescent wounded. But perhaps the most noteworthy was the National Frauendienst or Service for Women, organised the first day of the war. The relief given by the State to the wives and children of soldiers was distributed from stations in Berlin, and in the neighbourhood of each of these stations the Frauendienst established an office where women were always in attendance, ready to give help and advice to the soldiers' wives. There there were card-indexes of all the people within the district and of their needs. At the time I left Germany I believe that there were upwards of seven thousand women engaged in Berlin in social service, in instructing the women in the new art of cooking without milk, eggs or fat and seeing to it that the children had their fair share of milk. It is due to the efforts of these social workers that the rate of infant mortality in Berlin decreased during the war.

A war always causes a great unsettling in busi-

303

ness and trade; people no longer buy as many articles of luxury and the workers engaged in the production of these articles are thrown out of employment. In Germany, the National Women's Service, acting with the labour exchanges, did its best to find new positions for those thrown out of work. Women were helped over a period of poverty until they could find new places and were instructed in new trades.

Many women engaged in the work of sending packages containing food and comforts to the soldiers at the front and to the German prisoners of war in other countries.

Through the efforts of the American Association of Commerce and Trade, and the Embassy, a free restaurant was established in Berlin in one of the poorer districts. About two hundred people were fed here daily in a hall decorated with flags and plants. This was continued even after we left Germany.

At Christmas, 1916, Mrs. Gerard and I visited this kitchen with Mr. and Mrs. Wolf and General von Kessel, Commander of the Mark of Brandenburg, and one of his daughters. Presents were distributed to the children and the mothers received an order for goods in one of the department stores. The German Christmas songs were sung and when a little German child offered a prayer for peace, I do not think there was any

304

one present who could refrain from weeping.
Many of the German women of title, princesses, etc., established base hospitals of their
own and seemed to manage these hospitals with
success.

CHAPTER XVI

HATE

ON my way from Berlin to America, in February, 1917, at a dinner in Paris, I met the celebrated Italian historian, Ferrero. In a conversation with him after dinner, I reminded him of the fact that both he and a Frenchman, named Huret, who had written on America, had stated in their books that the thing which struck them most in the study of the American people was the absence of hate.

Ferrero recalled this and in the discussion which followed and in which the French novelist, Marcel Prevost, took part, all agreed that there was more hate in Europe than in America; first, because the peoples of Europe were confined in small space and, secondly, because the European, whatever his rank or station, lacked the opportunities for advancement and consequently the eagerness to press on ahead, and that fixing of the thought on the future, instead of the past, which formed part of the American character.

In a few hours in Europe it is possible to travel

in an automobile across countries where the people differ violently from the countries surrounding them, not only in language, customs and costumes, but also in methods of thought and physical appearance.

The day I left Berlin I went to see Herr von Gwinner, head of the Deutsche Bank, with reference to a charitable fund which had been collected for widows and orphans in Germany. In our talk, von Gwinner said that Europeans envied America because we seemed to be able to assimilate all those people who, as soon as they landed on our shores, sought to forget their old race hatreds and endeavoured, as speedily as possible, to adopt American clothes, language and thought. I told him I thought it was because in our country we did not try to force any one; that there was nothing to prevent a Pole speaking Polish and wearing Polish dress, if he chose; that the only weapon we used against those who desired to uphold the customs of Europe was that of ridicule; and that it was the repressive measures such as, for example, the repressive action taken by Prussia against the Poles and the Danes, the Alsatians and the Lorrainers, that had aroused a combative instinct in these peoples and made them cling to every vestige of their former nationality.

At first, with the coming of war, the concentrated hate of the German people seemed to be turned upon the Russians. Even Liebknecht, when he called upon me in order to show that he had not been shot, as reported in America, spoke of the perils of Czarismus and the hatred of the German people for the Russians. But later, and directed by the master hand of the governing class, all the hatred of the Germans was concentrated upon England.

The cartoon in *Punch* representing a Prussian family having its morning "Hate" was, in some aspects, not at all exaggerated. Hate in Germany is cultivated as a noble passion, and, during the war, divines and generals vied with each other in its praise. Early in 1917, the Prussian General in command at Limburg made a speech in which he extolled the advantages of hate and said that there was nothing like getting up in the morning after having passed a night in thought and dreams of hate.

The phrase "Gott strafe England" seemed to be all over Germany. It was printed on stamps to be affixed to the back of letters like our Red Cross stamps. I even found my German body servant in the Embassy affixing these stamps to the back of all letters, official and otherwise, that were sent out. He was stopped when discovered. Paper money was stamped with the words: "Gott strafe England," "und America" being

"Wilson and his Press is not America"

„Wilson und seine Presse ist nicht Amerika"

Eine amerikanische Kundgebung.

Am 27. Januar, dem Geburtstage des deutschen Kaisers, legten Amerikaner am Denkmale Friedrich des Großen einen Riesen-Lorbeerkranz mit einer deutschen und einer amerikanischen Fahne nieder. Letztere war in Trauerflor gehüllt. Friedrich der Große war einer der Ersten, der die mit Herzblut erkämpfte Unabhängigkeit der jungen Republik vom Joche Englands anerkannte. Den Dank Amerikas empfängt sein Nachkomme, Wilhelm II., in Form von heuchlerischen Phrasen und Waffenlieferungen an den Todfeind.

Photo Hilwa

An American Demonstration.

On the 27th of January, the birthday of the German Emperor, an immense laurel-wreath decorated with the German and American flags was placed by Americans at the foot of the monument to Frederick the Great. The American flag was enshrouded in black crape. Frederick the Great was the first to recognize the Independence of the young Republic, after it had won its freedom from the yoke of England, at the price of its very heart's blood through years of struggle. His successor, Wilhelm II., receives the gratitude of America in the form of hypocritical phrases and war supplies to his mortal enemy.

6

THIS PAGE FROM THE SCURRILOUS PUBLICATION OF MARTEN AND HIS COLLEAGUES SHOWS THE PHOTOGRAPH OF THE WREATH AND THE CRAPE-DRAPED AMERICAN FLAG

often added as the war progressed and America refused to change the rules of the game and stop the shipment of supplies to the Allies.

Every one is familiar with Lissauer's "Hymn of Hate." It is not extraordinary that one man in a country at war should produce a composition of this kind; but it is extraordinary as showing the state of mind of the whole country, that the Emperor should have given him the high order of the Red Eagle of the Second Class as a reward for having composed this extraordinary document.

Undoubtedly at first the British prisoners of war were treated very roughly and were starved and beaten by their guards on the way from the front to the concentration camps. Officers, objects usually considered more than sacred in Germany, even when wounded were subjected to brutal treatment and in the majority of their prisons were treated more like convicts than officers and gentlemen.

As the Germans gradually awoke to the fact that President Wilson was not afraid of the German vote and that the export of supplies from America would not be stopped, this stream of hate was turned on America. There was a belief in Germany that President Wilson was opposed by a majority of people of the United States, that he did not represent the real sentiment of

America, and that the sentiment there was favourable to Germany.

Unfortunately many Americans in Germany encouraged the German people and the German Government in this belief. Americans used to travel about, giving lectures and making speeches attacking their own country and their own President, and the newspapers published many letters of similar import from Americans resident in Germany.

One of the most active of these was a man named Maurice Somborn, a German American, who represented in Germany an American business house. He made it a practice to go about in Berlin and other cities and stand up in cafés and beer halls in order to make addresses attacking the President and the United States. So bold did he become that he even, in the presence of a number of people in my room, one day said that he would like to hang Secretary Bryan as high as Haman and President Wilson one foot higher. The American newspapers stated that I called a servant and had him thrown out of the Embassy. This statement is not entirely true: I selfishly kept that pleasure for myself.

The case of Somborn gave me an idea and I cabled to the Department of State asking authority to take up the passports of all Americans who abused their own country on the ground that they had violated the right, by their abuse, to the protection of a passport. The Department of State sustained my view and, by my direction, the consul in Dresden took up the passports of a singer named Rains and a gentleman of leisure named Recknagel who had united in addressing a letter to the Dresden newspapers abusing the President. It was sometime before I got Somborn's passport and I later on received from him the apologies of a broken and contrite man and obtained permission from Washington to issue him a passport in order to enable him to return to America.

Of course, these vilifiers of their own country were loud in their denunciations of me, but the prospect of losing the protection of their passports kept many of these men from open and treasonable denunciation of their own country.

The Government actually encouraged the formation of societies which had for their very object the scattering of literature attacking the President and the United States. The most conspicuous of these organisations was the so-called League of Truth. Permanently connected with it was an American dentist who had been in jail in America and who had been expelled from Dresden by the police authorities there. The secretary was a German woman who posed as an American, and had been on the stage as a snake dancer. The principal organiser was a German named Marten who had won the favour of the German authorities by writing a book on Belgium denying that any atrocities had taken place there. Marten secured subscriptions from many Germans and Americans resident in Germany, opened headquarters in rooms on the Potsdamerstrasse and engaged in the business of sending out pamphlets and leaflets attacking America. One of his principal supporters was a man named Stoddard who had made a fortune by giving travel lectures in America and who had retired to his handsome villa, in Meran, in Austria. Stoddard issued a pamphlet entitled, "What shall we do with Wilson?" and some atrocious attempts at verse, all of which were sent broadcast by the League of Truth.

This was done with the express permission of the German authorities because during the war no societies or associations of any kind could meet, be formed or act without the express permission and superintendence of both the military and police authorities. Any one who has lived in Germany knows that it would be impossible even in peace times to hang a sign or a wreath on a public statue without the permission of the local authorities; and yet on the Emperor's birthday, January twenty-seventh, 1916, this League of Truth was permitted to place an enormous

wreath, over four feet high, on the statue of
Frederick the Great, with an American flag
draped in mourning attached, and a silk banner
on which was printed in large letters of gold,
"Wilson and his press are not America." The
League of Truth then had a photograph taken
of this wreath which was sent all over Germany,
again, of course, with the permission of the
authorities. The wreath and attachments, in
spite of frequent protests on my part to Zimmermann and von Jagow, remained in this conspicuous position until the sixth of May, 1916. After
the receipt of the *Sussex* Note, I again called von
Jagow's attention to the presence of this wreath,
and I told him that if this continuing insult to
our flag and President was not taken away that
I would go the next day with a cinematograph
operator and take it away myself. The next day
the wreath had disappeared.

This League, in circulars, occasionally attacked me, and in a circular which they distributed shortly after my return to Germany at the
end of December, 1916, it was stated, "What do
you think of the American Ambassador? When
he came to Germany after his trip to America
he brought a French woman with him." And
the worst of this statement was that it was true.
But the League, of course, did not state that my
wife came with me bringing her French maid by

the express permission of the German Foreign Office.

I have had occasion many times to wonder at the curious twists of the German mind, but I have never been able to understand on what possible theory the German Government permitted and even encouraged the existence of this League of Truth. Certainly the actions of the League, headed by a snake dancer and a dentist, would not terrorise the American Congress, President Wilson or me into falling in with all the views of the German Government, and if the German Government was desirous of either the President's friendship or mine why was this gang of good-for-nothings allowed to insult indiscriminately their country, their President and their Ambassador?

One of the friends of Marten, head of this League, was (———) (————), a man who at the time he was an officer of the National Guard of the State of New York, accepted a large sum of money "for expenses" from Bernstorff.

Of course, in any country abroad acceptance by an officer of money from a foreign Ambassador could not be explained and could have only one result—a blank wall and firing party for the receiver of foreign pay. Perhaps we have grown so indulgent, so soft and so forgetful of the obligations which officers owe to their flag

314

and country that on (————)'s return from Germany he will be able to go on a triumphant lecture tour through the United States.

There was published in Berlin in English a rather ridiculous paper called the *Continental Times,* owned by an Austrian Jewess who had been married to an Englishman. The Foreign Office, after the outbreak of the war, practically took over this sheet by buying monthly many thousand copies. News coloured hysterically to favour the Central Empires was printed in this paper, which was headed "A Paper for Americans," under the editorship of an Englishman of decent family named Stanhope, who, of course, in consequence did not have to inhabit the prison camp of Ruhleben. (————) was a contributor to this newspaper, and scurrilous articles attacking President Wilson appeared. Finally (————) wrote a lying article for this paper in which he charged that Conger of the Associated Press had learned of Sir Roger Casement's proposed expedition; that Conger told me; that I cabled the news to Washington to the State Department; and that a member of President Wilson's Cabinet then gave the information to the British Ambassador. Later in a wireless which the Foreign Office permitted (————) to send Senator O'Gorman of New York,

(————) varied his lie and charged that I had sent the information direct to Great Britain.

The Continental Times was distributed in the prison camps and after (————)'s article I said to von Jagow, "I have had enough of this nonsense which is supported by the Foreign Office and if articles of the nature of (————)'s appear again I shall make a public statement that the prisoners of war in Germany are subjected to a cruel and unusual punishment by having the lying *Continental Times* placed in their hands, a paper which purports to be published for Americans but which is supported by the Foreign Office, owned by an Austrian and edited by a renegade Englishman!"

This *Continental Times* business again caused one to wonder at the German psychology which seems to think that the best way to make friends is to attack them. The author of "The Gentle Art of Making Enemies" must have attended a German school.

An Ambassador is supposed to be protected but not even when I filed affidavits in the Foreign Office, in 1916, made by the ex-secretary of the "League of Truth" and by a man who was constantly with Marten and the dentist, that Marten had threatened to shoot me, did the Foreign Office dare or wish to do anything against this ridiculous League. These affidavits were corroborated by a respectable restaurant keeper in Berlin and his assistants who testified that Marten with several ferocious looking German officers had come to his restaurant "looking" for me. I never took any precaution against these lunatics whom I knew to be a bunch of cowardly swindlers.

Marten and his friends were also engaged in a propaganda against the Jews.

The activities of Marten were caused by the fact that he made money out of his propaganda; as numerous fool Germans and traitorous Americans contributed to his war chest, and by the fact that his work was so favourably received by the military that this husky coward was excused from all military service.

It seemed, too, as if the Government was anxious to cultivate the hate against America. Long before American ammunition was delivered in any quantity to England and long before any at all was delivered to France, not only did the Government influence newspapers and official gazettes, but the official *Communiqués* alleged that quantities of American ammunition were being used on the West front.

The Government seemed to think that if it could stir up enough hate against America in Germany on this ammunition question the Americans would become terrorised and stop the shipment.

The Government allowed medals to be struck in honour of each little general who conquered a town—"von Emmich, conqueror of Liège," etc., a pernicious practice as each general and princeling wanted to continue the war until he could get his face on a medal—even if no one bought it. But the climax was reached when medals celebrating the sinking of the *Lusitania* were sold throughout Germany. Even if the sinking of the *Lusitania* had been justified only one who has lived in Germany since the war can understand the disgustingly bad taste which can gloat over the death of women and babies.

I can recall now but two writers in all Germany who dared to say a good word for America. One of these, Regierungsrat Paul Krause, son-in-law of Field Marshal Von der Goltz, wrote an article in January, 1917, in the *Lokal Anzeiger* pointing out the American side of the question of this munition shipment; and that bold and fearless speaker and writer, Maximilian Harden, dared to make a defence of the American standpoint. The principal article in one of the issues of his paper, *Die Zukunft,* was headed "If I were Wilson." After some copies had been sold the issue was confiscated by the police, whether at the instance of the military or at the instance of the Chancellor, I do not know. Every one had the impression in Berlin that this confiscation was by order of General von Kessel, the War Governor of the Mark of Brandenburg.

I met Harden before the war and occasionally conversed with him thereafter. Once in a while he gave a lecture in the great hall of the Philharmonic, always filling the hall to overflowing. In his lectures, which, of course, were carefully passed on by the police, he said nothing startling. His newspaper is a weekly publication; a little book about seven inches by four and a half, but wielding an influence not at all commensurate with its size.

The liberal papers, like the largest paper of Berlin, the *Tageblatt,* edited by Theodor Wolff, while not violently against America, were not favourable. But the articles in the Conservative papers and even some of the organs of the Catholic Party invariably breathed hatred against everything American.

In the Reichstag, America and President Wilson were often attacked and never defended. On May thirtieth, 1916, in the course of a debate on the censorship, Strasemann, of the National Liberal Party and of the branch of that party with Conservative leanings, violently opposed President Wilson and said that he was not wanted as a peacemaker.

Government, newspapers and politicians all united in opposing America.

I believe that to-day all the bitterness of the hate formerly concentrated on Great Britain has now been concentrated on the United States. The German-Americans are hated worse than the native Americans. They have deeply disappointed the Germans: first, because although German-Americans contributed enormously towards German war charities the fact of this contribution was not known to the recipients in Germany. Money sent to the German Red Cross from America was acknowledged by the Red Cross; but no publicity was given in Germany to the fact that any of the money given was from German-Americans. Secondly, the German-Americans did not go, as they might have done, to Germany, through neutral countries, with American passports, and enter the German army; and, thirdly, the most bitter disappointment of all, the German-Americans have not yet risked their property and their necks, their children's future and their own tranquillity, by taking arms against the government of America in the interest of the Hohenzollerns.

For years, a clever propaganda had been carried on in America to make all Germans there feel that they were Germans of one united nation, to make those who had come from Hesse and Bavaria, or Saxony and Württemberg, forget that as late as 1866 these countries had been overrun and conquered by Prussian militarism.

When Prince Henry, the Kaiser's brother, visited America, he spent most of his time with German-Americans and German-American societies in order to assist this propaganda.

Even in peace time, the German-American who returns to the village in which he lived as a boy and who walks down the village street exploiting himself and his property, does not help good relations between the two countries. Envy is the mother of hate and the envied and returned German-American receives only a lip welcome in the village of his ancestors.

Caricatures of Uncle Sam and of President Wilson were published in all German papers. A caricature representing our President releasing the dove of peace with one hand while he poured out munitions for the Allies with the other was the least unpleasant.

As I have said, from the tenth of August, 1914, to the twenty-fifth of September, 1915, the Emperor continually refused to receive me on the ground that he would not receive the Ambassador of a country which furnished munitions to the enemies of Germany; and we were thoroughly black-listed by all the German royalties. I did not see one, however humble, after the outbreak of the war, with the exception of Prince Max of Baden, who had to do with prisoners of war in Germany and in other countries. On one occasion I sent one of my secretaries to the palace of Princess August Wilhelm, wife of one of the Kaiser's sons, with a contribution of money for her hospital, she having announced that she would personally receive contributions on that day. She took the money from the secretary and spoke bitterly against America on account of the shipment of arms.

Even some boxes of cigarettes we sent another royalty at the front at Christmas time, 1914, were not acknowledged.

Dr. Jacobs, who was the correspondent in Berlin of *Musical America,* and who remained there until about the twenty-sixth of April, 1917, was called on about the sixteenth of April, 1917, to the Kommandantur and subjected to a cross-examination. During this cross-examination he was asked if he knew about the "League of Truth," and why he did not join that organisation. Whether it was a result of his non-joining or not, I do not know, but during the remainder of his stay in Berlin he was compelled to report twice a day to the police and was not allowed to leave his house after eight o'clock in the evening. The question, however, put to him shows the direct interest that the German authorities took in the existence of this malodorous organisation.

It appears in some of the circulars issued by the League of Truth that I was accused of giving American passports to Englishmen in order to enable them to leave the country.

After I left Germany there was an interpellation in the Reichstag about this, and Zimmermann was asked about the charge which he said he had investigated and found untrue.

In another chapter I have spoken of the subject of the selling of arms and supplies by America to the Allies. No German ever forgets this. The question of legality or treaties never enters his mind: he only knows that American supplies and munitions killed his brother, son or father. It is a hate we must meet for long years.

CHAPTER XVII

DIPLOMATIC NEGOTIATIONS (*Continued*)

A FEW days after the events narrated in Chapter XII, von Jagow called to see me at the Embassy and invited me to visit the Emperor at the Great General Headquarters; but he did not state why I was asked, and I do not know to this day whether the Chancellor and those surrounding the Emperor had determined on a temporary settlement of the submarine question with the United States and wished to put that settlement out, as it were, under the protection of the Emperor, or whether the Emperor was undecided and those in favour of peace wished me to present to him the American side of the question. I incline to the latter view. Von Jagow informed me that an officer from the Foreign Office would accompany me and that I should be allowed to take a secretary and the huntsman (*Leibjaeger*), without whom no Ambassador ever travels in Germany.

Mr. Grew, our counsellor, was very anxious to go and I felt on account of his excellent work, as well as his seniority, that he was entitled to be chosen. Lieutenant von Prittwitz, who was attached to the Foreign Office as a sort of special aide to von Jagow, was detailed to accompany us. We were given a special salon car and left on the evening of Friday, April twenty-eighth. As we neared the front by way of the line running through Saar Brucken, our train was often halted because of long trains of hospital cars on their way from the front to the base hospitals in the rear; and as we entered France there were many evidences of the obstinate fights which had raged in this part of the country in August, 1914. Parts of the towns and villages which we passed were in ruins, and rough trench lines were to be discerned on some of the hillsides. At the stations, weeping French women dressed in black were not uncommon sights, having just heard perhaps of the death, months before, of a husband, sweetheart or son who had been mobilised with the French army.

The fortress city of Metz through which we passed seemed to be as animated as a beehive. Trains were continuously passing. Artillery was to be seen on the roads and automobiles were hurrying to and fro.

The Great General Headquarters of the Kaiser for the Western Front is in the town of Charleville-Mézières, situated on the Meuse in the Department of the Ardennes, which Department at that time was the only French Department wholly in the possession of the Germans. We were received at the railway station by several officers and escorted in one of the Kaiser's automobiles, which had been set apart for my use, to a villa in the town of Charleville, owned by a French manufacturer named Perin. This pretty little red brick villa had been christened by the Germans, "Sachsen Villa," because it had been occupied by the King of Saxony when he had visited the Kaiser. A French family servant and an old gardener had been left in the villa, but for the few meals which we took there two of the Emperor's body huntsmen had been assigned, and they brought with them some of the Emperor's silver and china.

The Emperor had been occupying a large villa in the town of Charleville until a few days before our arrival. After the engineer of his private train had been killed in the railway station by a bomb dropped from a French aeroplane, and after another bomb had dropped within a hundred yards of the villa occupied by the Kaiser, he moved to a red brick château situated on a hill outside of Charleville, known as either the Château Bellevue or Bellaire.

Nearly every day during our stay, we lunched and dined with von Bethmann-Hollweg in the

villa of a French banker, which he occupied.
About ten people were present at these dinners,
the Chancellor's son-in-law, Zech, Prittwitz, two
experts in international law, both attached to the
Foreign Office, and, at two dinners, von Treutler,
the Prussian Minister to Bavaria, who had been
assigned to represent the Foreign Office near the
person of the Kaiser and Helfferich who, towards
the end of our stay, had been summoned from
Berlin.

I had been working hard at German and as von
Bethmann-Hollweg does not like to talk English
and as some of these persons did not speak that
language we tried to carry on the table conversation in German, but I know that when I tried to
explain, in German, to Helfferich the various tax
systems of America, I swam out far beyond my
linguistic depth.

During our stay here I received cables from
the Department of State which were transmitted
from Berlin in cipher, and which Grew was able
to decipher as he had brought a code book with
him. In one of these it was expressly intimated
that in any settlement of the submarine controversy America would make no distinction between armed and unarmed merchant ships.

We formed for a while quite a happy family.
The French owners of the villa seemed to
have had a fondness for mechanical toys. After

dinner every night these toys were set going, much to the amusement of von Bethmann-Hollweg. One of these toys, about two feet high, was a Hoochi-Koochi dancer and another successful one was a clown and a trained pig, both climbing a step ladder and performing marvellous feats thereon. Grew, who is an excellent musician, played the piano for the Chancellor and at his special request played pieces by Bach, the favourite composer of von Bethmann-Hollweg's deceased wife. One day we had tea in the garden of the villa formerly occupied by the Emperor, with the Prince of Pless (who is always with the Kaiser, and who seemed to be a prime favourite with him), von Treutler and others, and motored with Prince Pless to see some marvellous Himalayan pheasants reared by an old Frenchman, an ex-jailer, who seemed to have a strong instinct to keep something in captivity.

The Kaiser's automobile, which he had placed at my disposal, had two loaded rifles standing upright in racks at the right and left sides of the car, ready for instant use. On one day we motored, always, of course, in charge of the officers detailed to take care of us, to the ancient walled city of Rocroy and through the beautiful part of the Ardennes forest lying to the east of it, returning to Charleville along the heights above the valley of the Meuse.

AMBASSADOR GERARD AND HIS PARTY IN SEDAN

WITH GERMAN OFFICERS AND MEMBERS OF THE FRENCH FOOD COMMISSION BEFORE THE COTTAGE AT BAZEILLES, WHERE NAPOLEON III AND BISMARCK MET AFTER THE BATTLE OF SEDAN

The feeding of the French population, which is carried on by the American Relief Commission, was a very interesting thing to see and, in company with one of the members of the French committee, we saw the workings of this system of American Relief. We first visited a storehouse in Charleville, the headquarters for the relief district of which Charleville may be called the capital.

For relief purposes Northern France is divided into six districts. From the central distribution point in each district, food is sent to the commune within the district, the commune being the ultimate unit of distribution and each commune containing on the average about five hundred souls. We then motored to one of the communes where the distribution of food for the week was to take place that afternoon. Here in a factory, closed since the war, the people of the commune were lined up with their baskets waiting for their share of the rations. On entering a large room of the factory, each stopped first at a desk and there either paid in cash for the week's allowance of rations or signed an agreement to pay at some future date. The individuals who had no prospect of being able to pay received the rations for nothing. About one-third were in each class. The money used was not always French, or real money, but was, as a rule, the paper money issued in that part of Northern France by each town and redeemable after the war.

Signs were hung up showing the quantity that each person was entitled to receive for the next fifteen days and the sale price per kilo to each inhabitant. For instance, in this particular period for the first fifteen days of the month of May, 1916, each inhabitant could, in this district, receive the following allowances at the following rates:

ARTICLE	AMOUNT PER HEAD		PRICE
Flour	4 K. 500	The Kilogram	0 fr. 48
Rice	K. 500		0 fr. 55
Beans	K. 500		0 fr. 90
Bacon	K. 500		2 fr. 80
Lard	K. 250		2 fr. 30
Green Coffee	K. 250		1 fr. 70
Crystallized Sugar	K. 150		0 fr. 90
Salt	K. 200		0 fr. 10
Soap (hard)	K. 250		1 fr. 00

In addition to these articles each inhabitant of the commune which we visited, also received on the day of our visit a small quantity of carrot seed to plant in the small plot of ground which each was permitted to retain out of his own land by the German authorities.

The unfortunate people who received this allowance looked very poor and very hungry and very miserable. Many of them spoke to me, not only here but also in Charleville, and expressed their great gratitude to the American people for what was being done for them. Those in Charleville said that they had heard that I was in their town because of trouble pending between America and Germany. They said they hoped that there would be no war between the two countries because if war came they did not know what would become of them and that, in the confusion of war, they would surely be left to starve.

In Charleville notices were posted directing the inhabitants not to go out on the streets after, I think, eight o'clock in the evening, and also notices informing the population that they would be allowed a small quantity of their own land for the purpose of growing potatoes.

After visiting the factory building where the distribution of rations was taking place, we motored to Sedan, stopping on the way at the hamlet of Bazeilles, and visiting the cottage where Bismarck and Emperor Napoleon the Third had their historic interview after the battle of Sedan.

The old lady who owns this house received us and showed us bullet marks made on her house in the war of 1870, as well as in the present war. She apologised because she had had the windowpane, broken by a rifle shot in this war, replaced on account of the cold. As a girl, she had received Bismarck and Napoleon and had shown them to the room upstairs where they had held their consultation. I asked her which chair in this room Bismarck had sat in, and sat in it myself, for luck. I also contributed to the collection of gold pieces given to her by those who had visited her cottage.

In Sedan we visited an old mill where stores of the relief commission were kept, and in the mayor's office were present at a sort of consultation between the Prussian officers and members of the French Committee of Sedan in which certain details relative to the feeding of the population were discussed.

The relief work is not, of course, carried on right up to the battle line but we visited a small village not many kilometres in the rear of the German line. In this village we were, as before, shown the stores kept for distribution by the relief commission. As there were many soldiers in this village I said I thought that these soldiers must have stores of their own but, in order to be sure that they were not living on the supplies of the relief commission, I thought it only fair that I should see where the soldiers' stores were kept. I was taken across the railroad track to where their stores were kept and, judging from the labels on the barrels and boxes, I should say that a great many of these stores had come from Holland.

During this trip about the country, I saw a number of women and girls working, or attempting to work, in the fields. Their appearance was so different from that of the usual peasant that I spoke to the accompanying officers about it. I was told, however, that these were the peasants of the locality who dressed unusually well in that part of France. Later on in Charleville, at the lodging of an officer and with Count Wengersky, who was detailed to act as sort of interpreter and guide to the American Relief Commission workers, I met the members of the American Relief Commission who were working in Northern France and who had been brought on a special train for the purpose of seeing me to Charleville. This Count Wengersky spoke English well. Having been for a number of years agent of the Hamburg American Line in London, he was used to dealing with Americans and was possessed of more tact than usually falls to the lot of the average Prussian officer. We had tea and cakes in these lodgings, and then some of the Americans drew me aside and told me the secret of the peculiar looking peasants whom I had seen at work in the fields surrounding Charleville.

It seems that the Germans had endeavoured to

get volunteers from the great industrial towns of Lille, Roubeix and Tourcoing to work these fields; that after the posting of the notices calling for volunteers only fourteen had appeared. The Germans then gave orders to seize a certain number of inhabitants and send them out to farms in the outlying districts to engage in agricultural work. The Americans told me that this order was carried out with the greatest barbarity; that a man would come home at night and find that his wife or children had disappeared and no one could tell him where they had gone except that the neighbours would relate that the German non-commissioned officers and a file of soldiers had carried them off. For instance, in a house of a well-to-do merchant who had perhaps two daughters of fifteen and seventeen, and a man servant, the two daughters and the servant would be seized and sent off together to work for the Germans in some little farm house whose location was not disclosed to the parents. The Americans told me that this sort of thing was causing such indignation among the population of these towns that they feared a great uprising and a consequent slaughter and burning by the Germans.

That night at dinner I spoke to von Bethmann-Hollweg about this and told him that it seemed to me absolutely outrageous; and that, without consulting with my government, I was prepared to protest in the name of humanity against a continuance of this treatment of the civil population of occupied France. The Chancellor told me that he had not known of it, that it was the result of orders given by the military, that he would speak to the Emperor about it and that he hoped to be able to stop further deportations. I believe that they were stopped, but twenty thousand or more who had been taken from their homes were not returned until months afterwards. I said in a speech which I made in May on my return to America that it required the joint efforts of the Pope, the King of Spain and our President to cause the return of these people to their homes; and I then saw that some German press agency had come out with an article that I had made false statements about this matter because these people were not returned to their homes as a result of the representations of the Pope, the King of Spain and our President, but were sent back because the Germans had no further use for them. It seems to me that this denial makes the case rather worse than before.

At the Chancellor's house in the evenings we had discussions on the submarine situation and I had several long talks with von Bethmann-Hollweg alone in a corner of the room while the others listened to music or set the mechanical toys in motion. These discussions, without doubt, were reported to the Emperor either by the Chancellor or by von Treutler who at that time was high in favor with his Majesty.

I remember on one evening I was asked the question as to what America could do, supposing the almost impossible, that America should resent the recommencement of ruthless submarine warfare by the Germans and declare war. I said that nearly all of the great inventions used in this war had been made by Americans; that the very submarine which formed the basis of our discussion was an American invention, and so were the barbed wire and the aeroplane, the ironclad, the telephone and the telegraph, so necessary to trench warfare; that even that method of warfare had been first developed on something of the present scale in our Civil War; and that I believed that, if forced to it, American genius could produce some invention which might have a decisive effect in this war. My German auditors seemed inclined to believe that there was something in my contentions. But they said, "While possibly you might invent something in America, while possibly you will furnish money and supplies to the Allies, you have no men; and the public sentiment of your country is such that you will not be able to raise an army large enough to make any impression." I said that possibly if hostilities once broke out with the Germans, the

336

Germans might force us by the commission of such acts as had aroused Great Britain, to pass a law for universal military service. This proposition of mine was branded by the Germans as absolutely impossible; and, therefore, I am sure that the adoption by the United States of universal service in the first round of the war struck a very severe blow at the morale of Germany.

Von Bethmann-Hollweg always desired to make any settlement of the submarine question contingent upon our doing something against Great Britain; but I again and again insisted that we could not agree to do anything against some other power as a condition of obtaining a recognition of our rights from the German Empire.

During my stay at the General Headquarters, General Falkenhayn, although he was there at the time, carefully avoided me, which I took to be a sign that he was in favour of war with America. In fact, I heard afterwards that he had insisted on giving his views on the subject, but that a very high authority had told him to confine himself to military operations.

After we had been a day or so at Charleville, the Vice-Chancellor, Helfferich, arrived. I have always believed that he was sent for to add his weight to the arguments in favour of peace and to point out that it was necessary for Germany to have the friendship of America after the war, so as to have markets where she could place her goods. And I am convinced that at this time, at any rate, the influence of Helfferich was cast in the scale in favour of peace.

Finally, I was told that on the next day, which was Monday, May first, I was to lunch with the Emperor. Grew was invited to accompany me, and von Bethmann-Hollweg said that he would call for me about an hour before the time set for lunch as the Emperor desired to have a talk with me before lunch. In the afternoon an extract from the log of a German submarine commander was sent to me in which the submarine commander had stated that he had sighted a vessel which he could easily have torpedoed, but as the vessel was one hundred and twenty miles from land, he had not done so because the crew might not be able from that distance to reach a harbour. When the Chancellor called for me the following morning, he asked me if I had read this extract from the submarine officer's log, and noted how he had refrained from torpedoing a boat one hundred and twenty miles from land. I told the Chancellor that I had read the extract, but that I had also read in the newspaper that very morning that a ship had been torpedoed in stormy weather at exactly the same distance from land and the crew compelled to seek safety in the ship's boats; that, anyway, "one swallow did not make a summer," and that reports were continually being received of boats being torpedoed at great distances from land.

We then got in the motor and motored to the château about a mile off, where the Kaiser resided. We got out of the motor before going into the courtyard of the château, and immediately I was taken by the Chancellor into a garden on the gently sloping hillside below the château. Here the Emperor, dressed in uniform, was walking.

As I drew near the Emperor, he said immediately, "Do you come like the great pro-consul bearing peace or war in either hand?" By this he referred, of course, to the episode in which Quintus Fabius Maximus, chief of the Roman envoys sent to Hannibal in the Second Punic War, doubled his toga in his hand, held it up and said: "In this fold I carry peace and war: choose which you will have." "Give us which you prefer," was the reply. "Then take war," answered the Roman, letting the toga fall. "We accept the gift," cried the Carthaginian Senator, "and welcome."

I said, "No, your Majesty, only hoping that the differences between two friendly nations may be adjusted." The Emperor then spoke of what he termed the uncourteous tone of our notes, saying that we charged the Germans with

barbarism in warfare and that, as Emperor and
head of the Church, he had wished to carry on
the war in a knightly manner. He referred to
his own speech to the members of the Reichstag
at the commencement of the war and said that
the nations opposed to Germany had used unfair
methods and means, that the French especially
were not like the French of '70, but that their
officers, instead of being nobles, came from no
one knew where. He then referred to the efforts
to starve out Germany and keep out milk and said
that before he would allow his family and grand-
children to starve he would blow up Windsor
Castle and the whole Royal family of England.
We then had a long discussion in detail of the
whole submarine question, in the course of which
the Emperor said that the submarine had come
to stay, that it was a weapon recognised by all
countries, and that he had seen a picture of a
proposed giant submarine in an American paper,
the *Scientific American*. He stated that, anyway, there was no longer any international law.
To this last statement the Chancellor agreed.
He further said that a person on an enemy merchant ship was like a man travelling on a cart
behind the battle lines—he had no just cause of
complaint if injured. He asked me why we had
done nothing to Great Britain because of her al-

leged violations of international law—why we had not broken the British blockade.

In addition to the technical arguments based on international law, I answered that no note of the United States had made any general charge of barbarism against Germany; that we complained of the manner of the use of submarines and nothing more; that we could never promise to do anything to Great Britain or to any other country in return for a promise from Germany or any third country to keep the rules of international law and respect the rights and lives of our citizens; that we were only demanding our rights under the recognised rules of international law and it was for us to decide which rights we would enforce first; that, as I had already told the Chancellor, if two men entered my grounds and one stepped on my flowerbeds and the other killed my sister, I should probably first pursue the murderer of my sister; that those travelling on the seas in enemy merchant ships were in a different position from those travelling in a cart behind the enemy's battle lines on land because the land travellers were on enemy's territory, while those on the sea were on territory which, beyond the three-mile limit, was free and in no sense enemy's territory. We also discussed the position taken by the German Government in one of the *Frye* Notes, in which the German expert had taken the position that a cargo of food destined for an armed enemy port was presumed to be for the armies of the enemy, and therefore contraband. The Emperor spoke of the case of the *Dacia* with some bitterness, but when I went into an explanation the Chancellor joined in the conversation and said that our position was undoubtedly correct. I said that it was not our business to break the blockade—that there were plenty of German agents in the United States who could send food ships and test the question; that one ship I knew of, the *Wilhelmina,* laden with food, had been seized by the British, who then compromised with the owners, paying them, I believed, a large sum for the disputed cargo. And in taking up the doctrine of ultimate destination of goods, i.e., goods sent to a neutral country but really destined for a belligerent, I said I thought that during our Civil War we had taken against Great Britain exactly the same stand which Great Britain now took; and I said I thought that one of the decisions of our Supreme Court was based on a shipment to Matamoras, Mexico, but which the Supreme Court had decided was really for the Confederacy.

Discussing the submarine question, the Emperor and Chancellor spoke of the warning given in the *Lusitania* case; and I said: "If the Chancellor warns me not to go out on the Wilhelm-platz, where I have a perfect right to go, the fact that he gave the warning does not justify him in killing me if I disregarded his warning and go where I have a right to go." The conversation then became more general and we finally left the garden and went into the château, where the Emperor's aides and guests were impatiently waiting for lunch.

This conversation lasted far beyond lunch time. Anxious heads were seen appearing from the windows and terraces of the château to which we finally adjourned. I sat between the Emperor and Prince Pless. Conversation was general for the most of the time, and subjects such as the suffragettes and the peace expedition of Henry Ford were amusingly discussed.

After lunch, I again had a long talk with the Emperor but of a more general nature than the conversation in the garden.

That night about eleven o'clock, after again dining with the Chancellor, we left Charleville in the same special salon car, arriving at Berlin about four P. M. the next day, where at the station were a crowd of German and American newspaper correspondents, all anxious to know what had happened.

At this last dinner at the Chancellor's he took me off in a corner and said, "As I understand it, what America wants is cruiser warfare on the part of the sumbarines." And I said, "Yes, that is it exactly. They may exercise the right of visit and search, must not torpedo or sink vessels without warning, and must not sink any vessel unless the passengers and crew are put in a place of safety."

On the morning of the third of May, I heard that the German note had been drafted, but that it would contain a clause to the effect that while the German submarines would not go beyond cruiser warfare, this rule, nevertheless, would not apply to armed merchantmen.

As such a proposition as this would, of course, only bring up the subject again, I immediately ordered my automobile and called on the Spanish Ambassador, stating to him what I had heard about the contents of the note; that this would mean, without doubt, a break with America; and that, as I had been instructed to hand the Embassy over to him, I had come to tell him of that fact. I gave the same information to other colleagues, of course hoping that what I said would directly or indirectly reach the ears of the German Foreign Office. Whether it did or not, I do not know, but the *Sussex* Note when received did not contain any exception with reference to armed merchantmen.

With the receipt of the *Sussex* Note and the President's answer thereto, which declined assent to the claim of Germany to define its attitude toward our rights in accordance with what we might do in regard to the enforcement of our rights against Great Britain, the submarine question seemed, at least for the moment, settled. I, however, immediately warned the Department that I believed that the rulers of Germany would at some future date, forced by public opinion, and by the von Tirpitz and Conservative parties, take up ruthless submarine war again, possibly in the autumn but at any rate about February or March, 1917.

In my last conversation with von Bethmann-Hollweg before leaving the Great General Headquarters, when he referred to the cruiser warfare of the submarines, he also said, "I hope now that if we settle this matter your President will be great enough to take up the question of peace." It was as a result of intimations from government circles that, after my return to Berlin, I gave an interview to a representative of a Munich newspaper, expressing my faith in the coming of peace, although I was careful to say that it might be a matter of months or even years.

Thereafter, on many occasions the Chancellor impressed upon me the fact that America must do something towards arranging a peace and that if nothing was done to this end, public opinion in Germany would undoubtedly force a resumption of a ruthless submarine war.

In September of 1916, I having mentioned that Mrs. Gerard was going to the United States on a short visit, von Jagow insistently urged me to go also in order to make every effort to induce the President to do something towards peace; and, as a result of his urging and as a result of my own desire to make the situation clear in America, I sailed from Copenhagen on the twenty-eighth of September with Mrs. Gerard, on the Danish ship, *Frederick VIII,* bound for New York. I had spent almost three years in Berlin, having been absent during that time from the city only five or six days at Kiel and two week-ends in Silesia in 1914, with two weeks at Munich in the autumn, two days at Munich and two days at Parten-Kirchen in 1916, and two week-ends at Heringsdorf, in the summer of the same year, with visits to British prison camps scattered through the two and a half years of war.

On the *Frederick VIII* were Messrs. Herbert Swope of the *New York World* and William C. Bullitt of the *Philadelphia Ledger,* who had been spending some time in Germany. I impressed upon each of these gentlemen my fixed belief that Germany intended shortly, unless some definite move was made toward peace, to commence ruthless submarine war; and they made this view clear in the articles which they wrote for their respective newspapers.

Mr. Swope's articles which appeared in the *New York World* were immediately republished by him in a book called "Inside the German Empire." In Mr. Swope's book on page ninety-four, he says, "The campaign for the ruthless U-boat warfare is regarded by one man in this country who speaks with the highest German authority, as being in the nature of a threat intended to accelerate and force upon us a movement toward peace. Ambassador Gerard had his attention drawn to this just before he left Berlin but he declined to accept the interpretation."

On page eighty-eight he writes, "Our Embassy in Berlin expected just such a demonstration as was given by the U-53 in October when she sank six vessels off Nantucket, as a lesson of what Germany could do in our waters if war came."

On page seventy-four he says further, "Throughout Germany the objection for the resumption of ruthless U-boat warfare of the *Lusitania* type grows stronger day by day. The Chancellor is holding out against it, but how long he can restrain it no one can say. I left Germany convinced that only peace could prevent its resumption. And the same opinion is held by every German with whom I spoke, and it is held

347

also by Ambassador Gerard. The possibility was so menacing that the principal cause of the Ambassador's return in October was that he might report to Washington. The point was set out in press despatches at that time."

I wrote a preface to Mr. Swope's book for the express purpose of informing the American public in this way that I believed that Germany intended at an early date to resume the ruthless U-boat warfare.

Our trip home on the *Frederick VIII* was without incident except for the fact that on the ninth day of October, Swope came to the door of my stateroom about twelve o'clock at night and informed me that the captain had told him to tell me that the wireless had brought the news that German submarines were operating directly ahead of us and had just sunk six ships in the neighbourhood of Nantucket. I imagine that the captain slightly changed the course of our ship, but next day the odour of burning oil was quite noticeable for hours.

These Danish ships in making the trip from Copenhagen to New York were compelled to put in at the port of Kirkwall in the Orkney Islands, north of Scotland, where the ship was searched by the British authorities. On the occasion of our visit to Kirkwall, on this trip, a Swede, who had been so foolish as to make a sketch of the harbour and defences of Kirkwall from the top deck of the *Frederick VIII,* was taken off the boat by the British. The British had very cleverly spotted him doing this from the shore or a neighbouring boat, through a telescope.

Ships can enter Kirkwall only by daylight and at six o'clock every evening trawlers draw a net across the entrance to the harbour as a protection against submarines. A passage through this net is not opened until daylight the following morning.

Captain Thomson of the *Frederick VIII,* the ship which carried us to America and back to Copenhagen, by his evident mastery of his profession gave to all of his passengers a feeling of confidence on the somewhat perilous voyage in those dangerous waters.

When I reached America, on October eleventh, I was given a most flattering reception and the freedom of the City of New York. Within a few days after my arrival, the President sent for me to visit him at Shadow Lawn, at Long Branch, and I was with him for over four hours and a quarter in our first conference. I saw him, of course, after the election, before returning to Germany, and in fact sailed on the fourth of December at his special request.

Before I left I was impressed with the idea that he desired above all things both to keep and to make peace. Of course, this question of making peace is a very delicate one. A direct offer on our part might have subjected us to the same treatment which we gave Great Britain during our Civil War when Great Britain made overtures looking towards the establishment of peace, and the North answered, practically telling the British Government that it could attend to its own business, that it would brook no interference and would regard further overtures as unfriendly acts.

The Germans started this war without any consultation with the United States, and then seemed to think that they had a right to demand that the United States make peace for them on such terms and at such time as they chose; and that the failure to do so gave them a vested right to break all the laws of warfare against their enemies and to murder the citizens of the United States on the high seas, in violation of the declared principles of international law.

Nevertheless, I think that the inclination of the President was to go very far towards the forcing of peace.

Our trip from New York to Copenhagen was uneventful, cold and dark. We were captured by a British cruiser west of the Orkneys and taken in for the usual search to the port of Kirkwall where we remained two days.

The President impressed upon me his great interest in the Belgians deported to Germany. The action of Germany in thus carrying a great part of the male population of Belgium into virtual slavery had roused great indignation in America. As the revered Cardinal Farley said to me a few days before my departure, "You have to go back to the times of the Medes and the Persians to find a like example of a whole people carried into bondage."

Mr. Grew had made representations about this to the Chancellor and, on my return, I immediately took up the question.

I was informed that it was a military measure, that Ludendorf had feared that the British would break through and overrun Belgium and that the military did not propose to have a hostile population at their backs who might cut the rail lines of communication, telephones and telegraphs; and that for this reason the deportation had been decided on. I was, however, told that I would be given permission to visit these Belgians. The passes, nevertheless, which alone made such visiting possible were not delivered until a few days before I left Germany.

Several of these Belgians who were put at work in Berlin managed to get away and come to see me. They gave me a harrowing account of how they had been seized in Belgium and made to work in Germany at making munitions to be used probably against their own friends. I said to the Chancellor, "There are Belgians employed in making shells contrary to all rules of war and the Hague conventions." He said, "I do not believe it." I said, "My automobile is at the door. I can take you, in four minutes, to where thirty Belgians are working on the manufacture of shells." But he did not find time to go.

Americans must understand that the Germans will stop at nothing to win this war, and that the only thing they respect is force.

While I was in America von Jagow, as had been predicted by his enemies in Berlin, had fallen and Zimmermann had been given his place.

I remained a day in Copenhagen, in order to arrange for the transportation to Germany of the three tons of food which I had brought from New York, and, also, in order to lunch with Count Rantzau, the German Minister, a most able diplomat.

Therefore, the President's peace note arrived in Berlin just ahead of me and was delivered by Mr. Grew a few hours before my arrival. Joseph C. Grew, of Boston, was next in command during all my stay in Berlin. He most ably carried on the work of the Embassy during my absence on the trip to America, in the autumn of 1916; and at all times was of the greatest assistance to me. I hope to see him go far in his career.

This note was dated December eighteenth, 1916, and was addressed by the Secretary of State to the American Ambassadors at the capitals of the belligerent powers. It commenced as follows: "The President directs me to send you the following communication to be presented immediately to the Minister of Foreign Affairs of the government to which you are accredited.

"The President of the United States has instructed me to suggest to the (here is inserted a designation of the government addressed) a course of action in regard to the present war which he hopes that the government will take under consideration as suggested in the most friendly spirit, etc."

In the note which was sent to the Central Powers it was stated: "The suggestion which I am instructed to make, the President has long had it in mind to offer. He is somewhat embarrassed to offer it at this particular time because it may now seem to have been prompted by a desire to play a part in connection with the recent overtures of the Central Powers."

Of course, the President thus referred to the address made by Bethmann-Hollweg in the Reichstag in December, in which, after reviewing generally the military situation, the Chancellor said: "In a deep moral and religious sense of duty towards this nation and beyond it towards humanity, the Emperor now considers that the moment has come for official action towards peace. His Majesty, therefore, in complete harmony and in common with our Allies decided to propose to the hostile powers to enter peace negotiations." And the Chancellor continued, saying that a note to this effect had been transmitted that morning to all hostile powers, through the representatives of these powers to whom the interests and rights of Germany in the enemy States had been entrusted; and that, therefore, the representatives of Spain, the United States and Switzerland had been asked to forward the note.

Coincidently with this speech of the Chancellor's, which was December twelfth, 1916, the Emperor sent a message to the commanding generals reading as follows: "Soldiers! In agreement with the sovereigns of my Allies and with the consciousness of victory, I have made an offer of peace to the enemy. Whether it will be accepted is still uncertain. Until that moment arrives you will fight on."

I return to the President's note.

The President suggested that early occasion be sought to call out from all the nations now at war an avowal of their respective views as to the terms upon which the war might be concluded, and the arrangements which would be deemed satisfactory as a guarantee against its renewal.

He called the attention of the world to the fact that according to the statements of the statesmen of the belligerent powers, the objects which all sides had in mind seemed to be the same. And the President finally said that he was not proposing peace, not even offering mediation; but merely proposing that soundings be taken in order that all nations might know how near might be the haven of peace for which all mankind longed.

Shortly after the publication of this note Secretary Lansing gave an interview to the representatives of the American press in which he stated that America was very near war. This interview he later explained.

As soon as possible after my return to Berlin I had interviews with Zimmermann and the Chancellor. Zimmermann said that we were such personal friends that he was sure we could continue to work, as we had in the past, in a frank and open manner, putting all the cards upon the table and working together in the interests of peace. I, of course, agreed to this and it seemed, on the surface, as if everything would go smoothly.

Although the torpedoing without warning of

the *Marina,* while I was in the United States, had resulted in the death of a number of Americans on board, nevertheless there seemed to be an inclination on the part of the government and people of the United States to forget this incident provided Germany would continue to keep her pledges given in the *Sussex* Note. During all the period of the war in Germany I had been on good terms with the members of the government, namely, von Bethmann-Hollweg, von Jagow, Zimmermann and the other officials of the Foreign Office, as well as with Helfferich, Dr. Solf, the Colonial Minister, Kaempf, the President of the Reichstag and a number of the influential men of Germany such as von Gwinner, of the Deutsche Bank, Gutmann of the Dresdener Bank, Dr. Walter Rathenau, who for a long time was at the head of the department for the supply and conservation of raw materials, General von Kessel, Over-Commander of the Mark of Brandenburg, in spite of many tiffs with him over the treatment of prisoners, Theodor Wolff, editor of the *Tageblatt,* Professor Stein, Maximilian Harden and many others.

For a long time the fight waged by von Bethmann-Hollweg was America's fight and a fight for peace, so much so that the newspapers which attacked the Chancellor were the same ones which had attacked President Wilson, America and

Americans in general, and which had very often
included me in their attacks. During every crisis
between America and Germany I had acted with
von Jagow and Zimmermann in a most confidential way, looking forward always to one object,
namely, the preservation of peace between our
respective countries. Many suggestions were
made which, I think, materially aided up to that
time in the preservation of peace.

The Chancellor and the Foreign Office, however, through sheer weakness did nothing to prevent the insults to our flag and President perpe-
trated by the "League of Truth"; although both
under the law and the regulations of the "State
of Siege" this gang could not operate without
the consent of the authorities. So far as I was
concerned personally, a few extra attacks from
tooth carpenters and snake dancers meant nothing, but certainly aroused my interest in the workings of the Teutonic official brain.

On my return every one in official life,—von
Bethmann-Hollweg, Zimmermann, von Stumm
who succeeded Zimmermann, von der Busche,
formerly German Minister in the Argentine, who
had equal rank with Stumm in the Foreign Office
—all without exception and in the most convincing language assured me that cases like that of
the *Marina,* for example, were only accidents and
that there was every desire on the part of Ger-

many to maintain the pledges given in the *Sussex* Note.

And the great question to be solved is whether the Germans in making their offers of peace, in begging me to go to America to talk peace to the President, were sincerely anxious for peace, or were only making these general offers of peace in order to excuse in the eyes of the world a resumption of ruthless submarine warfare and to win to their side public opinion in the United States, in case such warfare should be resumed.

Had the decision rested with the Chancellor and with the Foreign Office, instead of with the military, I am sure that the decision would have been against the resumption of this ruthless war. But Germany is not ruled in war time by the civilian power. Hindenburg at the time I left for America was at the head of the General Staff and Ludendorf, who had been Chief of Staff, had been made the Quartermaster General in order that he might follow Hindenburg to General Headquarters.

Hindenburg, shortly before his battle of the Masurian Lakes, was a General living in retirement at Hanover. Because he had for years specialised in the study of this region he was suddenly called to the command of the German army which was opposing the Russian invasions. Ludendorf, who had been Colonel of a regiment at the attack on Liège, was sent with him as his Chief of Staff. The success of Hindenburg in his campaigns is too well known to require recapitulation here. He became the popular idol of Germany, the one general—in fact the one man—whom the people felt that they could idolise. But shortly before my trip to America an idea was creeping through the mind of the German people leading them to believe that Hindenburg was but the front, and that the brains of the combination had been furnished by Ludendorf. Many Germans in a position to know told me that the real dictator of Germany was Ludendorf.

My trip to America was made principally at the instance of von Jagow and the Chancellor, and, in my farewell talk with the Chancellor a few days before leaving, I asked if it could not be arranged, since he was always saying that the civilian power was inferior to that of the military, that I should see Hindenburg and Ludendorf before I left. This proposed meeting he either could not or would not arrange, and shortly after my return I again asked the Chancellor if I could not see, if not the Emperor, at least Hindenburg and Ludendorf, who the Chancellor himself had said were the leaders of the military, and, therefore, the leaders of Germany. Again I was put off.

In the meantime and in spite of the official

assurance given to me certain men in Germany, in a position to know, warned me that the government intended to resume ruthless submarine war. Ludendorf, they said, had declared in favour of this war and, according to them, that meant its adoption.

At first I thought that Germany would approach the resumption of ruthless submarine war *via* the armed merchantman issue.

The case of the *Yarrowdale* prisoners seemed to bear out this theory. A German raider captured and sunk a number of enemy vessels and sent one of the captured boats, the *Yarrowdale,* with a prize crew to Swinemunde. On board, held as prisoners, were a number of the crews of the captured vessels; and among those men I learned "under the rose," were some Americans. The arrival of the *Yarrowdale* was kept secret for some time, but as soon as I received information of its arrival, I sent note after note to the Foreign Office demanding to know if there were any Americans among the prisoner crews.

For a long time I received no answer, but finally Germany admitted what I knew already, that Americans taken with the crews of captured ships were being held as prisoners of war, the theory of the Germans being that all employed on armed enemy merchant ships were enemy combatants. I supposed that possibly Germany

might therefore approach the submarine controversy by this route and claim that armed merchantmen were liable to be sunk without notice.

Instructed by the State Department, I demanded the immediate release of the *Yarrowdale*
prisoners. This was accorded by Germany, but,
after the breaking of relations, the prisoners
were held back; and it was not until after we
left Germany that they were finally released.

I asked permission to visit these prisoners and
sent Mr. Ayrault and Mr. Osborne to the place
where I knew they were interned. The permission to visit them arrived, but on the same day
orders were given to remove the prisoners to
other camps. Mr. Osborne and Mr. Ayrault,
however, being on the ground, saw the prisoners
before their removal and reported on their conditions.

On January sixth the American Association
of Commerce and Trade gave me a dinner at the
Hotel Adlon. This was made the occasion of a
sort of German-American love-feast. Zimmermann, although he had to go early in the evening
to meet the Foreign Minister of Austria-Hun-
gary, was present; Helfferich, Vice-Chancellor
and Secretary of the Interior; Dr. Solf, the Colonial Minister; Sydow, Minister of Commerce;
Dernburg; von Gwinner of the Deutsche Bank;
Gutmann of the Dresdener Bank; Under Secre-

tary von der Busche of the Foreign Office; the Mayor and the Police President of Berlin; the President of the Berlin Chamber of Commerce; Under Secretary von Stumm of the Foreign Office; and many others of that office. There were present also Under Secretary Richter of the Interior Department; Lieutenant Colonel Doeutelmoser of the General Staff; the editors and proprietors of the principal newspapers in Berlin; Count Montgelas, who had charge of American affairs in the Foreign Office; naval officers like Captain Lans; the American correspondents in Germany; and Prince Isenburg; rubbing shoulders with the brewers, George Ehret and Krueger, of New York and Newark. There were literary lights like Ludwig Fulda, Captain Persius, Professor Hans Delbrück, Dr. Paasche, Vice-President of the Reichstag, and many others equally celebrated as the ones that I have named. Speeches were made by Mr. Wolf, President of the American Association of Commerce and Trade, Helfferich, Zimmermann, von Gwinner and me. A tone of the greatest friendliness prevailed. Zimmermann referred to our personal friendship and said that he was sure that we should be able to manage everything together. Helfferich in his speech said that I, by learning German and studying the life of the German people, was one of the few diplomats that

362

had come to Germany who had learned something of the real life and psychology of the Germans. Von Gwinner made a speech in English that would have done credit to any American after-dinner speaker; and I, in my short address, said that the relations between the two countries had never been better and that so long as my personal friends like Zimmermann and other members of the government, who I named, were in office, I was sure that the good relations between the two countries would be maintained. I spoke also of the sums of money that I had brought back with me for the benefit of the widows and orphans of Germany.

The majority of the German newspapers spoke in a very kindly way about this dinner and about what was said at it. Of course, they all took what I said as an expression of friendliness, and only Reventlow claimed that, by referring to the members of the government, I was interfering in the internal affairs of Germany.

The speeches and, in fact, this dinner constituted a last desperate attempt to preserve friendly relations. Both the reasonable men present and I knew, almost to a certainty, that return to ruthless submarine war had been decided on and that only some lucky chance could prevent the military, backed by the made public opinion, from insisting on a defiance of international law and the laws of humanity.

The day after the dinner von Bethmann-Hollweg sent for me and expressed approval of what I said and thanked me for it and on the surface it seemed as if everything was "as merry as a marriage bell." Unfortunately, I am afraid that all this was only on the surface, and that perhaps the orders to the submarine commanders to recommence ruthless war had been given the day preceding this love-feast.

The Germans believed that President Wilson had been elected with a mandate to keep out of war at any cost, and that America could be insulted, flouted and humiliated with impunity.

Even before this dinner we had begun to get rumours of the resumption of ruthless submarine war and within a few days I was cabling to the Department information based not upon absolute facts but upon reports which seemed reliable and which had been collected through the able efforts of our very capable naval attaché, Commander Gherardi.

And this information was confirmed by the hints given to me by various influential Germans. Again and again after the sixth of January, I was assured by Zimmermann and others in the Foreign Office that nothing of the kind was contemplated.

Now were the German moves in the direction of peace sincere or not?

From the time when von Bethmann-Hollweg first spoke of peace, I asked him and others what the peace terms of Germany were. I could never get any one to state any definite terms of peace and on several occasions when I asked the Chancellor whether Germany was willing to withdraw from Belgium, he always said, "Yes, but with guarantees." Finally in January, 1917, when he was again talking of peace, I said, "What are these peace terms to which you refer continually? Will you allow me to ask a few questions as to the specific terms of peace? First are the Germans willing to withdraw from Belgium?" The Chancellor answered, "Yes, but with guarantees." I said, "What are these guarantees?" He said, "We must possibly have the forts of Liège and Namur; we must have other forts and garrisons throughout Belgium. We must have possession of the railroad lines. We must have possession of the ports and other means of communication. The Belgians will not be allowed to maintain an army, but we must be allowed to retain a large army in Belgium. We must have the commercial control of Belgium." I said, "I do not see that you have left much for the Belgians except that King Albert will have the right to reside in Brussels with an honor guard." And the Chancellor said, "We cannot allow Belgium to be an outpost (*Vorwerk*) of England"; and I said, "I do not suppose the English, on the other hand, wish it to become an outpost of Germany, especially as von Tirpitz has said that the coast of Flanders should be retained in order to make war on England and America." I continued, "How about Northern France?" He said, "We are willing to leave Northern France, but there must be a rectification of the frontier." I said, "How about the Eastern frontier?" He said, "We must have a very substantial rectification of our frontier." I said, "How about Roumania?" He said, "We shall leave Bulgaria to deal with Roumania." I said, "How about Serbia?" He said, "A very small Serbia may be allowed to exist, but that is a question for Austria. Austria must be left to do what she wishes to Italy, and we must have indemnities from all countries and all our ships and colonies back."

Of course, "rectification of the frontier" is a polite term for "annexation."

On the twenty-second of January, 1917, our President addressed the Senate; and in his address he referred to his Note of the eighteenth of December, sent to all belligerent governments. In this address he stated, referring to the reply of the Entente Powers to his Peace Note of the eighteenth of December, "We are that much

366

nearer to the definite discussion of the peace which shall end the present war."

He referred to the willingness of both contestants to discuss terms of peace, as follows: "The Central Powers united in reply which stated merely that they were ready to meet their antagonists in conference to discuss terms of peace. The Entente Powers have replied much more definitely and have stated, in general terms, indeed, but with sufficient definiteness to imply details, the arrangements, guarantees and acts of reparation which they deem to be the indispensable conditions of a satisfactory settlement. We are that much nearer a definite discussion of the peace which shall end the present war." The President further referred to a world concert to guarantee peace in the future and said, "The present war must first be ended, but we owe it to candour and to a just regard for the opinion of mankind to say that so far as our participation in guarantees of future peace is concerned, it makes a great deal of difference in what way and upon what terms it is ended." He said that the statesmen of both of the groups of nations at war had stated that it was not part of the purpose they had in mind to crush their antagonists, and he said that it must be implied from these assurances that the peace to come must be "a peace without victory."

In the course of his address he said: "Statesmen everywhere are agreed that there should be a united, independent and autonomous Poland." In another place he said: "So far as practicable, moreover, every great people now struggling toward a full development of its resources and its powers should be assured a direct outlet to the highways of the sea." Where this cannot be done by cession of territory it can no doubt be arranged by the neutralisation of direct rights of way; and he closed by proposing in effect that the nations of the world should adopt the Monroe Doctrine and that no nation should seek to explain its policy for any other nation or people.

After the receipt of the Ultimatum of January thirty-first from Germany, the Chancellor, in a conversation I had with him, referred to this Peace Note of December eighteenth and to the speech of January twenty-second.

I must say here that on my return to Germany I went very far in assuring the Chancellor and other members of the Government of the President's desire to see peace established in the world; and I told them that I believed that the President was ready to go very far in the way of coercing any nation which refused a reasonable peace; but I also impressed on all the members of the Government with whom I came in contact my belief that the election had not in any way al-

COMITÉ D'ALIMENTATION DU NORD DE LA FRANCE

DISTRICT DE CHARLEVILLE 9

Le Comité du District informe les Habitants qu'il met à leur disposition pour la
PREMIÈRE quinzaine *du mois de* **MAI 1916**
les quantités de marchandises suivantes dans le tableau ci-dessous et aux prix fixés :

MARCHANDISES	QUANTITÉS A DISTRIBUER POUR LA QUINZAINE ET PAR HABITANT	PRIX DE VENTE AUX HABITANTS
1. Farine	4 k. 500	le kilog 0 fr. 48
Prix maximum du pain.		— 0 fr. 40
2. Riz.	0 k. 500	— 0 fr. 55
3. Haricots.	0 k. 500	— 0 fr. 90
4. Lard	0 k. 500	— 2 fr. 80
5. Saindoux	0 k. 250	— 2 fr. 30
6. Café vert	0 k. 250	— 1 fr. 70
7. Sucre cristallisé. . .	0 k. 150	— 0 fr. 90
8. Sel	0 k. 200	— 0 fr. 10
9. Savon dur	0 k. 250	— 1 fr.

En principe le ravitaillement doit être distribué à tous les habitants.
1° Au comptant à ceux qui peuvent payer;
2° A titre remboursable pour les personnes momentanément privées de ressources, avec signature d'un engagement de remboursement à la commune après la guerre;
3° Gratuitement aux indigents.
Le prix moyen de la vie est fixé à 1 franc par jour et par habitant. Un barème de classification a été établi en prenant ce chiffre pour base et peut être consulté à la Mairie.
Toute personne qui, le pouvant, se refuserait au paiement ou à la signature de l'engagement, peut être momentanément privée de ravitaillement, sauf le pain, jusqu'à ce qu'elle ait payé ou signé.
Les habitants sont libres de ne pas prendre toutes les denrées mises à leur disposition. Les parts non distribuées restent à la commune, qui peut ainsi soit constituer une réserve, soit faire des distributions supplémentaires dans la même forme que les distributions ordinaires.
Les habitants ne doivent pas prendre les denrées dont ils n'ont pas besoin. Il leur est formellement interdit de faire du commerce avec les denrées du Ravitaillement et notamment d'en céder à des commerçants pour les remettre en vente.
Les denrées provenant du Ravitaillement qui seront trouvées chez des commerçants seront saisies.

Le Gérant du District,   *Le Président du District,*
L. PILLOT   **G. CAMION**

Cette affiche doit être apposée avant la distribution.

A POSTER FROM THE CHARLEVILLE DISTRICT, SHOWING
THE ALLOTMENT OF FOOD TO EACH PERSON FOR THE
FIRST FIFTEEN DAYS OF MAY, 1916

tered the policy of the President, and I warned them of the danger to our good relations if ruthless submarine warfare should be resumed.

Von Bethmann-Hollweg, however, at this interview after the thirty-first of January, said that he had been compelled to take up ruthless submarine war because it was evident that President Wilson could do nothing towards peace. He spoke particularly of the President's speech of January twenty-second and said that in that speech the President had made it plain that he considered that the answer of the Entente Powers to his Peace Note formed a basis for peace, which was a thing impossible for Germany even to consider; and said further (and this was a criticism I heard not only from him, but also from many Germans), that when the President spoke of a united and independent Poland he evidently meant to take away from Germany that part of Poland which had been incorporated in the Kingdom of Prussia and give it to this new and independent Kingdom, thereby bringing the Eastern frontier of Germany within two hours by motor from Berlin; and that, further, when the President spoke of giving each nation a highway to the sea, he meant that the German port of Dantzig should be turned over to this new State of Poland, thereby not only taking a Prussian port but cutting the extreme East-

ern part of Prussia from the remainder of the
country. I said that these objections appeared
to me very frivolous; that the President, of
course, like a clever lawyer endeavouring to gain
his end, which was peace, had said that all parties were apparently agreed that there should
be a peace; that if Germany were fighting a
merely defensive war, as she had always claimed,
she should be greatly delighted when the
President declared that all the weight of America was in favor of a peace without victory,
which meant, of course, that Germany should
be secured from that crushing and dismember-
ment which Germany's statesmen had stated so
often that they feared. I said, further, that I
was sure that when the President spoke of the
united and independent State of Poland he had
not, of course, had reference to Poland at any
particular period of its history, but undoubtedly
to Poland as constituted by Germany and
Austria themselves; and that, in referring to the
right of a nation to have access to the sea, he
had in mind Russia and the Dardanelles rather
than to any attempt to take a Prussian port for
the benefit of Poland.

Von Bethmann-Hollweg said that one of the
principal reasons why Germany had determined
upon a resumption of ruthless submarine warfare
was because of this speech of the President to the

American Senate. Of course, the trouble with this feeling and the criticism of the President's speech made by the Chancellor is that the orders for the resumption of ruthless submarine warfare had been given long before the news of the speech came to Germany.

I had cabled the information collected by Commander Gherardi as to the orders given to submarines long before the date of the President's speech, and it happened that on the night after I had received the German note announcing this resumption I was taking a walk after dinner about the snow-covered streets of Berlin. In the course of this walk I met a young German woman of my acquaintance who was on intimate terms with the Crown Princess. She was on her way on foot from the opera house, where she had been with the Crown Princess, to the underground station, for by this time, of course, taxis had become an unknown luxury in Berlin, and I joined her. I told her of the Ultimatum which I had received at six o'clock that evening from Zimmermann and I told her that I was sure that it meant the breaking of diplomatic relations and our departure from Germany. She expressed great surprise that the submarine warfare was set to commence on the thirty-first of January and said that weeks before they had been talking over the matter at the Crown Princess's and that she had heard then that the orders had been given to commence it on the fifteenth. In any event it is certain that the orders to the submarine commanders had been given long prior to the thirty-first and probably as early as the fifteenth.

I sincerely believe that the only object of the Germans in making these peace offers was first to get the Allies, if possible, in a conference and there detach some or one of them by the offer of separate terms; or, if this scheme failed, then it was believed that the general offer and talk about peace would create a sentiment so favourable to the Germans that they might, without fear of action by the United States, resume ruthless submarine warfare against England.

A week or two before the thirty-first of January, Dr. Solf asked me if I did not think that it would be possible for the United States to permit the resumption of ruthless submarine warfare against Great Britain. He said that three months' time was all that would be required to bring Great Britain to her knees and end the war. And in fact so cleverly did von Tirpitz, Grand Admiral von Meuster, the Conservatives and the enemies of the Chancellor and other advocates of submarine war carry on their propaganda that the belief was ingrained in the whole of the German nation that a resumption of this ruthless war would lead within three months to what all Germans so ardently desired—peace. It was impossible for any government to resist the popular demand for the use of this illegal means of warfare, because army and navy and people were convinced that ruthless submarine war spelled success and a glorious peace.

But this peace, of course, meant only a German peace, a peace as outlined to me by the Chancellor; a peace impossible for the Allies and even for the world to accept; a peace which would leave Germany immensely powerful and ready immediately after the war to take up a campaign against the nations of the Western hemisphere; a peace which would compel every nation, so long as German autocracy remained in the saddle, to devote its best energies, the most fruitful period of each man's life, to preparations for war.

On January thirtieth, I received a definite intimation of the coming Ultimatum the next day and, judging that the hint meant the resumption of ruthless submarine war, I telegraphed a warning to the American Ambassadors and Ministers as well as to the State Department. On January thirty-first at about four o'clock in the afternoon I received from Zimmermann a short letter of which the following is a copy:

"The Secretary of State of the Foreign Office, Zimmermann, requests the honor of the visit of his Excellency, the Ambassador of the United States of America, this afternoon at six o'clock in the Foreign Office, Wilhelmstrasse 75/76.

"Berlin, the 31st January, 1917."

Pursuant to this letter, I went to the Foreign Office at six o'clock. Zimmermann then read to me in German a note from the Imperial Government, announcing the creation of the war zones about Great Britain and France and the commencement of ruthless submarine warfare at twelve P. M. that night. I made no comment, put the note in my pocket and went back to the Embassy. It was then about seven P. M. and, of course, the note was immediately translated and despatched with all speed to America.

After the despatch of the note I had an interview with the Chancellor in which he, as I have stated above, criticised both the Peace Note of December eighteenth as not being definite enough and the speech to the Senate of January twenty-second; and further said that he believed that the situation had changed, that, in spite of what the President had said in the note before the *Sussex* settlement, he was now for peace, that he had been elected on a peace platform, and that nothing would happen. Zimmermann at the time he delivered the note told me that this submarine warfare was a necessity for Germany, and that Germany could not hold out a year on the question of food. He further said, "Give us only two months of this kind of warfare and we shall end the war and make peace within three months."

Saturday, February third, the President announced to Congress the breaking of diplomatic relations with Germany. The news of this, of course, did not reach Berlin until the next day; and on this Saturday afternoon Mrs. Gerard and I had an engagement to go to the theatre with Zimmermann and Mrs. Friedlaender-Fuld-Mitford, a young lady whose father is considered the richest man in Berlin, and who had been married to a young Englishman, named Mitford, a son of Lord Redesdale. Through no fault on the lady's part, there had been an annulment of this marriage; and she was occupying a floor of her own in the handsome house of her father and mother on the Pariser-Platz in Berlin. We stopped for Mrs. Mitford and took her to the theatre where we saw a very clever play, I think by Thoma, called "Die Verlorene Tochter" (The Prodigal Daughter). Zimmermann did not come to the play but joined us later at the Friedlaender-Fuld House where we had a supper of four in Mrs. Mitford's apartments. After supper, while I was talking to Zimmermann, he spoke of the note to America and said: "During the past month, this is what I have been doing so often at the General Headquarters with the Emperor. I often thought of telling you what was going on as I used to tell you in the old days, but I thought that you would only say that such a course would mean a break of diplomatic relations, and so I thought there was no use in telling you. But as you will see, everything will be all right. America will do nothing, for President Wilson is for peace and nothing else. Everything will go on as before. I have arranged for you to go to the Great General Headquarters and see the Kaiser next week and everything will be all right."

The next day, Sunday, we had a German who is connected with the Foreign Office and his American wife to lunch, and another German who had been in America, also connected with the Foreign Office. Just as we were going in to lunch some one produced a copy of the *"B. Z."*, the noon paper published in Berlin, which contained what seemed to be an authentic account of the breaking of diplomatic relations by America. The lunch was far from cheerful. The Germans looked very sad and said practically nothing, while I tried to make polite conversation at my end of the table.

The next day I went over to see Zimmermann, having that morning received the official despatch from Washington, and told him that I had come to demand my passports.

Of course, Zimmermann by that time had received the news and had had time to compose himself. The American correspondents told me that when he saw them on the day before, he had at first refused to say anything and then had been rather violent in his language and had finally shown great emotion. I am sure, from everything I observed, that the break of diplomatic relations came as an intense surprise to him and to the other members of the government, and yet I cannot imagine why intelligent men should think that the United States of America had fallen so low as to bear without murmur this sudden kick in the face.

The police who had always been about our Embassy since the commencement of the war, were now greatly increased in numbers; and guarded not only the front of the house, but also the rear and the surrounding streets; but there was no demonstration whatever on the part of the people of Berlin. On Tuesday afternoon I went out for a walk, walking through most of the principal streets of Berlin, absolutely alone, and

on my return to the Embassy I found Count
Montgelas, who, with the rank of Minister, was
at the head of the department which included
American affairs in the Foreign Office. I asked
Montgelas why I had not received my passports,
and he said that I was being kept back because
the Imperial Government did not know what had
happened to Count Bernstorff and that there had
been rumours that the German ships in America
had been confiscated by our government. I said
that I was quite sure that Bernstorff was being
treated with every courtesy and that the German
ships had not been confiscated. I said, moreover,
"I do not see why I have to disprove your idea
that Bernstorff is being maltreated and the German ships confiscated. It seems to me it is for
you to prove this; and, at any event, why don't
you have the Swiss Government, which now represents you, cable to its Minister in Washington
and get the exact facts?" He said, "Well, you
know, the Swiss are not used to cabling."

He then produced a paper which was a re-af-
firmation of the treaty between Prussia and the
United States of 1799, with some very extraordinary clauses added to it. He asked me to read
this over and either to sign it or to get authority
to sign it, and said that if it was not signed it
would be very difficult for Americans to leave
the country, particularly the American corre-

spondents. I read this treaty over and then said, "Of course I cannot sign this on my own responsibility and I will not cable to my government unless I can cable in cipher and give them my opinion of this document." He said, "That is impossible." This treaty was as follows:

Agreement between Germany and the United States of America concerning the treatment of each other's citizens and their private property after the severance of diplomatic relations.

Article 1.

After the severance of diplomatic relations between Germany and the United States of America and in the event of the outbreak of war between the two Powers the citizens of either party and their private property in the territory of the other party shall be treated according to Article 23 of the treaty of amity and commerce between Prussia and the United States of 11 July, 1799, with the following explanatory and supplementary clauses.

Article 2.

German merchants in the United States and American merchants in Germany shall so far as the treatment of their persons and their property is concerned be held in every respect on a par with the other persons mentioned in Article 23. Accordingly they shall even after the period provided for in Article 23 has elapsed be entitled to remain and continue their profession in the country of their residence.

Merchants as well as the other persons mentioned in Article 23 may be excluded from fortified places or other places of military importance.

Article 3.

Germans in the United States and Americans in Germany shall be free to leave the country of their residence within the times and by the routes that shall be assigned to them by the proper authorities.

The persons departing shall be entitled to take along their personal property including money, valuables and bank accounts excepting such property the exportation of which is prohibited according to general provisions.

Article 4.

The protection of Germans in the United States and of Americans in Germany and of their property shall be guaranteed in accordance with the laws existing in the countries of either party. They shall be under no other restrictions concerning the enjoyment of their private rights and the judicial enforcement of their rights than neutral residents; they may accordingly not be transferred to concentration camps nor shall their private property be subject to sequestration or liquidation or other compulsory alienation except in cases that under the existing laws apply also to neutrals.

As a general rule, German property in the United States and American property in Germany shall not be subject to sequestration or liquidation or other compulsory alienation under other conditions than neutral property.

Article 5.

Patent rights or other protected rights held by Germans in the United States or Americans in Germany shall not be declared void; nor shall the exercise of such rights be impeded nor shall such rights be transferred to others without the consent of the person entitled thereto; provided that regulations made

380

exclusively in the interest of the State shall apply.

Article 6.

Contracts made between Germans and Americans either before or after the severance of diplomatic relations, also obligations of all kinds between Germans and Americans shall not be declared cancelled, void or in suspension except under provisions applicable to neutrals.

Likewise the citizens of either party shall not be impeded in fulfilling their liabilities arising from such obligations either by injunctions or by other provisions unless these apply also to neutrals.

Article 7.

The provisions of the sixth Hague Convention relative to the treatment of enemy merchant ships at outbreak of hostilities shall apply to the merchant vessels of either party and their cargo.

The aforesaid ships may not be forced to leave port unless at the same time they be given a pass recognised as binding by all the enemy sea powers to a home port or a port of an allied country or to another port of the country in which the ship happens to be.

Article 8.

The regulations of chapter 3 of the eleventh Hague Convention relative to certain restrictions in the exercise of the right of capture in maritime war shall apply to the captains, officers and members of the crews of merchant ships specified in Article 7 and of such merchant ships that may be captured in the course of a possible war.

Article 9.

This agreement shall apply also to the colonies and other foreign possessions of either party.

Berlin, February   , 1917.

I then said, "I shall not cable at all. Why do you come to me with a proposed treaty after we have broken diplomatic relations and ask an Ambassador who is held as a prisoner to sign it? Prisoners do not sign treaties and treaties signed by them would not be worth anything." And I also said, "After your threat to keep Americans here and after reading this document, even if I had authority to sign it I would stay here until hell freezes over before I would put my name to such a paper."

Montgelas seemed rather rattled, and in his confusion left the paper with me—something, I am sure, he did not intend to do in case of a refusal. Montgelas was an extremely agreeable man and I think at all times had correctly predicted the attitude of America and had been against acts of frightfulness, such as the torpedoing of the *Lusitania* and the resumption of ruthless submarine war. I am sure that a gentleman like Montgelas undertook with great reluctance to carry out his orders in the matter of getting me to sign this treaty.

I must cheerfully certify that even the most pro-German American correspondents in Berlin, when I told them of Montgelas' threat, showed the same fine spirit as their colleagues. All begged me not to consider them or their lib-

erty where the interests of America were involved.

As soon as diplomatic relations were broken,—
and I broke them formally not only in my conversation with Zimmermann of Monday morning but also by sending over a formal written
request for my passports on the evening of that
day,—our telegraph privileges were cut off. I was
not even allowed to send telegrams to the American consuls throughout Germany giving them
their instructions. Mail also was cut off, and
the telephone. My servants were not even permitted to go to the nearby hotel to telephone. In
the meantime we completed our preparations for
departure. We arranged to turn over American interests, and the interests of Roumania and
Serbia and Japan, to the Spanish Embassy; and
the interests of Great Britain to the Dutch. I
have said already that I believe that Ambassador
Polo de Bernabe will faithfully protect the interests of America, and I believe that Baron
Gevers will fearlessly fight the cause of the British prisoners.

We sold our automobiles; and two beautiful
prize winning saddle horses, one from Kentucky
and one from Virginia, which I had brought with
me from America, went on the stage,—that is, I
sold them to the proprietor of the circus in
Berlin!

The three tons of food which we had brought with us from America we gave to our colleagues in the diplomatic corps,—the Spaniards, Greeks, Dutch and the Central and South Americans. I had many friends among the diplomats of the two Americas who were all men of great ability and position in their own country. I think that most of them know only too well the designs against Central and South America cherished by the Pan-Germans.

Finally, I think on the morning of Friday, Mr. Oscar King Davis, correspondent of the *New York Times,* received a wireless from Mr. Van Anda, editor of the *New York Times,* telling him that Bernstorff and his staff were being treated with every courtesy and that the German ships had not been confiscated. In the evening our telephone was reconnected, and we were allowed to receive some telegrams and to send open telegrams to the consuls, etc. throughout Germany, and we were notified that we would probably be allowed to leave the next day in the evening.

Always followed by spies, I paid as many farewell visits to my diplomatic colleagues as I was able to see; and on Saturday I thought that, in spite of the ridiculous treatment accorded us in cutting off the mail and telephone and in holding me for nearly a week, I would leave in a sporting spirit: I therefore, had my servant telephone and ask whether Zimmermann and von Bethmann-Hollweg would receive me. I had a pleasant farewell talk of about half an hour with each of them and I expressly told the Chancellor that I had come to bid him a personal farewell, not to make a record for any White Book, and that anything he said would remain confidential. I also stopped in to thank Dr. Zahn, of the Foreign Office, who had arranged the details of our departure and gave him a gold cigarette case as a souvenir of the occasion. At the last moment, the Germans allowed a number of the consuls and clerks who had been working in the Embassy, and the American residents in Berlin, to leave on the train with us; so that we were about one hundred and twenty persons in all on this train, which left the Potsdamer station at eight-ten in the evening. The time of our departure had not been publicly announced, but although the automobiles, etc. in front of the Embassy might have attracted a crowd, there was no demonstration whatever; and, in fact, during this week that I was detained in Berlin I walked all over the city every afternoon and evening, went into shops, and so on, without encountering any hostile demonstration.

There was a large crowd in the station to see us off. All the Spanish Embassy, Dutch, Greeks and many of our colleagues from Central and

South America were there. There were, from the Foreign Office, Montgelas, Dr. Roediger, Prittwitz and Horstmann. As the train pulled out, a number of the Americans left in Berlin who were on the station platform raised quite a vigorous cheer.

Two officers had been sent by the Imperial Government to accompany us on this train; one, a Major von der Hagen, sent by the General Staff and the other, a representative of the Foreign Office, Baron Wernher von Ow-Wachendorf. It was quite thoughtful of the Foreign Office to send this last officer, as it was by our efforts that he had secured his exchange when he was a prisoner in England; and he, therefore, would be supposed to entertain kindly feelings for our Embassy.

I had ordered plenty of champagne and cigars to be put on the train and we were first invited to drink champagne with the officers in the dining car; then they joined us in the private salon car which we occupied in the end of the train. The journey was uneventful. Outside some of the stations a number of people were drawn up who stared at the train in a bovine way, but who made no demonstration of any kind.

We went through Württemburg and entered Switzerland by way of Schaffhausen. The two officers left us at the last stop on the German side. I had taken the precaution before we left Berlin to find out their names, and, as they left us, I gave each of them a gold cigarette case inscribed with his name and the date.

At the first station on the Swiss side a body of Swiss troops were drawn up, presenting arms, and the Colonel commanding the Swiss army (there are no generals in Switzerland), attended by several staff officers, came on the train and travelled with us nearly to Zürich.

I started to speak French to one of these staff officers, but he interrupted me by saying in perfect English, "You do not have to speak French to me. My name is Iselin, many of my relations live in New York and I lived there myself some years."

At Zürich we left the German special train, and were met on the platform by some grateful Japanese, the American Consul and a number of French and Swiss newspaper reporters, thus ending our exodus from Germany.

CHAPTER XVIII

LIBERALS AND REASONABLE MEN

I HAVE already expressed a belief that Germany will not be forced to make peace because of a revolution, and that sufficient food will be somehow found to carry the population during at least another year of war.

What then offers a prospect of reasonable peace, supposing, of course, that the Germans fail in the submarine blockade of England and that the crumbling up of Russia does not release from the East frontier soldiers enough to break the lines of the British and French in France?

I think that it is only by an evolution of Germany herself toward liberalism that the world will be given such guarantees of future peace as will justify the termination of this war.

There is, properly speaking, no great liberal party in the political arena in Germany. As I have said, the Reichstag is divided roughly into Conservatives, Roman Catholics, or Centrum, and Social Democrats. The so-called National Liberal party has in this war shown itself a branch of the Conservative party, and on some issues as bitter, as conservative, as the Junkers themselves. Herr Bassermann and Herr Stresemann have not shown themselves leaders of liberal thought, nor has their leadership been such as to inspire confidence in their political sagacity.

It was Stresemann who on May thirtieth, 1916, said in the Reichstag referring to President Wilson as a peacemaker, "We thrust the hand of Wilson aside." On the day following, the day on which the President announced to Congress the breaking of diplomatic relations, news of that break had not yet arrived in Berlin and Herr Stresemann on that peaceful Sunday morning was engaged in making a speech to the members of the National Liberal party in which he told them that as a result of his careful study of the American situation, of his careful researches into American character and politics, he could assure them that America would never break with Germany. As he concluded his speech and sat down amid the applause of his admirers, a German who had been sitting in the back of the room rose and read from the noon paper, the "B. Z.", a despatch from Holland giving the news that America had broken relations with Germany. The political skill and foresight of Herr Stresemann may be judged from the above incident.

The Socialists, or Social Democrats, more properly speaking, have shown themselves in opposition to the monarchical form of government in Germany. This has put them politically, militarily and socially beyond the pale.

After a successful French attack in the Champagne, I heard it said of a German woman, whose husband was thought to be killed, that her rage and despair had been so great that she had said she would become a Social Democrat; and her expression was repeated as showing to what lengths grief had driven her. This girl was the wife of an ordinary clerk working in Berlin.

The Social Democrats are not given offices, are not given titles: they never join the class of *"Rat,"* and they cannot hope to become officers of the army. Did not Lieutenant Forstner, the notorious centre of the Zabern Affair, promise a reward to the first one of his men who in case of trouble should shoot one "of those damn Social Democrats"?

There is, therefore, no refuge at present politically, for the reasonable men of liberal inclinations; and it is these liberal men who must themselves create a liberal party: a party, membership in which will not entail a loss of business, a loss of prospects of promotion and social degradation.

There are many such men in Germany to-day; perhaps some of the conservative Socialists will join such a party, and there are men in the government itself whose habits of mind and thought are not incompatible with membership in a liberal organisation. The Chancellor himself is, perhaps, at heart a Liberal. He comes of a banking family in Frankfort and while there stands before his name the "von" which means nobility, and while he owns a country estate, the whole turn of his thought is towards a philosophical liberalism. Zimmermann, the Foreign Secretary, although the mental excitement caused by his elevation to the Foreign Office at a time of stress, made him go over to the advocates of ruthless submarine war, lock, stock and barrel, is nevertheless at heart a Liberal and violently opposed to a system which draws the leaders of the country from only one aristocratic class. Dr. Solf, the Imperial Colonial Minister, while devoted to the Emperor and his family is a man so reasonable in his views, so indulgent of the views of others, and indulgent without weakness, that he would make an ideal leader of a liberalised Germany. The great bankers, merchants and manufacturers, although they appreciate the luscious dividends that they have received during the peaceful years since 1870, nevertheless feel under their skins the ignominy of living in a country where a class exists by birth, a class not even tactful enough to conceal its ancient contempt for all those who soil their hands by business or trade.

In fact such a party is a necessity for Germany as a buffer against the extreme Social Democrats.

At the close of the war the soldiers who have fought in the mud of the trenches for three years will most insistently demand a redistricting of the Reichstag and an abolition of the inadequate circle voting of Prussia. And when manhood suffrage comes in Prussia and when the industrial population of Germany gets that representation in the Reichstag out of which they have been brazenly cheated for so many years, it may well be that a great liberal party will be the only defence of private property against the assault of an enraged and justly revengeful social democracy.

The workingmen of Germany have been fooled for a long time. They constitute that class of which President Lincoln spoke, "You can fool some of the people all of the time"; and the middle class of manufacturers, merchants, etc. have acquiesced in the system because of the profits that they have made.

The difficulty of making peace with Germany, as at present constituted, is that the whole world feels that peace made with its present government would not be lasting; that such a peace would mean the detachment of some of the Allies from the present world alliance against Germany; preparation by Germany, in the light of her needs as disclosed by this war; and the declaration of a new war in which there would be no battle of the Marne to turn back the tide of German world conquest.

For a long time before this war, radicals in Great Britain pinned a great faith to the Socialist party of Germany. How little that faith was justified appeared in July and August of 1914 when the Socialist party tamely voted credits for the war; a war declared by the Emperor on the mere statement that it was a defensive war; declared because it was alleged that certain invasions of German territory, never since substantiated, had taken place.

The Socialist party is divided. It is a great pity that the world cannot deal with men of the type of Scheidemann, who, in other democracies, would appear so conservative as to be almost reactionary. But Scheidemann and his friends, while they have, in their attempted negotiations with the Socialists of other countries, the present protection of the Imperial Government, will have no hand in dictating terms of peace so long as that government is in existence. They are being used in an effort to divide the Allies.

As President Wilson said in his message to

Russia of May twenty-sixth, 1917: "The war has begun to go against Germany, and, in their desperate desire to escape the inevitable ultimate defeat, those who are in authority in Germany are using every possible instrumentality, are making use even of the influence of the groups and parties among their own subjects to whom they have never been just or fair or even tolerant to promote a propaganda on both sides of the sea which will preserve for them their influence at home and their power abroad, to the undoing of the very men they are using."

There is an impression abroad that the Social Democratic party of Germany, usually known abroad as the Socialist party, partakes of at least some of the characteristics of a great liberal party. This is far from being the case. By their acts, if not by their express declarations, they have shown themselves as opposed to the monarchical form of government and their leaders are charged with having declared themselves openly in favour of free love and against religion. The Roman Catholic Church recognises in Social Democracy its greatest enemy, and has made great efforts to counteract its advance by fostering a sort of Roman Catholic trades-union for a religious body of Socialists. The Social Democrat in Germany is almost an outcast. Although one third of the members of the Reichstag belong to this party, its members are never called to hold office in the government; and the attitude of the whole of the governing class, of all the professors, school-teachers, priests of both Protestant and Roman Catholic religions of the prosperous middle classes, is that of violent opposition to the doctrines of Social Democracy. The world must entertain no illusion that the Social Democratic leaders speak for Germany.

If the industrial populations had their fair share of representation in the Reichstag they might perhaps even control that body. But, as I have time and again reiterated, the Reichstag has only the power of public opinion; and the Germany of to-day is ruled by officials appointed from above downwards. All of these officials in Germany must be added to the other classes that I have mentioned. There are more officials there than in any other country in the world. As they owe their very existence to the government, they must not only serve that government, but also make the enemies of that government their own. Therefore, they and the circle of their connections are opponents of the Social Democrats.

All this shows how difficult it is at present for the men of reasonable and liberal views, who do not wish to declare themselves against both religion and morality, to find a political refuge.

The Chancellor, himself a liberal at heart, as

I have said, has declared that there must be changes in Germany. It is perhaps within the bounds of probability that a great new liberal party will be formed to which I have referred, composed of the more conservative Social Democrats, of the remains of the National Liberal and Progressive parties and of the more liberal of the Conservatives. The important question is then whether the Roman Catholic party or Centrum will voluntarily dissolve and its members cease to seek election merely as representatives of the Roman Catholic Church.

It is perhaps too much to expect that the Centrum party, as a whole and as at present constituted, will declare for liberalism and parliamentary government and for a fair redistricting of the divisions in Germany which elect members to the Reichstag, but there are many wise and far-seeing men in this party; and its leaders, Dr. Spahn and Erzberger, are fearless and able men.

For some years a movement has been going on in the Centrum party looking to this end. Many members believed that the time had come when it was no longer necessary that the Roman Catholics in order to safeguard their religious liberties continue the political existence of the Centrum, and attempts were made to bring about this change. It was decided adversely, however, by the Roman Catholics. But the question is not dead. Voluntary dissolution of the Centrum as a Roman Catholic party would immediately bring about a creation of a true liberal party to which all Germans could belong without a loss of social prestige, without becoming declared enemies of the monarchy and without declaring themselves against religion and morality.

At the Congress which will meet after the war it will be easy for the nations of the world to deal with the representatives of a liberal Germany, with representatives of a government still monarchical in form, but possessed of either a constitution like that of the United States or ruled by a parliamentary government. I believe that the tendency of German liberalism is towards the easiest transition,—that of making the Chancellor and his ministers responsible to the Reichstag and bound to resign after a vote of want of confidence by that body.

At the time of the Zabern Affair, Scheidemann claimed that the resignation of the Chancellor must logically follow a vote of want of confidence; and it was von Bethmann-Hollweg who refused to resign, saying that he was responsible to the Emperor alone. It requires no violent change to bring about this establishment of parliamentary government, and, if the members of the Reichstag should be elected from districts fairly constituted, the world would then be dealing with a liberalised Germany, and a Germany which has become liberalised without any violent change in the form of its government.

Of course, coincident with this parliamentary reform, the vicious circle system of voting in Prussia must end.

This change to a government by a responsible ministry can be accomplished under the constitution of the German Empire by a mere majority vote of the Reichstag and a vote in the Bundesrat, in which less than fourteen votes are against the proposed change in the constitution. This means that the consent of the Emperor as Prussian King must be obtained, and that of a number of the rulers of the German States.

In the reasonable liberalisation of Germany, if it comes, Theodor Wolff and his father-in-law, Mosse, will play leading parts. The great newspaper, the *Tageblatt,* which Mosse owns and Wolff edits, has throughout the war been a beacon light at once of reason and of patriotism. And other great newspapers will take the same enlightened course.

I am truly sorry for Georg Bernhard, the talented editor of the *Vossiche Zeitung,* who, a Liberal and a Jew, wears the livery of Junkerdom, —I am sure to his great distaste.

After I left Germany the *Vossiche Zeitung* made the most ridiculous charges against me, such as that I issued American passports to British subjects. The newspaper might as well have solemnly charged that I sent notes to the Foreign Office in sealed envelopes. Having charge of British interests, I could not issue British passports to British citizens allowed to leave Germany, but, according to universal custom in similar cases and the express consent of the Imperial Foreign Office, I gave these returning British, American passports superstamped with the words "British subject." A mare's nest, truly!

The fall of von Bethmann-Hollweg was a triumph of kitchen intrigue and of Junkerism. I believe that he is a liberal at heart, that it was against his best judgment that the ruthless submarine war was resumed, the pledges of the *Sussex* Note broken and Germany involved in war with America. If he had resigned, rather than consent to the resumption of U-boat war, he would have stood out as a great Liberal rallying point and probably have returned to a more real power than he ever possessed. But half because of a desire to retain office, half because of a mistaken loyalty to the Emperor, he remained in office at the sacrifice of his opinions; and when he laid down that office no title of Prince or even of Count waited him as a parting gift. In his retirement he will read the lines of Schiller—
favourite quotation in Germany—"Der Mol

hat seine Schuldigkeit gethan, der Mohr kann gehen." "The Moor has done his work, the Moor can go." And in his old age he will exclaim, as Shakespeare makes the great Chancellor of Henry the Eighth exclaim, "Oh Cromwell, Cromwell! Had I but served my God with half the zeal I served my King, He would not, in mine age, have left me naked to mine enemies." But this God is not the private War God of the Prussians with whom they believe they have a gentlemen's working agreement, but the God of Christianity, of humanity and of all mankind.

It would have been easier for Germany to make peace with von Bethmann-Hollweg at the helm. The whole world knows him and honours him for his honesty.

Helfferich remained as Vice-Chancellor and Minister of the Interior: a powerful, and agile intellect,—a man, I am sure, opposed to militarism. Reasonable in his views, one can sit at the council table with him and arrive at compromises and results, but his intense patriotism and surpassing ability make him an opponent to be feared.

Kühlmann has the Foreign Office. Far more wily than Zimmermann, he will continue to strive to embroil us with Japan and Mexico, but he will not be caught. Second in command in London, he reported then that England would enter the war. The rumours scattered broadcast, as he took office, to the effect that he was opposed to ruthless U-boat war were but evidences of a more skilful hand in a campaign to predispose the world in his favour and, therefore, to assist him in any negotiations he might have on the carpet. Beware of the wily Kühlmann!

Baiting the Chancellor is the favourite sport of German political life. No sooner does the Kaiser name a Chancellor than hundreds of little politicians, Reichstag members, editors, reporters and female intriguers try to drive him from office. When von Bethmann-Hollweg showed an inclination towards Liberalism, and advocated a juster electoral system for Prussia, the Junkers, the military and the upholders of the caste system joined their forces to those of the usual intriguers; and it was only a question of time until the Chancellor's official head fell in the basket.

His successor is a Prussian bureaucrat. No further description is necessary.

Of course no nation will permit itself to be reformed from without. The position of the world in arms with reference to Germany is simply this. It is impossible to make peace with Germany as at present constituted, because that peace will be but a truce, a short breathing space before the German military autocrats again send

the sons of Germany to death in the trenches
for the advancement of the System and the personal gloiy and advantage of stuffy old generals
and prancing princes.

The world does not believe that a free Germany will needlessly make war, believe in war
for war's sake or take up the profession of arms
as a national industry.

The choice lies with the German people. And
how admirably has our great President shown
that people that we war not with them but with
the autocracy which has led them into the
shambles of dishonour.

CHAPTER XIX

THE GERMAN PEOPLE IN WAR

WITH the declaration of war the ultimate power in Germany was transferred from the civil to the military authorities.

At five o'clock on the afternoon of Friday, and immediately after the declaration of a State of War, the Guard of the Grenadier Regiment Kaiser Alexander, under the command of a Lieutenant with four drummers, took its place before the monument of Frederick the Great in the middle of the Unter den Linden. The drummers sounded a ruffle on their drums and the Lieutenant read an order beginning with the words "By all highest order: A State of War is proclaimed in Berlin and in the Province of Brandenburg." This order was signed by General von Kessel as Over-Commander of the Mark of Brandenburg; and stated that the complete power was transferred to him; that the civil officials might remain in office, but must obey the orders and regulations of the Over-Commander; that house-searchings and arrests by officials thereto empowered could take place at any time; that strangers who could not show good reason for remaining in Berlin, had twenty-four hours in which to leave; that the sale of weapons, powder and explosives to civilians was forbidden; and that civilians were forbidden to carry weapons without permission of the proper authorities.

The same transfer of authority took place in each army corps—*Bezirk,* or province or district in Germany; and in each army corps district or province the commanding general took over the ultimate power. In Berlin it was necessary to create a new officer, the Over-Commander of the Mark, because two army corps, the third and the army corps of the guards, had their headquarters in Berlin. These army corps commanders were not at all bashful about the use of the power thus transferred to them. Some of them even prescribed the length of the dresses to be worn by the women; and many women, having followed the German sport custom of wearing knickerbockers in the winter sports resorts of Garmisch-Partenkirchen, the Generalkommando, or Headquarters for Bavaria issued in January, 1917, the following order: "The appearance of many women in Garmisch-Partenkirchen has excited lively anger and indignation in the population there. This bitterness is directed particularly against certain women, frequently of ripe age, who do not engage in sports, but nevertheless show themselves in public continually clad in knickerbockers. It has even happened that women so dressed have visited churches during the service. Such behaviour is a cruelty to the earnest minds of the mountain population and, in consequence, there are often many disagreeable occurrences in the streets. Officials, priests and private citizens have turned to the Generalkommando with the request for help; and the Generalkommando has, therefore, empowered the district officials in Garmisch-Partenkirchen to take energetic measures against this misconduct; if necessary with the aid of the police."

I spent two days at Garmisch-Partenkirchen in February, 1916. Some of the German girls looked very well in their "knickers," but I agree with the Generalkommando that the appearance of some of the older women was "cruelty" not only to the "earnest mountain population" but to any observer.

These corps commanders are apparently responsible direct to the Emperor; and therefore much of the difficulty that I had concerning the treatment of prisoners was due to this system, as each corps commander considered himself supreme in his own district not only over the civil and military population but over the prison camps within his jurisdiction.

On the fourth of August, 1914, a number of laws were passed, which had been evidently prepared long in advance, making various changes made necessary by war, such as alteration of the Coinage Law, the Bank Law, and the Law of Maximum Prices. Laws as to the high prices were made from time to time. For instance, the law of the twenty-eighth of October, 1914, provided in detail the maximum prices for rye in different parts of Germany. The maximum price at wholesale per German ton of native rye must not exceed 220 marks in Berlin, 236 marks in Cologne, 209 marks in Koenigsberg, 228 marks in Hamburg, 235 marks in Frankfort a/M.

The maximum price for the German ton of native wheat was set at forty marks per ton higher than the above rates for rye. This maximum price was made with reference to deliveries without sacks and for cash payments.

The law as to the maximum prices applied to all objects of daily necessity, not only to food and fodder but to oil, coal and wood. Of course, these maximum prices were changed from time to time, but I think I can safely state that at no time in the war, while I was in Berlin, were the simple foods more expensive than in New York.

The so-called "war bread," the staple food of the population, which was made soon after the commencement of the war, was composed partially of rye and potato flour. It was not at all unpalatable, especially when toasted; and when it was seen that the war would not be as short as the Germans had expected, the bread cards were issued. That is, every Monday morning each person was given a card which had annexed to it a number of little perforated sections about the size of a quarter of a postage stamp, each marked with twenty-five, fifty or one hundred. The total of these figures constituted the allowance of each person in grammes per week. The person desiring to buy bread either at a baker's or in a restaurant must turn in these little stamped sections for an amount equivalent to the weight of bread purchased. Each baker was given a certain amount of meal at the commencement of each week, and he had to account for this meal at the end of the week by turning in its equivalent in bread cards.

As food became scarce, the card system was applied to meat, potatoes, milk, sugar, butter and soap. Green vegetables and fruits were exempt from the card system, as were for a long time chickens, ducks, geese, turkeys and game. Because of these exemptions the rich usually managed to live well, although the price of a goose rose to ridiculous heights. There was, of course, much underground traffic in cards and sales of illicit or smuggled butter, etc. The police were very stern in their enforcement of the law and the manager of one of the largest hotels in Berlin was taken to prison because he had made the servants give him their allowance of butter, which he in turn sold to the rich guests of the hotel.

No one over six years of age at the time I left could get milk without a doctor's certificate. One result of this was that the children of the poor were surer of obtaining milk than before the war, as the women of the Frauendienst and social workers saw to it that each child had its share.

The third winter of the war, owing to a breakdown of means of transportation and want of laborers, coal became very scarce. All public places, such as theatres, picture galleries, museums, and cinematograph shows, were closed in Munich for want of coal. In Berlin the suffering was not as great but even the elephants from Hagenbeck's Show were pressed into service to draw the coal carts from the railway stations.

Light was economized. All the apartment houses (and all Berlin lives in apartment houses) were closed at nine o'clock. Stores were forbidden to illuminate their show windows and all theatres were closed at ten. Only every other street electric light was lit; of the three lights in each lamp, only one.

As more and more men were called to the front, women were employed in unusual work. The new underground road in Berlin is being built largely by woman labour. This is not so difficult a matter in Berlin as in New York, because Berlin is built upon a bed of sand and the difficulties of rock excavation do not exist. Women are employed on the railroads, working with pickaxes on the road-bed. Women drive the great yellow post carts of Berlin. There were women guards on the underground road, women conductors on the tramways and women even become motor men on the tramcars. Banks, insurance companies and other large business institutions were filled with women workers who invaded the sacred precincts of many military and governmental offices.

A curious development of the hate of all things foreign was the hunt led by the Police President of Berlin, von Jagow (a cousin of the Foreign Minister), for foreign words. Von Jagow and his fellow cranks decided that all words of foreign origin must be expunged from the German language. The title of the Hotel Bristol on the Unter den Linden disappeared. The Hotel Westminster on the same street became Linden-hof. There is a large hotel called "The Cumberland," with a pastry department over which there was a sign, the French word, *Confissérie*. The management was compelled to take this sign down, but the hotel was allowed to retain the name of Cumberland, because the father-in-law of the Kaiser's only daughter is the Duke of Cumberland. The word "chauffeur" was eliminated, and there were many discussions as to what should be substituted. Many declared for *Kraftwagenfuhrer* or "power wagon driver." But finally the word was Germanised as "Schauffoer." Prussians took down the sign, *Confektion*, but the climax came when the General in command of the town of Breslau wrote a confectioner telling him to stop the use of the word *"bonbon"* in selling his candy. The confectioner, with a sense of humour and a nerve unusual in Germany, wrote back to the General that he would gladly discontinue the use of the word *"bonbon"* when the General ceased to call himself "General," and called the attention of this high military authority to the fact that "General" was as much a French word as *"bonbon."*

Unusual means were adopted in order to get all the gold coins in the country into the Imperial Bank. There were signs in every surface and underground car which read, "Whoever keeps back a gold coin injures the Fatherland."

And if a soldier presented to his superiors a twenty mark gold piece, he received in return twenty marks in paper money and two days leave of absence. In like manner a school boy who turned in ten marks in gold received ten marks in paper and was given a half holiday. Cinematograph shows gave these patrons who paid in gold an extra ticket, good for another day. An American woman residing at Berlin was awakened one morning at eight o'clock by two police detectives who told her that they had heard that she had some gold coins in her possession, and that if she did not turn them in for paper money they would wreck her apartment in their search for them. She, therefore, gave them the gold which I afterwards succeeded in getting the German Government to return to her. Later, the export of gold was forbidden, and even travellers arriving with gold were compelled to give it up in return for paper money.

While, of course, I cannot ascertain the exact amounts, I found, nevertheless, that great quantities of food and other supplies came into Germany from Holland and the Scandinavian countries, particularly from Sweden. Now that we are in the war we should take strong measures and cut off exports to these countries which export food, raw material, etc. to Germany. Sweden is particularly active in this traffic, but I understand that sulphur pyrites are sent from Norway, and sulphuric acid made therefrom is an absolute essential to the manufacture of munitions of war.

Potash, which is found as a mineral only in Germany and Austria, was used in exchange of commodities with Sweden and in this way much copper, lard, etc. reached Germany.

Early in the summer of 1915, the first demonstration took place in Berlin. About five hundred women collected in front of the Reichstag building. They were promptly suppressed by the police and no newspaper printed an account of the occurrence. These women were rather vague in their demands. They called von Buelow an old fat-head for his failure in Italy and complained that the whipped cream was not so good as before the war. There was some talk of high prices for food, and the women all said that they wanted their men back from the trenches.

.   .   .   .   .   .

Early summer brought also a number of cranks to Berlin. Miss Jane Addams and her fellow suffragists, after holding a convention in Holland, moved on Berlin. I succeeded in getting both the Chancellor and von Jagow to consent to receive them, a meeting to which they looked forward with unconcealed perturbation.

However, one of them seems to have impressed Miss Addams, for, as I write this, I read in the papers that she is complaining that we should not have gone to war because we thereby risk hurting somebody's feelings.

. . . .

On July twenty-seventh, 1915, I reported that I had learned that the Germans were picking out the Revolutionists and Liberals from the many Russian prisoners of war, furnishing them with money and false passports and papers, and sending them back to Russia to stir up a revolution.

. . . .

A German friend of mine told me that a friend of his who manufactured field glasses had received a large order from the Bulgarian Government. This manufacturer went to the Foreign Office and asked whether he should deliver the goods. He was told not only to deliver them but to do it as quickly as possible. By learning of this I was able to predict long in advance the entry of Bulgaria on the side of the Central Powers.

. . . .

Even a year after the commencement of the war there were reasonable people in Germany. I met Ballin, head of the great Hamburg American Line, on August ninth. I said to him, "When are you going to stop this crazy fighting?" The next day Ballin called on me and said that the sensible people of Germany wanted peace and that without annexation. He told me that every one was afraid to talk peace, that each country thought it a sign of weakness, and that he had advised the Chancellor to put a statement in an official paper to say that Germany fought only to defend herself and was ready to make an honourable peace. He told me that the Emperor at that time was against the annexation of Belgium.

· · · · · · ·

In calculating the great war debt built up by Germany, it must not be forgotten that German municipalities and other political districts have incurred large debts for war purposes, such as extra relief given to the wives and children of soldiers.

· · · · · · ·

In November, 1915, there were food disturbances and a serious agitation against a continuance of the war; and, in Leipzig, a Socialist paper was suppressed.

· · · · · · ·

The greatest efforts were made at all times to get in gold; and some time before I left Germany an advertisement was published in the newspapers requesting Germans to give up their jewelry for the Fatherland. Many did so: among them, I believe, the Empress and other royalties.

· · · · · · ·

In December, 1915, a prominent banker in Berlin said to me that the Germans were sick of the war; that the Krupps and other big industries were making great sums of money and were prolonging the war by insisting upon the annexation of Belgium; and that the Junkers were also in favour of the continuance of the war because of the fact that they were getting four or five times the money for their products while their work was being done by prisoners. He said that the *Kaufleute* (merchant middle class) will have to pay the cost of the war and that the Junkers will not be taxed.

· · · · · · ·

In December, butter became very scarce and the women waiting in long lines before the shops often rushed the shops. In this month many copper roofs were removed from buildings in Berlin. I was told by a friend in the Foreign Office that the notorious von Rintelen was sent to America to buy up the entire product of the Dupont powder factories, and that he exceeded his authority if he did anything else.

In December, on the night of the day of the peace interpellation in the Reichstag a call was

415

issued by placards for a meeting on the Unter den Linden. I went out on the streets during the afternoon and found that the police had so carefully divided the city into districts that it was impossible for a crowd of any size to gather on the Unter den Linden. There was quite a row at the session in the Reichstag. Scheidemann, the Socialist, made a speech very moderate in tone; but he was answered by the Chancellor and then an endeavour was made to close the debate. The Socialists made such a noise, however, that the majority gave way and another prominent Socialist, Landsberger, was allowed to speak for the Socialists. He also made a reasonable speech in the course of which he said that even Socialists would not allow Alsace-Lorraine to go back to France. He made use of a rather good phrase, saying that the "Dis-United States of Europe were making war to make a place for the United States of America."

.   .   .   .   .   .

The banks sent out circulars to all holders of safe deposit boxes, asking them to disclose the contents. This was part of the campaign to get in hoarded gold.

.   .   .   .   .   .

In January, 1916, we had many visitors. S. S. McClure, Hermann Bernstein, Inez Milholland Boissevain—all of the Ford Peace Ship—appeared in Berlin. I introduced Mrs. Boissevain to Zimmermann who admired her extremely.

.   .   .   .

In January, 1916, I visited Munich and from there a Bavarian officer prison camp and the prison camp for private soldiers, both at Ingol-stadt. I also conferred with Archdeacon Nies of the American Episcopal Church who carried on a much needed work in visiting the prison camps in Bavaria.

.   .   .   .

The American Colony in Munich maintained with the help of friends in America, a Red Cross hospital under the able charge of Dr. Jung, a Washington doctor, and his wife. The nursing was done by American and German girls. The American Colony at Munich also fed a number of school children every day. I regret to say, however, that many of the Americans in Munich were loud in their abuse of President Wilson and their native country.

.   .   .   .

In March, 1916, I was sounded on the question of Germany's sending an unofficial envoy, like Colonel House, to America to talk informally to the President and prominent people. I was told that Solf would probably be named.

.   .   .   .

In 1916, the importation of many articles of

417

luxury into Germany was forbidden. This move was naturally made in order to keep money in the country.

. . . .

A Dane who had a quantity of manganese in Brazil sold it to a Philadelphia firm for delivery to the United States Steel Company. The German Government in some way learned of this and the Dane was arrested and put in jail. His Minister had great difficulty, in getting him out.

. . . .

Liebknecht, in April of 1916, made matters lively at the Reichstag sessions. During the Chancellor's speech, Liebknecht interrupted him and said that the Germans were not free; next he denied that the Germans had not wished war; and, another time, he called attention to the attempts of the Germans to induce the Mohammedan and Irish prisoners of war to desert to the German side. Liebknecht finally enraged the government supporters by calling out that the subscription to the loan was a swindle.

. . . .

After the *Sussex* settlement I think that the Germans wished to inaugurate an era of better feeling between Germany and the United States. At any rate, and in answer to many anonymous attacks made against me, the *North German Gazette*, the official newspaper, published a sort of

certificate from the government to the effect that
I was a good boy and that the rumours of my
bitter hostility to Germany were unfounded.

.   .   .   .

In May, 1916, Wertheim, head of the great
department store in Berlin, told me that they had
more business than in peace times.

.   .   .   .

Early in June I had two long talks with Prince
von Buelow. He speaks English well and is suspected by his enemies of having been polishing
it up lately in order to make ready for possible
peace conferences. He is a man of a more active
brain than the present Chancellor, and is very
restless and anxious in some way to break into
the present political situation.

.   .   .   .

In June, the anonymous attacks on von Bethmann-Hollweg by pamphlet and otherwise, incensed him to such a degree that he made an open
answer in the Reichstag and had rather the best
of the situation. Many anonymous lies and rumours were flying about Berlin at this period, and
even Helfferich had to deny publicly the anonymous charges that he had been anonymously
attacking the Chancellor.

.   .   .   .

In July, the committee called the National
Committee for an Honourable Peace was formed

with Prince Wedel at its head. Most of the people in this League were friends of von Bethmann-Hollweg, and one of the three real heads was the editor of the *Frankfurter Zeitung,* the Chancellor's organ. It was planned that fifty speakers from this committee would begin to speak all over Germany on August first, but when they began to speak their views were so dissimilar and the speeches of most of them so ridiculous that the movement failed.

.   .   .   .

In August, I spent two Saturdays and Sundays at Heringsdorf, a summer resort on the Baltic. Before going there I had to get special permission from the military authorities through the Foreign Office, as foreigners are not allowed to reside on the coast of Germany. Regulations that all windows must be darkened at night and no lights shown which could be seen from the sea were strictly enforced by the authorities.

There are three bathing places. In each of them the bath houses, etc. surround three sides of a square, the sea forming the fourth side. Bathing is allowed only on this fourth side for a space of sixty-five yards long. One of these bathing places is for women and one for men, and the third is the so-called Familienbad (family bath) where mixed bathing is allowed. German women are very sensible in the matter of their bathing costumes and do not wear the extraordinary creations seen in America. They wear bathing sandals but no stockings, and, as most of them have fine figures but dress badly, they appear at their best at Heringsdorf. Both sea and air seemed somewhat cold for bathing. On account of their sensible dress, most of the German women are expert swimmers.

I noticed one very handsome blonde girl who sat on her bathing mantle exciting the admiration of the beach because of her fine figure. She suddenly dived into the pockets of the bathing mantle and produced an enormous black bread sandwich which she proceeded to consume quite unconsciously, after which she swam out to sea. No healthy German can remain long separated from food; and I noticed in the prospectus of the different boarding-houses at Heringsdorf that patrons were offered, in addition to about four meals or more a day, an extra sandwich to take to the beach to be consumed during the bathing hour.

．　．　．　．　．　．　．

There is a beautiful little English church in Berlin which was especially favoured by the Kaiser's mother during her life. Because of this, the Kaiser permitted this church to remain open, and the services were continued during the war. The pastor, Rev. Mr. Williams, obtained permission to visit the British prisoners, and most devotedly travelled from one prison camp to another. Both he and his sister, whose charitable work for the British deserves mention, were at one time thrown into jail, charged with spying.

.   .   .   .

I at first attended the hybrid American church, but when, in 1915, I think, the committee hired a German *woman* preacher I ceased to attend. The American, the Reverend Dr. Crosser, who was in charge when I arrived in Berlin left, to my everlasting regret, in the spring before the war.

.   .   .   .   .   .

Poor Creelman, the celebrated newspaper correspondent, died in Berlin. We got him in to a good hospital and some one from the Embassy visited him every day.

The funeral services were conducted in the American Church by the Rev. Dr. Dickie, long a resident of Berlin, whose wife had presented the library to the American church. The Foreign Office sent Herr Horstmann as its representative.

.   .   .   .   .   .

While to-day all royalties and public men pose for the movies, Czar Ferdinand of Bulgaria and his family are probably the first royalties to act in a cinematograph. In 1916, there was released in Berlin a play in which Czar Ferdinand of Bulgaria, his wife and two daughters by a former wife appeared, acting as Bulgarian royalties in the development of the plot.

.   .   .   .

The difference between von Jagow and Zimmermann was that von Jagow had lived abroad, had met people from all countries and knew that there was much to learn about the psychology of the inhabitants of countries other than Germany. Zimmermann, in the early part of his career, had been consul at Shanghai; and, on his way back, had passed through America, spending two days in San Francisco and three in New York. He seemed to think that this transcontinental trip had given him an intimate knowledge of American character. Von Jagow, on the other hand, almost as soon as war began, spent many hours talking to me about America and borrowed from me books and novels on that country. The novel in which he took the greatest interest was "Turmoil," by Booth Tarkington.

.   .   .   .

I think there must have been a period quite recently when the German Government tried to imbue the people with a greater degree of frightfulness, because all of us in visiting camps, etc.

observed that the *landsturm* men or older soldiers were much more merciful than the younger ones.

. . . .

Alexander Cochran, a New York yachtsman, volunteered to become a courier between the London Embassy and ours. On his first trip, although he had two passports (his regular passport and a special courier's passport), he was arrested and compelled to spend the night on the floor of the guard-room at the frontier town of Bentheim. This ended his aspirations to be a courier. He is now a commander in the British Navy, having joined it with his large steam yacht, the *Warrior* some time before the United States entered the war. In the piping times of peace he had been the guest of the Emperor at Kiel.

. . . .

A British prisoner, who escaped from Ruhleben, was caught in a curious manner. Prisoners in Ruhleben received bread from outside, as I have explained in the chapter on prisoners of war. This bread is white, something unknown in Germany since the war. The escaped prisoner took with him some sandwiches made of the bread he had received in Ruhleben and most incautiously ate one of these sandwiches in a railway station. He was immediately surrounded by a crowd of Germans anxious to know where he had obtained the white bread, and, in this way, was detected and returned to prison.

.   .   .   .

On our way out in September, 1916, we were given a large dinner in Copenhagen by our skilful minister there, the Hon. Maurice F. Egan, who has devoted many years of his life to the task of adding the three beautiful Danish islands to the dominions of the United States. He is an able diplomat, very popular in Copenhagen, where he is dean of the diplomatic corps. At this dinner we met Countess Hegerman-Lindencron, whose interesting books, "The Sunny Side of Diplomatic Life" and "The Courts of Memory," have had a large circulation in America. In Copenhagen, too, both on the way out and in, we lunched with Count Rantzau-Brockedorff, then German Minister there. Count Rantzau is skilful and wily, and not at all military in his instincts; and, I should say, far more inclined to arrive at a reasonable compromise than the average German diplomat. He is a charming International, with none of the rough points and aggressive manners which characterise so many Prussian officials.

.   .   .   .

In judging the German people, we must re-

member that, while they have made great progress in the last forty years in commerce and
chemistry, the very little liberty they possess is
a plant of very recent growth. About the year
1780, Frederick the Great having sent some
money to restore the burned city of Greiffenberg,
in Silesia, the magistrates of that town called
upon him to thank him. They kneeled and their
spokesman said, "We render unto your Majesty
in the name of the inhabitants of Greiffenberg,
our humble thanks for the most gracious gift
which your Majesty deigned to bestow in aid
and to assist us in rebuilding our homes.

"The gratitude of such dust as we, is, as we
are aware, of no moment or value to you. We
shall, however, implore God to grant your Majesty His divine favours in return for your royal
bounty."

Too many Germans, to-day, feel that they are
mere dust before the almost countless royalties
of the German Empire. And these royalties are
too prone to feel that the kingdoms, dukedoms
and principalities of Germany and their inhabitants are their private property. The Princes
of Nassau and Anspach and Hesse, at the time
of our Revolution, sold their unfortunate subjects to the British Government to be exported
to fight the Americans. Our American soil
covers the bones of many a poor German peasant

426

who gave up his life in a war from which he gained nothing.

.   .   .   .

When Frederick the Great, the model and exemplar of all German royalties, died in 1786, he disposed of the Kingdom of Prussia in his will as if it had been one of his horses. "I bequeath unto my dear nephew, Frederick William, as unto my immediate successor, the Kingdom of Prussia, the provinces, towns, palaces, forts, fortresses, all ammunition and arsenals, all lands mine by inheritance or right of conquest, the crown jewels, gold and silver service of plate in Berlin, country houses, collections of coins, picture galleries, gardens, and so forth." Contrast this will with the utterances of Washington and Hamilton made at the same time!

In the Grand Duchies of Mecklenburg, serfdom was not abolished until 1819.

.   .   .   .

The spies and the influencers of American correspondents made their headquarters at a large Berlin hotel. A sketch of their activities is given by de Beaufort in his book, "Behind the German Veil."

.   .   .   .

Among the American correspondents in Berlin during the war great credit should be given to Carl W. Ackerman and Seymour B. Conger, correspondents of the United and Associated Presses respectively, who at all times and in spite of their surroundings and in the face of real difficulties preserved their Americanism unimpaired and refused to succumb to the alluring temptations held out to them. I do not mean to imply that the other correspondents were not loyal, but the pro-Germanism of many of them unfortunately gave the Imperial Foreign Office and the great general staff a wrong impression of Americans. It is the splendid patriotism under fire of Ackerman and Conger that deserves special mention.

CHAPTER XX

LAST

I WAS credited by the Germans with having hoodwinked and jollied the Foreign Office and the Government into refraining for two years from using illegally their most effective weapon.

This, of course, is not so. I always told the Foreign Office the plain simple truth and the event showed that I correctly predicted the attitude of America.

Our American national game, poker, has given us abroad an unfair reputation. We are always supposed to be bluffing. A book was published in Germany about the President called, "President Bluff."

I only regret that those high in authority in Germany should have preferred to listen to pro-German correspondents who posed as amateur super-Ambassadors rather than to the authorised representatives of America. I left Germany with a clear conscience and the knowledge that I had done everything possible to keep the peace.

An Ambassador, of course, does not determine the policy of his own country. One of his principal duties, if not the principal one, is to keep his own country informed—to know beforehand what the country to which he is accredited will do, and I think that I managed to give the State Department advance information of the moves of the rulers of Germany.

I had the support of a loyal and devoted staff of competent secretaries and assistants, and both Secretaries Bryan and Lansing were most kind in the backing given by their very ably organised department.

I sent Secretary Lansing a confidential letter every week and, of course, received most valuable hints from him. Secretary Lansing was very successful in his tactful handling of the American Ambassadors abroad and in getting them to work together as cheerful members of the same team.

When I returned to America, after living for two and a half years in the centre of this world calamity, everything seemed petty and small. I was surprised that people could still seek little advantages, still be actuated by little jealousies and revenges. Freed from the round of daily work I felt for the first time the utter horror and uselessness of all the misery these Prussian military autocrats had brought upon the world; and what a reckoning there will be in Germany some day when the plain people realise the truth, when they learn what base motives actuated their rulers in condemning a whole generation of the earth to war and death!

Is it not a shame that the world should have been so disturbed; that peaceful men are compelled to lie out in the mud and filth in the depth of raw winter, shot at and stormed at and shelled, waiting for a chance to murder some other inoffensive fellow creature? Why must the people in old Poland die of hunger, not finding dogs enough to eat in the streets of Lemberg? The long lines of broken peasants in Serbia and in Roumania; the population of Belgium and Northern France torn from their homes to work as slaves for the Germans; the poor prisoners of war starving in their huts or working in factories and mines; the cries of the old and the children, wounded by bombs from Zeppelins; the wails of the mothers for their sons; the very rustling of the air as the souls of the ten million dead sweep to another world,—why must all these horrors come upon a fair green earth, where we believed that love and help and friendship, genius and science and commerce, religion and civilisation, once ruled?

It is because in the dark, cold Northern plains of Germany there exists an autocracy, deceiving a great people, poisoning their minds from one generation to another and preaching the virtue and necessity of war; and until that autocracy is either wiped out or made powerless, there can be no peace on earth.

The golden dream of conquest was almost accomplished. A little more advance, a few more wagon loads of ammunition, and there would have been no battle of the Marne, no Joffre, a modern Martel, to hammer back the invading hordes of barbarism.

I have always stated that Germany is possessed yet of immense military power; and, to win, the nations opposed to Germany must learn to think in a military way. The mere entrance, even of a great nation like our own, into the war, means nothing in a military way unless backed by military power.

And there must be no German peace. The old *régime,* left in control of Germany, of Bulgaria, of Turkey, would only seek a favourable moment to renew the war, to strive again for the mastery of the world.

Fortunately America bars the way,—America led by a fighting President who will allow no compromise with brutal autocracy.

THE END

432

I

10/VIII
14

Gebühren: M. Pf.

Telegraphie des Deutschen Reichs.

Befördert den 191.
Uhr M. mitt. in Ltg.

Angenommen durch: von an
burch

Nr. mit W. 191. ben / um Uhr Min. mitt.

Telegramm

Sr. Majestät des Kaisers und Königs.

1) H.R.H. Prince Henry was received by his Majesty King George V. in London who empowered him to transmit to me verbally that England would remain neutral if war broke out on the Continent involving Germany & France, Austria & Russia. This message was telegraphed to me by my brother from London after his conversation with H. M. the King, & repeated verbally on the 29th of July

2) My Ambassador in London transmitted a message from Sir E. Grey to Berlin saying that only in case France was likely to be crushed England would interfere.

3) On the 30th my ambassador in London reported that Sir E. Grey in course of a "private" conversation told him, that if the conflict remained localized between Russia — not Servia — & Austria

V17

THIS AND THE FOLLOWING FIVE PAGES ARE A FAC-SIMILE
REPRODUCTION OF THE TELEGRAM IN THE KAISER'S OWN
HANDWRITING WHICH HE GAVE AMBASSADOR GERARD TO
CABLE TO PRESIDENT WILSON (SEE **PAGE 200**)

433

Telegraphie des Deutschen Reichs.

Befördert den ___ / ___ 191 ___
Uhr ___ M. ___ mitt. in Ltg.

Angenommen durch: ___

Pf.

von

an

durch

Nr. ___ mit ___ W. 191 ben ___ / ___ um ___ Uhr ___ Min. ___ mitt.

Telegramm

Sr. Majestät des Kaisers und Königs.

England would not move, but if we "mixed" in the fray
she would take quick decisions + grave measures". I. e.
if I left my Ally Austria in the lurch to fight alone
England would not touch me.

4) This communication being directly counter to the Kings
message to me Itelegraphed to H. M^{ty} thanking himfor
this message through my Brother, & begging him to
use all his power to keep France + Russia - his Allies —
from making any warlike preparations calculated to
disturb my work of mediation. Stating that I was in
constant communication with H. M. th. Cz. In the
evening the King kindly answered that he had ordered
V. l.—

Gebühren:

ℳ. ____ Pf.

Angenommen durch:

____

Telegraphie des Deutschen Reichs.

vor

Befördert den ____ / ____ 191 __

Uhr ____ ℳ. ____ mitt. in Stg.

an ____

durch ____

Nr. ____ mit ____ W. 191 __ ben / ____ um ____ Uhr ____ Min. ____ mitt.

Telegramm

Sr. Majestät des Kaisers und Königs.

his Government to use every possible influence with his
allies to refrain from taking any provocative military measures
At the same time H.M. asked I should transmit to Vienna
the British proposal that Austria was to take Belgrade
+ a few other Servian towns + a strip of country as a
"main-mise" to make sure that the Servian promises
on paper should be fullfulled in reality. This proposal
was in the same moment telegraphed to me from Vienna
for London, quite in conjunction with the British proposal
besides I had telegraphed to H.M. the Zar the same as an
idea of mine, before I recieved the two Communications from
Vienna + London. As both were of the same opinion, I

VII

435

Gebühren: **Telegraphie des Deutschen Reichs.**   Befördert den ..../........191

.... M .... Pf.   .... Uhr .... M........ mitt. in Ltg.

Angenommen durch: von   an

durch

Nr. .... mit .... W. 191.. den ..../........ um .... Uhr .... Min. ...... mitt.

Telegramm

Sr. Majestät des Kaisers und Königs.

4) I immediately transmitted the telegrams vice versa
to Vienna & London. I felt that I was able to tide
the question over & was happy at the peaceful outlook.

5) While I was preparing a note to H. M. the Czar the
next morning, to inform him that Vienna, London, &
Berlin were agreed about the treatment of affairs
I received the telegram from H. E the Chancellor that
in the night before the Czar had given the order
to mobilise the whole of the Russian Army, which was
of corse also meant against Germany, whereas up till then
the southern Armies had been mobilised against Austria.

6) In a telgram from London my Ambassador, by another

Telegraphie des Deutschen Reichs.

Gebühren:

_____ M _____ Pf.

Angenommen durch:

von

Besördert den _____ / _____ 191__

Uhr _____ M. _____ mitt. in Vg.

ca

durch

Nr. _____ mit _____ W. 191 den _____ / _____ um _____ Uhr _____ Min. _____ mitt.

Telegramm

Sr. Majestät des Kaisers und Königs.

informed me he understood British Government would
guarantee neutrality of France, & wished to know wetter
Germany would refrain from attack. I telegraphed to H. M.
the King personally that, Mobilization being already carried
out could not be stopped, but if H. M. could guarantee
with his armed forces the neutrability of France I would
refrain from attacking her, leave her alone, & employ my
troops elsewere. H. M. answered that he thought my
offer was based on a misunderstanding; & as far as I can
make out Sir E. Grey never took my offer into serious
consideration. He never answered it. Instead he declared England
had to defend Belgian neutrality, which had to be violated by

V 1 a

Telegraphie des Deutschen Reichs.

Gebühren:

_____ M _____ Pf.

Angenommen durch:

von

Befördert den _____ / _____ 191_

Uhr _____ M. _____ mitt. in Ltg.

an

durch

Nr. _____ mit _____ B. 191_ ben _____ / _____ um _____ Uhr _____ Min. _____ mitt.

Telegramm

Sr. Majestät des Kaisers und Königs.

Germany on strategical grounds, knowledge having been received that France was already preparing to enter Belgium & the King of the Belgians having refused my petition for a free passage under garantees of his country's freedom I am most grateful for the President's message

William I. R.

438

Der Staatssekretär des
Auswärtigen Amts
Zimmermann, bittet
Seine Exzellenz den Bot-
schafter der Vereinigten
Staaten von Amerika,
Herrn Gerard, um die
Ehre seines Besuches
Heute Nachmittag um
6 Uhr im Auswärtigen
Amt, Wilhelmstraße 75/76.

Berlin, den 31. Januar 1917.

FAC-SIMILE OF SECRETARY OF STATE ZIMMERMAN'S RE-
QUEST TO AMBASSADOR GERARD TO CALL, IN ORDER TO
RECEIVE THE ANNOUNCEMENT OF RUTHLESS SUBMARINE
WARFARE AGAINST THE ALLIES

Kauffahrteischiffe beim Ausbruch der Feindseligkeiten finden auf die beiderseitigen Kauffahrtei-schiffe und deren Ladungen Anwendung.

at outbreak of hostilities shall apply to the merchant vessels of either party and their cargo.

Die bezeichneten Schiffe dürfen zum Auslaufen aus dem Hafen nur gezwungen werden, wenn ihnen gleichzeitig ein von den sämtlichen feindlichen Seemächten als verbindlich anerkannter Passierschein nach einem Hafen des eigenen oder eines verbündeten Landes oder nach einem anderen Hafen des Aufenthalts-landes angeboten wird.

The aforesaid ships may not be forced to leave port unless at the same time they be given a pass recognized as binding by all the enemy seapowers to a home port or a port of an allied country or to another port of the country in which the ship happens to be.

Artikel 8.

Die Bestimmungen des ariten Kapitels des elften Haager Abkommens über gewisse Beschran-kungen in der Ausübung des Beuterechts im Seekrieg finden auf den Kapitan, die Offiziere und die Mitglieder der Mann-schaft der im Artikel 7 be-zeichneten sowie der im Laufe eines

Article 8.

The regulations of chapter 3 of the eleventh Hague Conven-tion relative to certain restric-tions in the exercise of the right of capture in maritime war shall apply to the captains, of-ficers and members of the crews of merchant ships specified in article 7 and of such merchant ships

eines etwaigen Krieges weggenom-
menen Kauffahrteischiffe Anwendung.

ships that may be captuned in
the course of a possible war.

Artikel 9.
Diese Verständigung er-
streckt sich auch auf die Ko-
lonien und sonstigen auswärtigen Besitzungen der beiden Tei-
le.

Article 9.
This agreement shall apply
also to the colonies and other
foreign possessions of either
party.

Berlin, den   Februar 1917.

Berlin, February   1917.

Die ganze Berichterstattung über den letzten
Luftangriff seitens der Engländer hat sich, wie gewohnt,
darauf beschränkt, die übliche Anzahl von Menschenleben
als einzige Opfer des Angriffs anzugeben und die materiel-
len Schäden als völlig belanglos hinzustellen. Alle Bemühungen, durch weitgehende Absperrungsmaßnahmen und Ent-
hebung der Berichterstattung die tatsächlich verursachten
Schäden der Öffentlichkeit vorzuenthalten, sind auch dieses Mal erfolglos geblieben. Zerstörungen, wie sie namentlich der letzte Angriff im Gefolge gehabt hat, lassen sich
auf die Dauer eben nicht verschleiern. Der ganze Umfang
~~der der ganze Umfang~~ der Schäden läßt sich zwar noch nicht
im Entferntesten übersehen, doch genügt das, was bisher
bekannt geworden ist, vollauf, um zu erkennen, daß der
Luftangriff vom 13./14. X. alle bisherigen an Wirkung weit-
aus übertroffen hat.

Es wurden erfolgreich beworfen:

1. Die Londoner Hafenanlagen (die sogenannten Docks)
und ihre anliegenden Stadtteile

Im Einzelnen.

In den East India Docks brannte ein großer Schup-
pen, der zum Teil Munition und anderes Kriegsmaterial ent-
hielt, vollständig nieder.

In den London Docks wurden die Kaimauern und
Lagerhäuser auf weite Strecken niedergelegt. Mehrere Schiffe wurden getroffen, zum Teil völlig vernichtet.

In den Victoria Docks geriet ein großer Baum-
wollspeicher in Brand und wurde völlig zerstört.

Die in der Nähe der Docks gelegenen Straßen,
insbesondere die St. George Street und die Leman Street
haben schwer gelitten.

2.) Die City und das Zeitungsviertel sind mit
besonders gutem Erfolge angegriffen worden.

Insbesondere wurden mit Bomben belegt:

Der mit Geschützen versehene Tower nebst Towerbrücke,
die Chancery Lane,
die Liverpol Street,   In diesen Straßen sind zahl-
die Morgate Street,   reiche Häuser zerstört worden,
die Bishopsgate,   zum Teil ganze Häuserblocks.
die Altgate,
die Minories.

Im Einzelnen.

Die South Western Bank brannte bis auf die Grund-
mauern nieder. Erhebliche Summen an Geld und Wertpapieren
sollen vernichtet worden sein. Unter den Trümmern wurde
noch tagelang nach Geld und Papieren gesucht. Auch eine
Filiale der London Bank wurde eingeäschert.

Im Zeitungsviertel wurde das Gebäude der Morning
Post besonders schwer beschädigt.

Der Untergrund- und Eisenbahnbetrieb durch London mußte infolge von Zerstörungen teilweise eingestellt
werden.

Vor-

1.) **Woolwich.**
Im Arsenal sind schwere Beschädigungen angerichtet worden. Ein Teil ganz neuer Maschinen und Einrichtungen ist vernichtet worden

2.) **Enfield.**
Eine Batterie mit Scheinwerfern, von der die Luftschiffe heftiges Feuer bekommen hatten, wurde mit Bomben belegt und zum Schweigen gebracht. Die Scheinwerfer erloschen zum Teil unmittelbar nach den ersten Bombenwürfen.

3) **Hampton**
Die Pump- und Kraftstation wurde beworfen. Bei der guten Beobachtungsmöglichkeit wurden gute Treffergebnisse festgestellt

4) **Croydon**
Es wurde eine Reihe großer Fabrikanlagen beworfen und mehrere große Brände beobachtet

5.) **Kentistown** (Im Norden Londons)
Hier wurde eine besonders starke Scheinwerferbatterie ausgiebig mit Bomben belegt und zahlreiche Treffer beobachtet. Nach einem mitten in der Batterie gelegenen Treffer erlosch sofort eine Reihe von Scheinwerfern

6.) **Jn Westham und Eastham** wurden große Fabrik- und Eisenbahnanlagen beworfen Es konnte sehr guter Erfolg festgestellt werden

7) **Ipswich.**
Es wurde eine Batterie beworfen, deren Feuer nach wenigen Bombenwürfen merklich schwächer wurde

Die Luftschiffe wurden während des ganzen Angriffs außerordentlich heftig beschossen Aus allen Teilen Londons hagelte es Schrapnells und Sprenggranaten. 4 Flugzeuge bemühten sich, die Abwehr der Luftschiffe zu unterstützen, ohne jedweden Erfolg Zahllose Scheinwerfer beleuchteten aus allen Stadtteilen die Luftschiffe taghell. Eins der Luftschiffe nahm sich die Zeit, die Scheinwerfer zu zählen. Es zählte über 26 Die Engländer werden sich unter diesen Umständen nicht darüber beklagen dürfen, wenn wir ihre Kapitale als einen außerordentlich gut befestigten Platz ansehen und dementsprechend behandeln.

Text nicht wörtlich, jedoch soweit Zahlen und Tatsachen in Frage kommen, zu benutzen.

———

WE, the citizens of the United States of America, appeal in the name of justice and humanity, in the name of neutrality and future peace to the people, to the law makers, and the government of our country, to prevent the export from our shores of one single weapon, or of one pound of powder, to deal death in Europe. We recognise the fact, that the export is legally permissible through private firms, but nevertheless know, that our executive and our legislature can stop such export by a determined course of strict neutrality, a neutrality which is actuated by righteousness and sustained by public opinion.

The President of the United States has prevented the loan of money to France, and thereby our country has set its own precedent of what is just and right. This precedent binds us in legal opinion, as well as in the estimate of the world, to pursue in the greater matter, as in the lesser, a course of indubitable neutrality. Never in the history of nations, have orders of such gigantic proportions been accepted by any country as those now being executed in America for the continuance of the European war.

Do you know this fact?
Where are our peace societies?
Where are our women's organisations?
Where are our Churches?

No matter with whom we Americans, either individually, or as a nation sympathize politically, the statement up to the present time has been true, that we, as a nation, have been first and foremost in forwarding the peace-movements of the world. Are we willing to resign our prestige as a Peace-Maker? International business relations between our country and Europe have been extended and cordial. We protest against their destruction for the benefit of a few! Are we, for the sake of present business profit, willing to draw upon ourselves an enduring heritage of hatred? Generations will not suffice to wipe away the stain we bring upon ourselves! Men are dying on ghastly battle-fields for their ideals. Cannot we work and suffer for our ideal of the integrity of America? Guns, cannon, cartridges, dynamite, bombs are going from our manufactures not only to England, to France, and to Russia, but also to Japan. We are fortifying not only Europeans against each other, we are fortifying others against ourselves. Is this done with the consent of the entire American people? In case of any future struggle forced upon our own land, picture clearly the possible destruction brought upon us, did any neutral country of Europe take the position of neutrality we assume to-day. Does the American nation desire to resign the future security of its own citizens?

We protest against this destruction of American integrity, of American business interests, of American security, as a consequence of this one-sided neutrality! We protest not only in the interest of America, but above all, in the name of humanity, against a prolongation by our country of this hideous warfare. America's unlimited supply of death dealing machinery will cause an indefinite prolongation of this murder of mankind. When the war cloud lifts, our own land will be stained with the blood of our European brothers! Our actual military participation in this war, means Europe's last man! We protest in the name of international relationship and honor; we protest in the name of suffering womankind; we protest in the name of helpless children; we protest in the name of all that lives and breathes against any participation by our country in this human carnage!

We believe that, as a nation, we are not willing to resign our legacy of righteousness received from the Pilgrim Fathers. We believe that, as a nation, we desire to retain our political prestige as an arbiter of peace. We believe that now, if ever, is the time for action! In this belief we send our protest and our appeal to every American who loves his country and desires the welfare of the world!

Signed by American Citizens resident in Europe, whose signatures are being sent to the State Department in Washington

A PETITION TO THE PRESIDENT OF THE UNITED STATES, CIRCULATED FOR SIGNATURES AMONG THE AMERICANS IN EUROPE, OSTENSIBLY TO PROTEST AGAINST THE AMERICAN MANUFACTURE OF MUNITIONS OF WAR

Worte in die Zeit

Flugblätter 1914 von Ernst Lissauer

✠ Die Hälfte des Reinertrags ist für die Kriegerwaisen bestimmt. ✠

Erstes Blatt

> Und ward mir nicht gegeben, mitzuschlagen,
> Gewehr und Säbel in stürmender Hand,
> Sei mir vergönnt, ein kämpfend Wort zu sagen.
> O nimm auch diese Gabe an, mein Land!

Zum Geleit

Es gilt in diesem Kriege nicht nur Großmacht und Vormacht, nicht nur Gebiete und Kohlenstationen, nicht nur Handel und Siedelung; es gilt Bestand und Dauer des einigen Volkes, Wahrung und Wirkung der deutschen Kultur, die eben in eine neue Phase voller Triebkraft und Fülle wuchs. Dieser Krieg verklärt sich mit Geiste, und wiederum: die Geister waffnen sich. Der Geist der Volkheit, aus großer Geschichte her, in große Geschichte hin, bläst über den Massen, über den Waffen dieser Zeit. Und ist heute auch das Wort gering hinter der Tat, zu jeglicher Zeit ist das Wort verrucht, das nicht schlagendes Herz und greifende Hände hat: in solchem Sinn wollen diese Worte mit Hand anlegen.

Haßgesang gegen England

> Was schiert uns Russe und Franzos',
> Schuß wider Schuß und Stoß um Stoß!
> Wir lieben sie nicht,
> Wir hassen sie nicht,
> Wir schützen Weichsel und Wasgaupaß, —
> Wir haben nur einen einzigen Haß,
> Wir lieben vereint, wir hassen vereint,
> Wir haben nur einen einzigen Feind:
>
> Den ihr alle wißt, den ihr alle wißt,
> Er sitzt geduckt hinter der grauen Flut,
> Voll Neid, voll Wut, voll Schläue, voll List,
> Durch Wasser getrennt, die sind dicker als Blut.
> Wir wollen treten in ein Gericht,
> Einen Schwur zu schwören, Gesicht in Gesicht,

Am Mittwoch, den 4. Februar d. J., wird bei Ihren Kaiserlichen und Königlichen Majestäten im Weißen Saale des Königlichen Schlosses hierselbst ein **Ball** stattfinden, zu welchem die Einladungen durch die Hoffouriere und durch Karten erfolgen.*)

Die Damen erscheinen in langen ausgeschnittenen Kleidern **(keine viereckigen Ausschnitte und keine langen Aermel)**, mit hellen Glacé-Handschuhen, die Herren vom Zivil in Gala mit weißen Unterkleidern (Kniehosen, Schuhe und Strümpfe), die Herren vom Militär im Hofball-Anzuge, mit Ordensband.

Diejenigen Herren, welche zur Anlegung einer Uniform nicht berechtigt sind und demnach früher im schwarzen Frack, und weißer Krawatte erschienen, haben nunmehr die Befugnis, das vorgeschriebene Hofkleid zu tragen.

Für die Allerhöchsten und Höchsten Herrschaften ist die Anfahrt **gegen 8½ Uhr** vom Lustgarten her durch **Portal Nr. 5** bei der Wendeltreppe und **die Versammlung** im Kurfürstenzimmer.

Die Obersten Hof-, die Ober-Hof-, die Vize-Ober-Hof- und die Hof-Chargen, die General-Adjutanten, die Generale und Admirale à la suite und die Flügel-Adjutanten Seiner Majestät, der Minister des Königlichen Hauses und der Geheime Kabinettsrat, sowie die Gefolge der Allerhöchsten und der Höchsten Herrschaften nehmen dieselbe Anfahrt und versammeln sich um <u>8¼ Uhr</u> im Königszimmer; die Damen treten in die boisierte Galerie ein.

Alle anderen Gäste sind zu **8 Uhr** eingeladen.

Die Vorfahrt ist:

für die Fürsten, die Mitglieder des diplomatischen Corps und die Exzellenzen-Damen und Herren vom Lustgarten her durch **Portal Nr. 5** bei der Wendeltreppe,

für die Damen — soweit sie nicht zu den vorstehend bezeichneten Gästen gehören — und die sie begleitenden Herren vom Lustgarten her im **Portal Nr. 4,** an der Theatertreppe, von wo der Eintritt durch den Kapitel-Saal genommen wird, und

für die anderen Herren vom Zivil und Militär von der Schloßfreiheit her durch **Portal Nr. 3** bei der gegenüber der Wache belegenen Höllentreppe (Eintritt durch die Bilder-Galerie).

Die Versammlung ist:

für die Prinzen und Prinzessinnen aus souveränen neufürstlichen Häusern, sämtliche Damen, die Chefs der fürstlichen und ehemals reichsständischen gräflichen Häuser, die Diplomaten, die Exzellenzen und die tanzenden Herren im Weißen Saale;

die anderen eingeladenen Herren in der Weißen-Saal- und in der Bilder-Galerie.

Die noch vorzustellenden Damen versammeln sich im Ausbau der Bilder-Galerie (früheres Königinnengemach).

*) **Es wird dringend ersucht, im Behinderungsfalle die Absage <u>umgehend</u> an das Ober-Hofmarschallamt gelangen lassen zu wollen.**

Um **10³/₄ Uhr** wird ein Souper stattfinden und zwar im Marinesaal und im Königinnen-Zimmer:

für die Allerhöchsten und Höchsten Herrschaften,
und für diejenigen Eingeladenen, denen es besonders angesagt werden wird;

in der Schwarzen Adler-Kammer und der Roten Sammet-Kammer:

für die Hofstaaten;

im Gardes du Corps-Saale und den anliegenden Räumen:
für die tanzenden Damen und Herren und
alle einzelnen jüngeren Herren;
(Zugang eine Treppe tiefer über die Weiße Saal-Treppe)

im Braunschweigischen Saal, in der Braunschweigischen Galerie, in der Braunschweigischen Kammer, in den Königin-Elisabeth-Kammern und -Wohnung und im Elisabeth-Saal:

für die außerdem Eingeladenen.

Ende des Festes **gegen 12¹/₂ Uhr.**

Die **Abfahrt** ist **nach Wahl** bei der Wendeltreppe, oder im **Portal Nr. 4** bei der Theatertreppe in der Richtung nach dem Lustgarten, oder von der Bilder-Galerie aus über die Höllentreppe **durch Portal Nr. 3** nach der Schloßfreiheit.

Berlin, den 31. Januar 1914.

Der Ober-Hof- und Haus-Marschall
Freiherr von Reischach.

Die zur **Abholung** kommenden Wagen dürfen nur **vom Schloßplatz her** durch die **Portale I und II** in die **Schloßhöfe** einfahren.

W. Moeser Buchdruckerei, Hofbuchdrucker Sr. Majestät des Kaisers und Königs, Berlin S.

Zweite

Extra-Ausgabe

Berliner Lokal-Anzeiger

An jeder Anschlagsäule ist die nächste Geschäftsstelle des „Berliner Lokal-Anzeigers" angegeben.

32. Jahrgang. Freitag, 31. Juli. **1914.**

Deutschlands letztes Wort an Rußland.

Noch einmal, ehe die Waffen sprechen, gibt Deutschland dem russischen Reiche auf seine Herausforderung großmütig eine kurze Frist, sich zu besinnen und die drohende Katastrophe abzuwenden. Eine soeben erscheinende Sonderausgabe der Norddeutschen Allgemeinen Zeitung bringt folgende halbamtliche, für die Beurteilung der augenblicklichen Lage hochwichtige Mitteilung:

Nachdem die auf einen Wunsch des Zaren selbst unternommene Vermittlungsarbeit von der russischen Regierung durch allgemeine Mobilmachung der russischen Armee und Marine gestört worden ist, hat die Regierung Seiner Majestät des Kaisers heute in St. Petersburg wissen lassen, daß die deutsche Mobilmachung in Aussicht steht, falls Rußland nicht binnen zwölf Stunden seine Kriegsvorbereitungen einstellt und hierüber eine bestimmte Erklärung abgibt. Gleichzeitig ist an die französische Regierung eine Anfrage über ihre Haltung im Falle eines deutschrussischen Krieges gerichtet worden.

Zu diesen allerletzten Schritt hat der Kaiser sich ebenso gedacht, an ihn in unserer ersten Extraausgabe veröffentlichten Aussprache an die Volksmenge seine immer noch nicht abgeschwächene Bemühungen erwähnte, die Gegner zum Einlenken zu bringen, so weit hin nunmehr in kürzester Frist entscheiden, ob Rußland leichtfertig den Weltkrieg heraufbeschwören oder aber die gerechte Forderung Deutschlands erfüllen und seine Rüstungen einstellen wird.

Die Vorgeschichte des Konflikts.

Nachdem Seine Majestät der Kaiser den Kriegszustand für das Reich erklärt hat, ist der Zeitpunkt gekommen, die Vorgänge, die zu diesem Entschluß geführt haben, in breiter Lage vorzuhalten.

Seit Jahren hat Oesterreich-Ungarn gegen Bestrebungen zu kämpfen, die mit verbrecherischen Mitteln unter Duldung und Förderung der serbischen Regierung auf die Revolutionierung und Losreißung des südslawischen Landesteile Oesterreich-Ungarns hinarbeiten. Die Gewinnung dieser Gebiete ist ein unverhülltes Ziel der serbischen Politik. Diese glaubt dabei auf den Rückhalt Rußlands rechnen zu können. Im Gedanken, daß ihr Rußland die Aufgabe des jetzigen Moments zu lösen imstande ist, jede Gedanken ist durch Rußland Bemühungen, einen Bund der Balkanstaaten zustande zu bringen, Nahrung gegeben. Die großslawische Propaganda ist schließlich in der Ermordung des österreichisch-ungarischen

Thronfolgers und seiner Gemahlin grell hervorgetreten.

Die Oesterreich-Ungarische Monarchie entschloß sich deshalb, gegen ihren Bestand als Großmacht gerichteten verbrecherischen Treiben am Ende zu machen. Die mußte sich dabei ergeben, ob Rußland tatsächlich die Rolle des Beschützers der Südslawen als bisher des Beschützers der Oesterreich-Ungarischen Monarchie durchzuführen willens war. In diesem Falle kam im Lebensinteresse Deutschlands in Frage die ungebrochene Bestand der und verbündeten Monarchie, deffen wir bei Erhaltung unserer eigenen Großmachtstellung inmitten des Gegner von Ost und West bedürfen.

Oesterreich-Ungarn hat sich vornherein auf den Standpunkt gestellt, daß die Auseinandersetzung mit Serbien eine Angelegenheit sei, die nur Oesterreich-Ungarn und Serbien angehe. Unsere Bahrung dieses Standpunktes haben wir mit der größten Hingabe an allen Bemühungen teilgenommen, die auf Erhaltung des europäischen Friedens gerichtet waren. Oesterreich-Ungarn gab hierzu die Handhabe, daß es mehrerlei erklärte, daß es auf eine Eroberungen am Bestand Serbiens nicht antasten wolle. Diese Erklärungen ist namentlich in Petersburg mit Nachdruck zur Kenntnis gebracht worden. Unseren Bundesgenossen haben wir geraten, daß er ihr Würde der Monarchie vereinbar erschien, die ungeklärte Bestand des Verfahren gegenüber Serbien.

Bereits am 26. Juli lagen zuverlässige Meldungen über russische Rüstungen am Oesterreich-Ungarns gerichteten Grenze vor. Die ungeklärte Bestand der und die anhalten mußte, zu erklären. Vorbereitende militärische Maßnahmen Rußlands zwingen uns zu Gegenmaßregeln. Diese müssen in der Mobilisierung der Armee bestehen. Die Mobilisierung aber bedeutet den Krieg. Wir können nicht annehmen, daß Rußland einen europäischen Krieg entfesseln wolle. Am nächsten Tage erklärte der russische Kriegsminister unseren Militärattaché, daß noch keine Mobilmachung eingegangen. Wie Bord aufgebot Oesterreich-Ungarn die serbische Grenze übernehmen, wurden die auf Oesterreich-Ungarn gerichteten Militärbezirke mobilisiert, nämlich die Korps aus Kiew, Odessa, Moskau, Kasan. Jedoch hieben auch die nördlichen Front liegenden. Jedoch hieben auch den deutschland gerichteten Militärbezirken vorbereiten, daß auch an den deutschen Militärattaché erneut beruhigende Erklärungen gegeben, daß die Mitteilungen des Kriegsministers als noch voll zu der jetzt bestehend bezeichneten.

Am 29. Juli ging ein

Telegramm des Zaren

an den Kaiser ein, in welchem er in eindringlicher Bitte ausdrück, der Kaiser möge ihm in diesem ernsten Augenblick helfen. Er bitte ihn, um dem Unglück eines europäischen Krieges vorzubeugen, alles ihm mögliche zu tun, um den Bundesgenossen davon zurückzuhalten, zuweit zu gehen. Mit noch längerem Telegramm, daß er die Aufgabe des Vermittlers und der am Appell zur seine Freundschaft und Hilfe bereitwillig übernehmen könne. Dem entsprechende Aktion im Sinne des Kaisers war eingeleitet. Während dieZeit im Gange war, ließ die offizielle Nachricht ein, daß Rußland gegen Oesterreich-Ungarn mobil machte. Sofort hieraus wies der Kaiser den Zaren in einem weiteren Telegramm darauf hin, daß durch die russische Mobilmachung gegen Oesterreich-Ungarn seine auf Bitten des Zaren übernommene Vermittlertolle gefährdet, wenn nicht unmöglich, gemacht würde. Trotzdem wurde die in Wien eingeleitete Aktion fortgesetzt, wobei in England gemacht, in ähnlicher Richtung sich bewegende Schritte bei der deutschen Regierung unternommen worden.

Ueber diese Vermittlungsvorschläge sollte heute in Wien die Entscheidung fallen. Noch bevor sie ist, erhielt die deutsche Regierung die offizielle Nachricht, daß der Mobilmachungsbefehl für das gesamte russische Armee und Flotte ergangen ist. Darauf richtete der Kaiser ein letztes Telegramm an den Zaren, in dem er bemerkte, daß die Verantwortung für die Sicherheit des Reiches ihm zu die äußerste Grenze den Mobilmachungen ergangen. Wollte er im Frage zu Verantwortung für das Unheil, daß jetzt der Welt drohte. Er habe die Freundschaft mit dem Zaren und den russische Reich stets treu gehalten. Der Friede Europas könne jetzt noch erhalten werden, wenn Rußland sich entschließe, Deutschland und Oesterreich-Ungarn zu bedrohen.

Während also die deutsche Regierung auf Ersuchen Rußlands vermittelte, machte Rußland seine gesamten Streitkräfte mobil und bedrohte damit die Sicherheit des deutschen Reiches, von dem bis zu dieser Stunde noch keinerlei außergewöhnliche militärische Maßregeln getroffen waren.

Zur Erklärung des Kriegszustandes.

Die kriegsmäßige Grenzsicherung des Rußlands bedroht die öffentliche Sicherheit im Reichsgebiet. Gemäß Artikel 68 der Reichsverfassung ist daher von Seiner Majestät dem Kaiser der Kriegszustand erklärt worden. Die gleiche Anordnung ist im bald Bayern für den Bereich. Dieser Erlaß dient dem zur Königreich Bayern gerichteten. Diese Maßregel dient der ungestörten Durchführung der Mobilmachung und der Abwehr gegen feindliche Unternehmungen im Inland. Wah-

rend in früheren Kriegen zunächst nur die Sicherheit der Grenzgebiete bedroht war, ist bei dem Stande der modernen Kriegstechnik auch die Sicherheit im Innern des Landes bedroht, daß allein infolge der Entwicklung des Luftschiffe- und des Automobilwesens. Es liegt die Gefahr vor, daß der Ausbruch der Feindseligkeiten in Inneren des Landes mittels Luftschiffahrt, Eisenbahnen, Brücken, Stationen unserer drahtlose Telegraphie, Luftschiffstationen usw. versucht wird. Diese kann durch Polizei, selbst durch Militär nicht verhindert werden. Die sorgsamste Bewachung aller dieser Bauten im den gewünschten Grad von Kriegsschäden. Erreicht muß die Bedeutung dazu einrichtischer Vorbeugungen gegen Rußland getroffen, Störung und unfähige Grenzteilmessungen im Innern Landes verhindert werden. Die Verbereitungen der bewaffneten Macht müssen auf die Weise geschützt und die möglichste Störung hintergehalten sein. „Alle Kräfte des Volkes, die staatlichen Einrichtungen müssen an den Dienst der öffentlichen Wohlfahrt in den Dienst der Landesverteidigung gestellt werden. Die vorbildliche und unfähige Durchführung aller zum Schutze des heimischen Gebietes bestimmten Gebot es der, wenn nur verdienst, wenn die militärischen Gewalt an die Militärbefehlshaber übergeht.

Im Einklang der Presse sowie des Vereins- und Versammlungsfreiheit werden Schranken auferlegt werden. Die Forderungen betreffend werden. Die sorgsamste Bewachung und eine Maßregel auferlegt wird, daß die Interessen der Kriegsführung bei allen nur unabhängig, gefördert werden. Bei der Verhängung des Kriegszustandes gibt es all dieser Maßnahmen die rechtliche Grundlage.

Im Hinblick auf den Ernst der Stunde wird darauf vertraut, daß die Verhängung des Kriegszustandes in allen Kreisen der Bevölkerung als eine Maßregel aufgefaßt wird, die der Zweibestes des Landesverteidigung geschaffen werden. Die Bevölkerung wird daher der immer verbundenen Beschränkungen mit williger trägen, mit verminderung ungeschunener Müßigkeit des Landes und Bluts. Die Verteidigung des Vaterlandes den letzt Zivilangelegenheit gilt es hier für ob, die Treue hält, die es ihr Vaterland schuldet, und die dem Militärbefehlshaber und den Behörden vollkommen gehorsam zu gehandhabt werden, den für immer nach jedenfalls Mann hinaus seiner persönlichen Freiheit die beschränkt und seine der Frühlingen ist öffentliches Leben und Geschäft ungehindert fortgehen.

Verlobung des Prinzen Adalbert.

Wie uns soeben erzählen, hat sich Prinz Adalbert von Preußen, der dritte Sohn unseres Kaiserpaares, mit der Prinzessin Adelheid von Sachsen-Meiningen verlobt.

Prinzessin Adelheid Ena Antoine Elisabeth von Sachsen-Meiningen ist die älteste Tochter des Prinzen Friedrich von Sachsen-Meiningen geboren 12. Oktober 1891 und der Gemahlin Adelheid Prinzessin zur Lippe geb. 22. Juni 1870 geboren. Ihre älteste Schwester Feodora ist seit 1910 mit dem Großherzog Wilhelm Ernst von Sachsen verheiratet.

Die Kaiserliche Familie nahm heute im Schlosse von Berlin das heilige Abendmahl.

 Druck und Verlag von August Scherl G.m.b.H., Berlin SW, Zimmerstraße 36/41. — Verantwortlich für die Redaktion: Hans Sartorius, Berlin.

A BERLIN EXTRA.   GERMANY DISCLAIMS RESPONSIBILITY FOR THE WAR

that he had yet achieved the philosophic breadth of that poet's maturity— but the intensity with which he called for comradeship and celebrated freedom struck a new high in the rich tradition of English lyricism. He was born in 1909, attended Oxford, was closely associated with the Auden-Day Lewis group and with left-wing politics, travelled widely on the Continent; served as a fire-warden during the London blitz of 1940–42. The fluid-image technique of the oft-quoted

> Eye, gazelle, delicate wanderer,
> Drinker of horizon's fluid line . . .

has been criticized as symptomatic of the excess of ambiguity which is Spender's most obvious weakness. Sensitivity, verging on the feminine, a distrust of his own sentiment which too often leads to involved circum-locution—these tendencies cannot efface the singing strength of a dozen unsurpassed outpourings. Spender's latest work, of which "Spiritual Exercises" is characteristic, is more intellectual and embraces the influences of Hölderlin and Rilke (whose *Duino Elegies* Spender translated in 1939).

WALLACE STEVENS, who was born in Pennsylvania in 1879, and educated at Harvard, lives in Connecticut where he is presently vice-president of the Hartford Accident and Indemnity Company. More than any other modern poet, he has constructed a complete dream world. But he insists, like Bishop Berkeley, that this world of ideas is the real one; and while the tools he uses have been fancy, barbaric color, irony, abstraction and archaism, it must be admitted that the mortar itself has been the incongruous data of contemporary urban life. *Harmonium, Ideas of Order* and *The Man with the Blue Guitar* are among his contributions to a difficult genre.

ALLEN TATE was born in Kentucky in 1899 and lives in Tennessee. His *Selected Poems* were recently published and he is the author of *Reactionary Essays* as well as biographies of Jefferson Davis and Stonewall

Jackson. A Southern Agrarian in his politics, Tate's writing primly combines the "wit" of Pope and Donne with the uneasy modern conscience of the early T. S. Eliot. In 1945 Tate assumed the editorship of the *Sewanee Review.*

DYLAN THOMAS was born in Wales in 1914 and began to be recognized in the late thirties as the creator of a new poetic language that might supplant the dominant Auden-Spender-MacNeice canon. Thomas's vocabulary was non-political and lyrical, rich with new words and strong feelings, full of a mysticism of the body that suggested the work of such men as Matta and Tchelitchew in paint. Thomas defines poetry as "the rhythmic, inevitably narrative, movement from an over-clothed blindness to a naked vision," and poetic activity as "the physical and mental task of constructing a watertight compartment of words, preferably with a main moving column." Rejected for service in World War II, Thomas worked for the BBC. His poems and stories have been published in the United States by New Directions.

DUNSTAN THOMPSON's first book, *Poems* (1943), was rich with the scarcely assimilated influences of Conrad Aiken, George Barker and Dylan Thomas, but it had a richness of its own that made it memorable: its author showed surprising skill in the handling of the most difficult metrical patterns and he was not afraid to let an Elizabethan delight in words and a youthfully elegiac fascination with death carry him away. Thompson was born in Connecticut in 1918, was educated in England and France and at Harvard, published the experimental *Vice Versa* with Harry Brown, was serving overseas with the Army when his book came out.

WALTER JAMES TURNER was born in Australia in 1889 and lives in England, where he has been literary, musical and dramatic critic on such journals as the *London Mercury* and the *Daily Herald.* He has written novels, plays, satire and criticism. His poems, partly delightful fantasy, part an attempt to fix the poetry of science, are comparable, especially in their compact phrasing, to those of Wallace Stevens.

MARK VAN DOREN, the poet of a distinguished literary family, was born in Illinois in 1894, and divides his time between New York City, where he teaches and lectures, and Cornwall, Connecticut, where he has a farm. His work at St. John's College led to the provocative educational tract, *Liberal Education* (1943). For his *Collected Poems* (1939), Van Doren had won the Pulitzer Prize, and his *Anthology of World Poetry* (1929) and *The Oxford Book of American Prose* (1932) remain standard works. Van Doren's poems, drawing heavily on the American tradition and influenced by Robert Frost, are wonderfully skillful, observant, taut, and dry. Without innovation in matter or manner, they are never banal, often witty, and sometimes exciting. The two in this volume are from *Our Lady Peace and Other War Poems* (1942).

BARTOLOMEO VANZETTI was born in Italy in 1888. He landed at Ellis Island at the age of 20 and during the years until his arrest in 1919, he worked in stone-pits, brickyards, construction gangs and ice-works; finally as a carpenter and fish-peddler. A passionate student and thinker during this period (*The Divine Comedy* and Renan's *Jesus* were his favor-ite books) he turned from the Catholicism of his upbringing to theories of radical social change. It was as a philosophic anarchist and an active labor leader that he was framed on a murder charge with Nicola Sacco during the post-war Red-hysteria. He spent seven years in jail and was electrocuted August 22, 1927.

JOSÉ GARCIA VILLA, mystic and painter, is a naive poet whose first book, *Have Come, Am Here*, (1942) was poorly served by the sophisticated writers like Marianne Moore and Mark Van Doren who praised it un-critically. At their best the poems disclosed a childlike vision expressing itself through enchanting incantation. At their worst phrases like "To make icecream chrysantheme/Mix Christ and chrysanthemums," "God fears the poems of/Such as I!" and "O withouten her night-rose/I be forlornly aloss aloss" revealed a lamentable lack of intellectual discipline and taste. In a pretentious end-note Villa announced his discovery of "reversed consonance" (example, rhyming 'light' with 'tall'), a device which indicated more ingenuity than ear. He was born in Manila, Philippines, on a date which he refuses to reveal. His *Selected Poems*, with a preface by Edith Sitwell, will be published in England in 1946.

ROBERT PENN WARREN was born in Kentucky in 1905 and attended Vanderbilt in 1921. After leaving there he studied and taught at the University of California, Yale, Oxford (Rhodes Scholar), Vanderbilt, Louisiana State and the University of Minnesota. He left the latter for a year in 1944 to serve as Curator of Poetry at the Library of Congress. The influence of the Fugitive Group at Vanderbilt, and especially of John Crowe Ransom, nailed his decision to forsake science in favor of poetry. He became a contributor to the Southern Agrarian anthologies, served spells as editor of the *Southern Review* and *Kenyon*, wrote an impressive novel, *Night Rider* (1938), and two books of poems, *XXXVI Poems* (1935) and *Eleven Poems on the Same Theme* (1942). His *Selected Poems* were published in 1944. Warren's verse reflects conflict of spirit to the point of sometimes seeming deliberately rough and sometimes tortured; but it is always sharp and jewelled with memorable images. The early "Pondy Woods" and the late "Ballad of Billie Potts" are landmarks testifying to the successful collaboration of Warren the novelist and Warren the poet.

JOHN WHEELWRIGHT was born in Boston in 1897 and died there, in an automobile accident, in 1940. His *Selected Poems* were published by New Directions in 1941; his collected poetry is in preparation. In his preface to the former, R. P. Blackmur explains the difficulties in Wheelwright's style and context. Of the former: "He held lines to be in balance, to continue or to complete a pattern, if the major stresses came out even. The number of unstressed syllables did not count, but their cumulative value did count; hence scansion was variable even within a poem." Of the latter: "Like Blake, he saw truth in minute particulars, and . . . relished the particulars whether he saw any truth in them or not. He had a kind of naive or direct-eyed shrewdness that made of the oldest orthodoxy a fresh heresy, and rendered the immediate observation as absolute insight, and permitted him to mock both." Wheelwright was an architect and a wit, a recluse and a man who got bounced from bars, a Boston Brahmin and a Socialist who ran for office, and his verse is rich with this variety and paradox.

E. B. WHITE was born in Mt. Vernon, New York, in 1899 and edited the *New Yorker* in that lively magazine's formative years. Thereafter he wrote a column, *One Man's Meat*, for Harper's and recently a best-selling juvenile, *Stuart Little*. If wittier, more apparently effortless comedy has been achieved in our time than the ballad satirizing Rivera's attempt to paint Lenin on the walls of Mr. Rockefeller's City—this anthologist would like to see it. Yet, when pressed for an explanation, Mr. White said· "Writing light verse is very heavy work indeed; I get just as exhausted as the major poets."

OSCAR WILLIAMS began writing poetry for the second time in 1937. His first book, *The Golden Darkness*, was published in 1921 when he was 22 years of age by the Yale University Press. During the intervening years, he says, he "neither wrote nor read," but worked as an advertising promotion expert for a number of firms, his last assignment being Chairman for Advertising of the State Democratic Party of Florida in 1936. In 1940 *The Man Coming Toward You* was published and in 1945 *That's All That Matters*. The second book revealed some progress in Williams' effort to sustain beyond the image and single line his macabre imagination.

WILLIAM CARLOS WILLIAMS was born in 1883 and lives at Rutherford, New Jersey, where he practises medicine. The prose of his novel, *White Mule*, and the short stories, *Life Along the Passaic*, has been called "surgical"—both for its precision and its insistence upon physical detail. But in Williams' poems, which have agitated literary circles for two decades, there is an additional quality—the bird-like lyricism of the usually clipped lines, in which "anti-poetic" language is deliberately used to achieve contrast and new poetic meaning.

EDMUND WILSON, the present book editor of *The New Yorker* and by many considered the foremost literary critic in the United States, was born in 1895 in New Jersey, attended Princeton, and has written a great variety of books, first poetry and novel (*Poets, Farewell!, I Remember Daisy*), then criticism and travelogue (*Axel's Castle, The American Jitters*), social history and satire (*To the Finland Station, Notebooks of Night*). The celebrated parody of MacLeish was published in the last named book, after its initial appearance in *The New Yorker*, and is as interesting for what it reveals of Wilson's animus against poetry as for what it ridicules in MacLeish.

THOMAS WOLFE's writings have been twice presented as poetry in the six years since he died in 1938. In 1939 Scribners published *The Face of a Nation*, straight highlights from the novels, and in 1945 *A Stone, A Leaf, A Door*, in which Sgt. John S. Barnes had arranged some of the great passages in line and stanza. The controversy had raged during his life, and still rages: Was Wolfe essentially a writer of prose who lacked the discipline to cut away what he called "this constant and almost intolerable effort of memory and desire"? Or was he in fact a poet whose definition of poetry had been too narrow to enable him to perform without the incumbrances of the novel in his proper medium? Wolfe himself testifies to the latter view: "I'd rather be a poet than anything else in the world. God, what I wouldn't give to be a poet!" He was born in North Carolina in 1900, attempted playwriting at the University of North Carolina and at Harvard, taught at New York University, travelled in Europe, felt the influence of Joyce and saw his first novel, *Look Homeward, Angel*, pulled into shape by Maxwell Perkins. *Of Time and the River* appeared in 1935, *Story of a Novel* in 1936, *The Web and the Rock* in 1939 and *You Can't Go Home Again* in 1940.

ELINOR WYLIE was born in New Jersey in 1885 and died in New York in 1928. Her family, like her poetry, was aristocratic. She lived in England for some years, after shocking Washington society with a succession of impulsive marriages. Her novels, as well as her poems, won an early distinction for their meticulous grace and exquisite subjective perceptions. As the influence of "metaphysical" poets like Donne became more pronounced, and her emotional life deepened, Elinor Wylie came very close to giving her intensely personal idiom a universal elevation. But in spite of her fine craftsmanship, this poet is destined to remain an essentially feminine talent.

W. B. YEATS may be properly compared to Goethe for the increasing development of his art during a long lifetime, and for the energy with which, almost single-handed, he stimulated the birth of a whole national literature. Born in Ireland in 1865, living at times in Paris and London, Yeats was associated with Oscar Wilde, Millarmé and George Moore as a young man; later, as dramatist, with Synge, O'Casey and Lady Gregory; then with Joyce and AE and Pound; finally with Eliot and Auden and Turner. His early poems were dreamily impressionistic. He was a mystic, and even devoted himself to spiritualism for a while. Then he stripped his verse of vague ornament, originating a conversational, but always precise style, to convey more intellectual concepts. Yeats died in 1939. His *Last Poems*, full of defiant passion, political intransigeance and lyrical autumn, is an astonishing performance. His epitaph, from the poem "Under Ben Bulben," reads:

> Cast a cold eye
> On life, on death.
> Horseman, pass by!

ALPHABETICAL LIST OF POETS

INDEX OF FIRST LINES

MODERN LIBRARY GIANTS

A series of sturdily bound and handsomely printed, full-sized library editions of books formerly available only in expensive sets. These volumes contain from 600 to 1,400 pages each.

THE MODERN LIBRARY GIANTS REPRESENT A
SELECTION OF THE WORLD'S GREATEST BOOKS

The Best of the World's Best Books
COMPLETE LIST OF TITLES IN
THE MODERN LIBRARY

A series of handsome, cloth-bound books, formerly available only in expensive editions.

MISCELLANEOUS